MIGRATION AND SOCIAL WORK

Research in Social Work series

Series Editors: **Anna Gupta**, Royal Holloway, University of London, UK and **John Gal**, Hebrew University of Jerusalem, Israel

Published together with The European Social Work Research Association (ESWRA), this series examines current, progressive and innovative research applications of familiar ideas and models in international social work research.

Also available in the series:

Social Work Research Using Arts-Based Methods
Edited by **Ephrat Huss** and **Eltje Bos**

Critical Gerontology for Social Workers
Edited by **Sandra Torres** and **Sarah Donnelly**

Involving Service Users in Social Work Education, Research and Policy
Edited by **Kristel Driessens** and **Vicky Lyssens-Danneboom**

Adoption from Care
Edited by **Tarja Pösö**, **Marit Skivenes** and **June Thoburn**

Interprofessional Collaboration and Service User Participation
Edited by **Kirsi Juhila**, **Tanja Dall**, **Christopher Hall** and **Juliet Koprowska**

The Settlement House Movement Revisited
Edited by **John Gal**, **Stefan Köngeter** and **Sarah Vicary**

Find out more at:

policy.bristoluniversitypress.co.uk/
research-in-social-work

Research in Social Work series

Series Editors: **Anna Gupta**, Royal Holloway, University of London, UK and **John Gal**, Hebrew University of Jerusalem, Israel

---

Forthcoming in the series:

Migration and Social Work

Edited by **Emilio J. Gómez-Ciriano, Elena Cabiati** and **Sofia Dedotsi**

Find out more at:

policy.bristoluniversitypress.co.uk/research-in-social-work

Research in Social Work series

Series Editors: **Anna Gupta**, Royal Holloway, University of London, UK and **John Gal**, Hebrew University of Jerusalem, Israel

---

International Editorial Board:

Andrés Arias Astray, Complutense University of Madrid, Spain
Isobel Bainton, Policy Press, UK
Inge Bryderup, Aalborg University, Denmark
Tony Evans, Royal Holloway, University of London, UK
Hannele Forsberg, University of Tampere, Finland
John Gal, Hebrew University of Jerusalem, Israel
Anna Gupta, Royal Holloway, University of London, UK
Todd I. Herrenkohl, University of Michigan, US
Ephrat Huss, Ben-Gurion University of the Negev, Israel
Stefan Köngeter, Eastern Switzerland University of Applied Science (OST), Switzerland
Manohar Pawar, Charles Sturt University, Australia
Ian Shaw, National University of Singapore and University of York, UK
Alessandro Sicora, University of Trento, Italy
Darja Zaviršek, University of Ljubljana, Slovenia

Find out more at:

policy.bristoluniversitypress.co.uk/research-in-social-work

MIGRATION AND SOCIAL WORK
Approaches, Visions and Challenges

Edited by
Emilio José Gómez-Ciriano, Elena Cabiati
and Sofia Dedotsi

First published in Great Britain in 2024 by

Policy Press, an imprint of
Bristol University Press
University of Bristol
1-9 Old Park Hill
Bristol
BS2 8BB
UK
t: +44 (0)117 374 6645
e: bup-info@bristol.ac.uk

Details of international sales and distribution partners are available at
policy.bristoluniversitypress.co.uk

© Bristol University Press 2024

British Library Cataloguing in Publication Data
A catalogue record for this book is available from the British Library

ISBN 978-1-4473-6180-0 hardcover
ISBN 978-1-4473-6181-7 paperback
ISBN 978-1-4473-6182-4 ePub
ISBN 978-1-4473-6183-1 ePdf

The right of Emilio José Gómez-Ciriano, Elena Cabiati and Sofia Dedotsi to be identified as editors of this work has been asserted by them in accordance with the Copyright, Designs and Patents Act 1988.

All rights reserved: no part of this publication may be reproduced, stored in a retrieval system, or transmitted in any form or by any means, electronic, mechanical, photocopying, recording, or otherwise without the prior permission of Bristol University Press.

Every reasonable effort has been made to obtain permission to reproduce copyrighted material. If, however, anyone knows of an oversight, please contact the publisher.

The statements and opinions contained within this publication are solely those of the editors and contributors and not of the University of Bristol or Bristol University Press. The University of Bristol and Bristol University Press disclaim responsibility for any injury to persons or property resulting from any material published in this publication.

Bristol University Press and Policy Press work to counter discrimination on
grounds of gender, race, disability, age and sexuality.

Cover design: Bristol University Press
Front cover image: iStock/prettyboy80

Contents

List of figures		ix
Notes on contributors		x
Introduction Emilio José Gómez-Ciriano, Elena Cabiati and Sofia Dedotsi		1
1	The contribution of social work research to promote migration and asylum policies in Europe Emilio José Gómez-Ciriano	5
2	Participatory art in social work: from humanitarianism to humanisation of people on the move Darja Zaviršek	25
3	Grasping at straws: social work in reception and identification centres in Greece Marina Rota, Océane Uzureau, Malte Behrendt, Sarah Adeyinka, Ine Lietaert and Ilse Derluyn	47
4	Migrant girls' experiences of integration and social care in Sweden Elin Ekström	64
5	"Come to my house!": Homing practices of children in Swiss asylum camps Clara Bombach	80
6	Transnational dynamics of family reunification: reassembling social work with refugees in Belgium Pascal Debruyne, Kaat Van Acker, Dirk Geldof and Mieke Schrooten	95
7	Open or closed doors? Accessibility of Italian social work organisations towards ethnic minorities Elena Cabiati	112
8	Refugee children and families in the Republic of Ireland: the response of social work Muireann Ní Raghallaigh	126
9	Sense of place, migrant integration and social work Susan Levy and Maura Daly	146

| 10 | "If not now, when?": Reclaiming activism into social work education – the case of an intercultural student-academic project with refugees in the UK and Greece
Sofia Dedotsi and Ruth Hamilton | 161 |
| --- | --- | --- |
| 11 | EU border migration policy and unaccompanied refugee minors in Greece: the example of Lesvos and Samos hotspots
Marina Rota, Ine Lietaert and Ilse Derluyn | 177 |

Epilogue: Time to listen, time to learn, time to challenge … because there is hope
Emilio José Gómez-Ciriano, Elena Cabiati and Sofia Dedotsi — 198

Index — 201

List of figures

1.1	Four elements influencing knowledge	9
2.1	Marko Kočevar, EU flag, 2015	27
2.2	Marko Kočevar, Fences, 2015	28
2.3	Marko Kočevar, 'I feel Slovenia', 2015	28
2.4	IRWIN, State in Time, Lagos, 2010	38
2.5	IRWIN, State in Time, London, 2012	39
2.6	NSK passport holders, London, 2007	40
9.1	The Indicators of Integration Framework	148
9.2	New Scots Refugee Integration Strategy 2018–2022	153

Notes on contributors

Sarah Adeyinka is a researcher at Ghent University where she earned her Doctorate in Educational Sciences. She is part of the European Research Commission-funded ChildMove Project and conducted research on the impact of transit experiences on the wellbeing on unaccompanied minors. Her part of the project is focused on young female Nigerians who were trafficked into Italy for sexual exploitation. She has worked in the field of humanitarian aid for over 12 years with a focus on people in vulnerable situations. This included working onboard two Search and Rescue vessels in the central Mediterranean. Alongside a colleague, she conducted a study on the wellbeing of Nigerian and Ghanaian women working in prostitution in the Schaerbeek municipality of Brussels which resulted in a book. She is also Founder and Board Chair of CoCreate VZW, Belgium and CoCreate Humanitarian Aid Foundation, Nigeria.

Malte Behrendt graduated with a degree in Clinical Psychology in 2015. During an internship with an NGO in Colombia, he was able to gather first work and research experiences with minors in situations of extreme violence and displacement. Following his graduation, he started working in an emergency shelter for unaccompanied refugee minors in Berlin as a psychologist and social worker. Shortly thereafter he started training as a psychological psychotherapist at 'Zentrum Überleben' – an NGO specialising in the treatment of victims of torture. He worked as a PhD student in the ERC-funded research project 'ChildMove' at Ghent University for four years and has since graduated.

Clara Bombach has an MA in Social and Cultural Anthropology and is a doctoral student at Zurich University, and Educational Science and Senior Researcher at Marie Meierhofer Children's Institute, Zurich, Switzerland. Bombach is a qualitative researcher in the field of family and childhood studies, doing biographical research on the life trajectories of formerly placed children in care. She is involved in the scientific reappraisal efforts regarding compulsory social measures and placements in Switzerland until 1981. For her ethnographic doctoral thesis she studies the everyday lives of children and their parent(s) in so-called refugee community centres. In her committee work (for example, interest group Quality4Children), she is committed to the implementation of the United Nations Children's Rights in child and youth welfare services.

Elena Cabiati is Associate Professor at the Università Cattolica del Sacro Cuore, Italy, where she coordinates the Bachelor Programme in Social Work.

She teaches the methodology of social work, intercultural social work and the management of social welfare organisations. Her main research interests are: social work and migration, the involvement of experts by experience in social work education, child protection and management of social services. She is a registered social worker with fieldwork experience in child protection as both a practitioner and middle manager. She is Board Member of the European Social Work Research Association.

Maura Daly has worked as a social worker for 30 years. She completed her PhD on the social work professional identity in 2018 and has worked as a lecturer at the University of Dundee since then. She is the convenor for practice learning in social work and her main area of teaching is in preparing students for practice learning. Her main area of research for the past five years has been on a longitudinal study of the experiences of newly qualified social workers, which has just been completed. Maura and her husband are carers. They have provided respite care for a young man with disabilities since 2003 and have journeyed with him from pre-school to independent living. They have been foster carers since 2016 for a young man who fled war-torn Ethiopia as an unaccompanied minor and have written an autoethnographic account of this experience.

Pascal Debruyne has a PhD in Political and Social Sciences, Master's in Moral Philosophy and a Bachelor in Social Work. His research focuses on themes such as asylum and migration, urban superdiversity and informal social work and the politics of social work. He is currently a researcher at the Odisee University College of Applied Sciences, at the Center of Family Sciences. His current research focuses on the family reunification of refugees in Belgium.

Sofia Dedotsi is Assistant Professor at the Department of Social Work, University of West Attica, Greece. She is a qualified social worker, with field experience in child protection and family support in the UK and Greece. She has been teaching different social work courses in universities in Greece and the UK since 2010. Her research interests include social work anti-oppressive practices, social work education, migration and social policy. She gained the Advanced Award in Social Work from the PQ Consortium for Wales (2009) and was also an elected Board Member of ESWRA (2014–19), where she took the position of Vice-Chair (2017–19). She is a member of the Editorial Board of the *European Social Work Research Journal* and she has published in several academic journals, books and conferences as well as given guest lectures in universities across Europe.

Ilse Derluyn is Full Professor at the Department of Social Work and Social Pedagogy at Ghent University. Her main research topics concern the psychosocial wellbeing of war-affected children, young refugees and migrants, unaccompanied refugee minors and victims of trafficking. She is widely published and is also active in training and support for practitioners. She also gives counselling to refugees. Ilse is European Research Council grant holder of the research project ChildMove and coordinates the H2020-project RefugeesWellSchool. She is Director of the Centre for the Social Study of Migration and Refugees at Ghent University and Co-director of the Centre for Children in Vulnerable Situations.

Elin Ekström is a PhD student in social work. Her research focuses on processes of inclusion and exclusion among youth. Part of her studies seek to explore how females, so-called 'unaccompanied refugee minors', experienced their first years after seeking refuge in Sweden.

Dirk Geldof is Professor of Sociology at the Faculty of Design Sciences at the University of Antwerp. He is Lecturer and Senior Researcher at the Centre of Family Studies, Odisee University of Applied Sciences Brussels and Lecturer in the International Crossing Border Program at the Karel de Grote University College, Antwerp. His research focuses on migration, super-diversity and refugees.

Emilio José Gómez-Ciriano is Associate Professor at the Department of Social Work, Universidad de Castilla-La Mancha, Spain. He was previously a lawyer and worked for non-governmental organisations (NGOs) in migration and human rights issues at a Spanish level but also at a European and International level (United Nations). He has a PhD in Social Anthropology and a Bachelor in Social Work and specialised in economic social and cultural rights at Abo Akademi University, Finland. He is currently Head of the research group Alter-Accion. He has led some EU-funded research projects and others funded by the Spanish Government. He has done research as a guest researcher at the College of Europe and KU Leuven University, Belgium, Manchester Metropolitan University, the University of Salford, the Pontifical University of Salamanca and the National Distance Education University, Spain. He has also lectured in universities in Ecuador, the Netherlands, the UK and Finland and is responsible for Human Rights of Justice and Peace Spain. Currently he is on the Editorial Board of three journals and is the Secretary of the European Social Work Research Association.

Ruth Hamilton is a registered social worker and practised as a social worker and probation officer before becoming a researcher and social work lecturer. She has worked in several higher education institutions (HEI) in England delivering pre- and post-qualifying programmes and worked as a social work consultant delivering continued professional development to social workers in local authorities across the UK. Most recently she has been Head of Subject for Social Work at Northumbria University and Chair of Social Work Education North-East, a collaboration of six HEIs. She has worked on a variety of local and national research projects in health and social care including projects focused on sexual violence and the use of arts in community health projects. Her current research interests include pedagogical issues in social work education focusing on widening participation, student identity, developing research minded practitioners and critical consciousness, social activism and the refugee crises.

Susan Levy is Senior Lecturer in the School of Humanities, Social Sciences and Law, and Director of Professional Doctorates at the University of Dundee, Scotland. Her research centres on the role of the arts and embedding cultural diversity within social work, along with making visible and integrating different knowledges into practice. She is a co-editor of the forthcoming *Routledge Handbook of African Social Work Education* (2023).

Ine Lietaert holds a PhD in Social Work, studying the return and reintegration processes of assisted return migrants. She works as Assistant Professor at the United Nations University-CRIS, where she coordinates the Migration and Social research cluster, and at the Department of Social Work and Social Pedagogy at Ghent University, Belgium. She focuses on the impact of international/regional and national policies on social work and social support practices, with particular focus on the governance of 'mobile' groups in vulnerable situations, such as asylum seekers, return migrants, (internally) displaced persons and refugees. She also focusses on the impact of mobility and different types of borders and policies on migrants' lives, including their feeling of belonging, their copying strategies and their access to services, investigated through a socio-spatial research approach. She teaches international social work at Ghent University and is (co)supervising various research projects.

Muireann Ní Raghallaigh is Associate Professor of Social Work at University College Dublin (UCD), Ireland and programme director for UCD's Professional Masters in Social Work. She worked previously as a social worker with unaccompanied asylum-seeking children. She has conducted research in relation to the experiences of unaccompanied minors in foster care, refugees transitioning from Ireland's 'direct provision' accommodation system, refugee children arriving through resettlement schemes and refugee family reunification. She is currently involved in a project which explores ethical considerations in research with refugee populations. She previously served on the Board of Directors of the Irish Refugee Council and is currently co-chair of UCD's University of Sanctuary Committee.

Marina Rota is Sociologist with Postgraduate Studies in Criminology in Greece and Belgium. She holds a PhD in Sociology from Panteion University of Social and Political Sciences, Athens, and completed graduate seminars in social street work. Marina has worked in the migration and asylum as a field worker since 1995, mainly with unaccompanied refugee minors and child victims of human trafficking. She has also worked with different organisations including Doctors of the World, Doctors without Borders and the International Organization for Migration Department of Migration and Health. For the last 16 years, she has been training frontline professionals in identifying and supporting people in vulnerable situations and victims of trafficking. She was part of the ChildMove project at Ghent University from 2017 until 2022 where she worked as a researcher.

Mieke Schrooten is Professor of Social Work at the University of Antwerp and Odisee University of Applied Sciences, Brussels. She is affiliated with the Center for Research on Environmental and Social Change, University of Antwerp and the Social Work Research Centre, Odisee University of Applied Sciences. Her main topics of interest are mobility, transnational social work and informal social work practices.

Océane Uzureau holds a Master's in Migration Studies. She is a PhD candidate in Social Work and Welfare Studies at Ghent University and a researcher on the European Research Council-funded ChildMove project. She collaborated with the Observatory of the Migration of Minors, University of Poitiers in action research projects with unaccompanied minors in France. Her research interests focus on unaccompanied minors' migration and mobilities within Europe, social support while on the move, border experiences and graffiti analysis in transit migration hubs.

Kaat Van Acker is a social worker and experiential psychotherapist. She obtained her PhD in Psychology at KU Leuven in 2012 for a study on acculturation attitudes of Flemish majority members. Between 2013 and 2015, she worked as a social worker with asylum-seeking families in individual housing facilities. In 2015, she joined Odisee University of Applied Sciences as a lecturer and researcher while maintaining a position at KU Leuven as a research fellow and lecturer. Her current research primarily concerns refugee families, in particular refugee family wellbeing and reception infrastructures. As a psychotherapist, she also regularly works with refugees facing trauma and adaptation difficulties.

Darja Zaviršek is Professor at the University of Ljubljana, Faculty of Social Work and Chair of the Department of Social Justice and Inclusion and Professor at the University of Applied Science Alice Salomon Berlin. She was the chair of the International doctoral network in social work, and founded the East European subregional Association of the Schools of Social Work as part of the International Association of Schools of Social Work (IASSW) and is President and Board Member of the IASSW. She published several books and articles related to disability and gender studies, the history of social work and critical social studies. In 2016 she was the Hokenstad Lecture Awardee and in 2022 she got the IASSW Eileen Younghusband Memorial Award for achievements in social work teaching and research.

Introduction

Emilio José Gómez-Ciriano, Elena Cabiati and Sofia Dedotsi

Social work research on migration is still at a preliminary stage of development in comparison with other social sciences disciplines. Across Europe, the topic doesn't receive priority in the agenda, the dialogue is often left to individual sensitivities, and social policies, social work organisations and social education programs don't yet express the attention that this important topic reality deserves. However, migration and social work are closely interrelated.

Against this, the importance to discuss about the role, the peculiarities, the challenges and opportunities of social work with migrant people, also through research lenses, is increasingly necessary.

In recent years, social work research has experienced a remarkable development due to two main factors: on one side, the growing consciousness, by an increasing number of social workers, of the pivotal role of social work as a human rights-based profession and discipline with all it entails. On the other side, the positionality of social work research sharing a common ground of methodology and literature with the rest of social science disciplines while holding a unique knowledge base derived from its hybrid condition of being both a profession and an academic discipline. Therefore, as in a mutual and dialogical relationship, professional interventions with migrant people in need can be nurtured not only by academic research but also by the practitioners' critical reflection on their work at the very grassroot level, which, in turn, feeds academic research and theoretical perspectives.

Many social workers are not familiarised with migration as a phenomenon, and lack competences that would enable them to make better interventions when taking care of migrant people in the generic sense. Some of them do not only critically examine migration as a phenomenon but also engage with migrant people at the various stages of the migration or asylum-seeking process. Social workers, as helping professionals, welcome migrant people in need, intervening in all the stages in which being migrant or asylum seeker means to live in poverty or to be homeless, having to deal with huge difficulties without a supportive network, being a child or a young person without a family, being ill and with no access to the necessary care, being voiceless and subjected to violence, being discriminated and marginalised in society.

In this scenario, social workers guide helping processes at case, group and community level, advocating for human rights matters, and standing alongside migrant people in need, social workers identify, collect, analyse and denounce oppressive practices, human rights violations as well as share good practices that can contribute to social cohesion in the communities. This is something that the editors of the book have identified amongst the different chapters.

The main aim of this book is to identify the reality of migration and asylum in Europe through the lenses of the research done by social work academics from nine different countries. Each national context has a differentiated political, civic, organisational and academic culture that influences the way migrants and refugees are perceived and treated, despite the fact that they are part of the European Union (with the exceptions of the UK and Switzerland), with common frameworks related to migration and asylum at academic level (research 4 refugees, Erasmus +, Horizon Europe), at integration level (European website on integration, European Pact on Migration and Asylum) and at financial level (EMIF).

This book aims to provide a European perspective by collating these different perspectives for social work research on migration and asylum. It is the result of a joint work developed by a group of social work academics and researchers across Europe, most of whom are members of the Special Interest Group (SIG) on social work research on migration and asylum (SWIM) of the European Social Work Research Association (ESWRA). The SIG was stablished in 2016 with the aim to provide a social work research contribution on migration, in the broad sense, including ethnic minority persons, immigrants, asylum seekers and refugees, people with migration backgrounds, unaccompanied minors, and also by discussing the role of social work on different but interlocked perspectives: research, education, social policies and practices.

The core idea of the book editors is that we can rely on research to develop transformative research processes and that there are studies, innovations and experiences within the European context that we can learn from. As the subtitle of the book suggests, the contribution of each author offers knowledge and shares experiences on approaches, visions and challenges about social work and migration.

The book is organised into 11 chapters. Chapter 1 by Emilio José Gómez-Ciriano focuses on the contribution of social work research to promote migration and asylum policies in Europe. Looking at the contribution of social work pioneers, the author reflects on what is needed to raise awareness on items that can be challenging for social work research from a critical perspective.

Chapter 2 by Darja Zaviršek discusses how social workers and educators can use artistic work to address the humanitarian crises of migration and the societal anaesthesia attached to it. The chapter presents and analyses from a social work perspective some important Slovenian artists whose work is related to migration.

Chapter 3 by Marina Rota, Océane Uzureau, Malte Behrendt, Sarah Adeyinka, Ine Lietaert and Ilse Derluyn discusses challenges and peculiarities of social work with refugees in the first reception and identification centres (IRC) in Greece, highlighting how social workers, often without the necessary tools, are called upon to provide quality services, deal with crises and solve problems by combining assistance to the individual with the protection of the whole camp population.

Chapter 4 by Elin Ekstron explores migrant girls' expectations and perceptions of receiving social care in Sweden, exploring experiences giving and receiving social care from an intersectional perspective.

Chapter 5 by Clara Bombach is based in Switzerland. This chapter presents a research project conducted with children living in a Swiss cantonal asylum centre.

Chapter 6 presents a research project on family reunification of Syrian, Afghan and Iraqi refugees in Belgium and focuses on the dynamics of family reunification ('doing family at a distance'), specifically looking at lifeworld-dynamics of family relations beyond boundaries, connecting families between 'here and there'. The Belgian authors, Pascal Debruyne, Kaat Van Acker, Dirk Geldof and Mieke Schrooten, offer important knowledge on social work within transnational dynamics of family reunification of refugees.

Chapter 7 presents a reflection on the culture of social work organisations, starting from the idea that organisations do not operate the same way for everyone and can involuntarily discriminate against ethnic minority people. The author, Elena Cabiati, discusses the topic from an Italian perspective, highlighting factors of exclusion/inclusion.

Chapter 8 by Muireann Ní Raghallaigh explores the role of social work in relation to children and families from refugee backgrounds in the Republic of Ireland. Drawing on Irish and international research, the chapter argues that social workers in Ireland and elsewhere are very well placed to work with refugee children and their families in a systemic way.

Chapter 9 by Susan Levy and Maura Daly explores approaches to the integration of migrants broadly and specifically within Scotland. The chapter is contextualised within cultural social work, working with difference, and developing a sense of place and wellbeing to achieve sustainable and inclusive cities.

Chapter 10 discusses the need for a more political and activist social work education, based on a collaborative project between students and staff on migration, everyday bordering and (anti-)oppressive social work practices. Reflections of the authors, Sofia Dedotsi and Ruth Hamilton, arise from a project that involved students from a university in the North East of England.

Chapter 11 discusses EU border migration policy and unaccompanied minors in Greece through the example of Lesvos and Samos 'hotspots'. The authors, Marina Rota, Ine Lietaert and Ilse Derluyn, confront the policy-making with the reality to answer the question of EU policy on the living conditions of unaccompanied minors.

We are at the beginning of a long path in which we can learn how to better develop helping processes, how social work organisations can increase accessibility and sensitivities, how to teach and learn content through anti-discriminatory and human rights approaches, how social policies can avoid reproducing oppressive dynamics, how to protect and advocate for vulnerable people without paternalistic and assimilationist expectations and how to take a stand coherent with social work principles.

The recent events that have taken place in Ukraine with the invasion of its territory by Russian troops and the increasing numbers of displaced people knocking at the doors of European Union countries not only represent an ethical challenge for the social work profession as a whole, but specifically for social work research. And it is necessary to face it in order to implement the fairer and most respectful and human rights-based policies on migration and asylum in Europe.

This book represents a European source of learning and inspiration for all those who feel that from a practice, research and educational perspective, Social work with migrant people involves political, societal, human and relational challenges to be faced.

The editors of this book wish to express their gratitude to Policy Press for making this book possible. They also want to dedicate this book to all the people (particularly migrants, asylum seekers and refugees) that struggle for their dignity and their rights.

1

The contribution of social work research to promote migration and asylum policies in Europe

Emilio José Gómez-Ciriano

Inspirational thoughts from social work pioneers

'Nothing could be worse than the fear that one has given up too soon, and left one unexpended effort that could have saved the world.'

Jane Addams

From its very beginnings, social work has been inextricably linked with migration. The extent to which interventions with migrants were implemented in the early 20th century is highlighted throughout the pages of Mary Richmond's *Social Diagnosis* (1917) and Jane Addams' *Twenty years at Hull House* (1910) as one of the main activities of social work pioneers. The awareness of the working conditions of migrants and how they suffered exploitation, oppression and racism outraged social work pioneers, and motivated them to challenge and condemn the injustice behind the ideology that supported the status quo. However, they soon realised that their condemnation would not be effective unless it was supported by reliable data.

The chapter titled *Pioneer labor legislation in Illinois* from the book *Twenty years at Hull House* (Addams 1910, 2010: 132) clearly illustrates this idea and provides important pointers on how to lobby for political change.

First pointer: awareness, outrage and ethical commitment are key elements for change, but they are not enough

The settlement house in Chicago, Hull House, was deliberately set up in an immigrant quarter. The decision was made with the aim of establishing a good relationship with neighbours so that Hull House members could empathise with them and understand their context at the very grassroots level.

> Between Halsted Street and the river live about ten thousand Italians – Neapolitans, Sicilians and Calabrians, with an occasional Lombard or Venetian. To the south on Twelfth Street are many Germans, and

side streets are given over almost entirely to Polish and Russian Jews. Still farther south, these Jewish colonies merge into a huge Bohemian colony, so vast that Chicago ranks as the third Bohemian city in the world. To the northwest are many Canadian-French, clannish in spite of their long residence in America, and to the north are Irish and first-generation Americans. (Addams, 1910, 2010: 64)

Awareness can only be achieved by being in touch with reality and, in this case, paved the way to outrage and ethical commitment, which necessarily (and previously) requires the willingness of the practitioner to place herself out of her comfort zone to enable her to challenge uncontested narratives. At this point, it is important to highlight that this awareness is not achieved all at once but needs to be fostered over time to avoid being obscured by middle-class bourgeois temptations.

Second pointer: the need to collect valuable information

In order to promote substantial change, the Hull House pioneers had to take a step further and go beyond the general impressions they obtained via direct contact with their neighbours to collect information "carefully" (in Jane Addams' own words), which meant selecting and analysing data to make it fit for purpose.

> While we found many pathetic cases of child labour and hard-driven victims of the sweating system who could not possibly earn enough in the short, busy season to support themselves during the rest of the year, it became evident that we must add carefully collected information to our general impression of neighbourhood conditions if we would make it of any genuine value. (Addams, 1910, 2010: 134)

The adverb 'carefully', used in relation to information, was used both in relation to the amount and the quality of the information. In the paragraph, she suggests a series of pointers to raise important issues that could be useful today, such as: What purpose does the research serve? Who is the final owner of the research? To what extent do researchers have room for manoeuvre if they wish to give their research a differentiated and challenging direction?

Third pointer: putting research into practice

Once the information had been carefully collected, it had to be managed properly and purposefully to give it genuine value. The pioneers did this via a combination of audacity and wisdom. The chapter just referenced in

Twenty years at Hull House explains how Florence Kelley, a resident of Hull House, who was also a renowned social reformer, convinced the members of the governing body of the State of Illinois to investigate the sweating system and the situation of child labour in factories.

> Mrs Florence Kelley, an early resident of Hull House, suggested to the Illinois State Bureau of Labor that they investigate the sweating system in Chicago with its attendant child labour. The head of the Bureau adopted the suggestion and engaged Mrs Kelley to make the investigation. (Addams, 1910, 2010: 134)

The persuasiveness of Florence Kelley, on one side, and the fact that she was commissioned by the Bureau to act on its behalf, on the other, were crucial elements for a positive outcome of the research aims. Being able to construct alternative narratives and arguments based on ethical convictions substantiated by good research strengthens the persuasiveness of the argument as it emanates from a position of authenticity, which is difficult to refute.

Fourth pointer: what is not communicated does not exist

Once the report was finished, Florence Kelley presented it to the Illinois Bureau and, again, owing to her excellent communication skills, a committee was appointed to investigate her findings in depth. During the process, Hull House residents followed the work of the committee and met with their members at Hull House when it was concluded.

> After dining with members of the special committee at Hull House headquarters, Jane Addams expressed: 'our hopes ran high, and we believed that at last some of the worst ills under which our neighbors were suffering would be brought to an end'. (Addams, 1910: 134)

Indeed, meeting *key people* (committee members) *at the right place* (Hull House) and at the *right time* (when the committee members had finished their inspection) was crucial, as was networking with other entities, not just for enriching one's own views but to increase visibility and strengthen lobbying work.

> I remember that I very much disliked the word ''lobby', and still more the prospect of the lobbying itself, and we insisted that well-known Chicago women should accompany this first little group of settlement folk who with trade-unionists moved upon the state capitol on behalf of factory legislation. (Addams, 1910, 2010: 135)

Consequently, it is important to put research to work to promote real change. However, to what extent is it possible to transfer the lessons from Hull House to the present day?

Updating pioneers' tips: knowledge, empathy, emotion and action

By mirroring the pioneers' experience at Hull House, it is possible to highlight points that could be helpful for today's social work researchers. First, to what extent are academic teaching-learning programmes (including placement programmes) oriented in a way that promote critical reflection through direct contact of students with the reality of migrants and asylum seekers? To what extent does this extend to social work research? Second, to what extent do academia, public institutions and NGOs contribute to developing cross-cutting skills and competences that are essential for social workers in their relationship with migrants and asylum seekers? Third, to what extent are social workers aware of the importance of research as a useful tool to influence politics and produce changes?

Empathy, knowledge and awareness

Empathy, and knowledge 'qualified' the research that was performed at Hull House. Audacity, persuasiveness, cultural sensitivity, communication skills and networking were also crucial for becoming politically influential. Here, we focus on empathy, knowledge, and skills and competences.

The etymology of the term 'empathy' comes from the Greek *empatheia* which means passion and pain at the same time. According to this etymology, an emphatic person is one who is passionate about others and concerned by their pain. Levinas interprets empathy as a combination of proximity and responsibility. For Levinas, being responsible means to make oneself available for service to others in such a way that one's own life is intrinsically linked with that of others (Levinas, 1985: 97).

In turn, the etymology of the word 'knowledge' comes from the Old English word *cnāwan* which means to acknowledge or recognise.

As a result, empathy and knowledge are at the very grassroots of any initiative aimed at transforming reality through social work and social work research.

However, in social work research, knowledge does not come exclusively from a single source. Pawson et al (2003) identify five sources of knowledge in social work:

- *Organisational knowledge*: knowledge that comes from the organisation, which may include agency policies and protocols. Defined as that gained

from governance and regulation activities in the organisation of social work processes.
- *Practitioner knowledge*: knowledge that is built on the experience of practitioners, which covers that gained from experience in their day-to-day role as a social worker. Pawson explains that this knowledge tends to be personal, tacit and specific to a particular context.
- *Service user knowledge*: knowledge that comes from service users, which is that gained from being at the receiving end of social worker interventions. Pawson highlights how this knowledge has been traditionally undervalued and under-represented.
- *Academic knowledge*: knowledge that is provided by Academia. That which is taught and learned in Academia, disseminated through classes, conferences and seminars and also made available in journal articles, books, reports and evaluations.
- *Political knowledge/policy knowledge*: knowledge that comes from the broader community.

These five sources of knowledge may be present, to a greater or lesser extent, in social work research. However, as knowledge is not neutral (Kolakosky, 1975: 76; Marin, 1975: 89, 90), academia, public institutions and organisations play an important role by being willing (or not) to promote (or not) ways of doing research that can be (or not) reliable and rigorous enough to be suitable for social transformation where appropriate.

Awareness built on empathy and knowledge could motivate social workers to take more responsibility by adopting anti-oppressive research approaches driven by moral and ethical codes that explicitly challenge sources of privilege or power based on unjustifiable evidence (McLaughlin, 2012). As we are dealing with migrants and refugees, the degree of intercultural

Figure 1.1: Four elements influencing knowledge

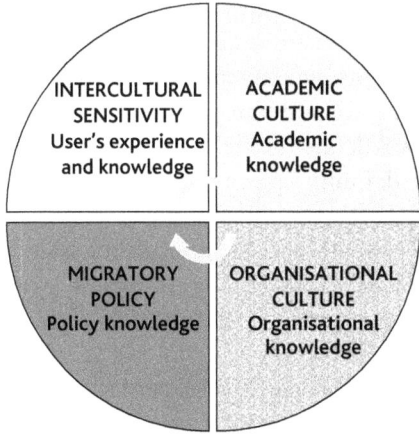

sensitivity that exists in society and the welcoming (or not) attitude towards migrants and refugees stipulated in governmental policy are also important.

Figure 1.1 shows how, in the current context of neoliberalism (grey), intercultural sensitivity (white), academic culture (light grey), migratory policy (dark grey) and organisational culture (spotted grey) interact with each other by influencing the different areas of knowledge, and how awareness is built on the different compositions (or quality) of knowledge. Consequently, authentic knowledge about migration should comprise the content taught at university, an organisational culture that favours practice-based research, an accurate idea of how migration policy works and is oriented and, last but not least, the existence of intercultural sensitivity.

Intercultural sensitivity is defined by Chen and Starosta (1996) as the 'ability to develop positive emotion towards understanding and appreciating cultural differences that promote appropriate and effective behavior in intercultural communication' (Chen and Starosta, 1996). It influences how migrants and refugees settle in reception countries, whether they feel integrated or not, and their relationship with the system (especially with the visible face of the system – officers and social workers). It also shapes their experience and knowledge as users in the context of reception countries. Intercultural sensitivity goes hand-in-hand with the concept of cultural humility coined by Tervalon and Murray-Garcia (1998) and defined as:

> Lifelong commitment to self-evaluation and self-critique, to redressing power imbalances in patient-physician dynamic, and to developing mutually beneficial and nonpaternalistic clinical and advocacy partnership with communities on behalf of individuals and defined populations. (Tervalon and Murray-Garcia, 1998: 123)

Academic culture refers to the 'attitudes, values and ways of behaving that are shared by people who work or study at universities' (Brick, 2009) lecturers, researchers and students. Academic culture has a decisive impact on academic knowledge both in teaching and researching but also in the values that future social workers will acquire and transmit.

Organisational culture is defined as a set of shared assumptions that guide actions in organisations by defining appropriate behaviour for various situations (Ravasi and Schultz, 2006). Organisational culture affects the way people and groups interact with each other, users and stakeholders. Organisational culture influences the extent to which employees identify with their organisation (Schrodt, 2002) and, as mentioned earlier, affects organisational knowledge.

Neoliberal paradigm in social work is defined by Cummins (2018) as a 'cult of managerialism' and an increase in audit and risk management culture that challenges traditional social work approaches and values (Cummins, 2018: 102).

In turn, Di Rosa et al (2019) speak about the trend of 'managerialisation' and the threat for the social worker who risks 'becoming inflexible working in purely bureaucratic posts, forsaking the fostering of social rights and the wellbeing of the individual and his community' (Di Rosa et al, 2019: 120).

Migration policy deals with the norms that rule the transit of people across borders from one country to another and also with the situation of people who intend to work and stay in a country for different reasons, and their relationship with receiving societies. In his renowned article, 'Network, Linkages, and Migration Systems', Fawcett (1989) understands by *migration system* two or more places linked by a flow or counterflow of people and creates 'a conceptual framework that identifies twelve types of linkages in migration systems that are applicable to various forms of migration' (Fawcett, 1989: 671).

Academia and social work research on migration and asylum

What is researched and taught on migration in academia not only frames the *acquis* of what *social workers-to-be* (either academics or practitioners) will acquire for the future, but also the implicit worldview of teaching and research in this area. Authors such as Boccagni and Righard (2020) consider that 'it is far from desirable that social workers cope with [the] complexity' that migration entails 'by learning-on-the-job' (Boccagni and Righard, 2020: 380). Unfortunately, in many faculties, explicit content relating to dealing with migration is still residual and limited to the 'corner of peculiarities' (Van Ewijk, 2010: 182).

Many authors have alerted to the risk posed by academics who do not question governmental narratives on migration and asylum, and how such views are predominant in the faculties in which future practitioners will train. They also alert to the fact that these views are exported to the organisations practitioners work for, which, in turn, strengthen organisational cultures that are embedded with methodological nationalism. In the article titled *The role of critical social work education in improving ethical practices with refugees and asylum seekers* (Morley et al, 2020) Candice Le, a social worker employed as an immigration officer by the Australian Government from 2013 to 2015, explains how she had passively assumed the hegemonic discourse on migration for many years until she began to reflect critically on her work after studying an MA in Social Work Studies.

> This incident did not really become critical to me until I developed a critical framework during my Master of Social Work Studies. Previously, I did not regard my role as problematic. It was only by becoming aware of power, privilege and oppression that I started to reflect on my role, with considerable shock, and regret. ... Since studying social work, however, I have recognised the broader social

and political contexts of asylum seeking and forced migration. (Morley et al, 2020: 409)

Therefore, it is essential for academia to provide students with a critical understanding on social work with migrants and refugees. 'A critical social work education may assist graduates to genuinely work toward social justice' (Morley et al, 2020). This can be achieved in many ways: by introducing students to reports and studies dealing with migration and by involving migrant users in teaching (Beresford and Boxall, 2012: 156) and/or research (McLaughlin, 2009, 2012). The challenge for students concerns strong interdisciplinarity work and also becoming involved in face-to-face interactions, which lie at the heart of social work.

Academia should provide students with tools to raise awareness and reflect on their experience of structural inequalities by emphasising emotional aspects (Robinson and Masocha, 2017). zavirsek agrees on this point by considering that, in order to develop empathy towards migrants, students should be provided with tools that enable them to reconstruct unchallenged narratives if necessary. However, this would still not be enough given that they often lack emotional experiences linked to migration (Zaviršek, 2017: 235).

Social work research on migration is mainly centred on academia and its topics generally coincide with the research priorities of funding institutions (EU, Governments, among others). Academic environments in which researchers operate are not always willing to support the involvement of users, community groups or practitioners (McRoy et al, 2012; Palinkas and Soydan, 2012; Teater, 2017). As McLaughlin and Teater state: 'Academic institutions place significant importance to research influence and not so much to practice influence.' As a result, academics often prefer to perform research that is likely to be published in high impact factor journals than in other spheres that may be not as rewarding (McLaughlin and Teater, 2017: 70). Universities also exert pressure on authors as a requirement for promotion. In comparison with other branches of social sciences and humanities, it should be noted that social work is not yet acknowledged by funding institutions and other social sciences and humanities disciplines as a scientific discipline. This circumstance might have an effect on the number of research projects that are led by social workers.

Organisational culture and social work research on migration and asylum

There is also research – although to a lesser extent – from practitioners who reflect on their practice and document their findings, insights, and intuitions on migration. This happens when the institutions they work for promote the type of philosophy that encourages such interaction. It also happens when academic researchers prioritise the influence of practice over the influence of research (Mc Laughlin and Teater, 2017: 70).

However, for this to happen it is essential that practitioners are not put under pressure or bureaucratised. Unfortunately, that is not the case in most situations in which 'organizational contexts are imbued with hegemonic assumptions [on migration] and blindly adopt dominant and managerial practices [and regulations]' (Morley et al, 2020: 406).

Sometimes organisational rules are so overwhelming that they are uncritically assumed by a large majority of practitioners. There is little room for manoeuvre to challenge the current state of affairs, especially when – as previously mentioned – educating and training in migration and asylum is absent in the content taught in many schools and faculties. As a result, critical and self-reflective social work does not exist, and 'defensive social work' defined by Banks (2012) as that which 'follow the rules, carry out tasks and fulfil their obligations defined by their organization and the law, takes the floor with the risks it entails' (Morley et al, 2020: 410).

As Morley et al state, 'social workers need the autonomy to contest human rights violations to which they bear witness'. They also need the knowledge and skills provided by university to build said autonomy on strong pillars and strategies to resist pressures that dilutes the quality of their practice-based research (Lymbery and Butler, 2004).

Practice-based research in migration and asylum provides the contents of investigation with coherence, and research-based practice helps to refine procedures and improve intervention. However, for this to be a success, there needs to be a good, synergic connection between academia and organisations and this hardly ever happens. The fact is that neither academia nor organisations usually provide social workers with the tools and knowledge needed for the critical thinking that may eventually provoke change.

At the right moment in the right place? Social workers influencing politics: the role of research

Social work pioneers influenced policymakers by cleverly managing empathy, audacity, persuasiveness, communication and teamworking. These skills are nowadays defined by the World Health Organisation (WHO), the Organisation for Economic Co-operation and Development (OECD) and the European Union as 'soft skills', 'transversal skills' and 'key competences for lifelong training', respectively. Their attainment is crucial for raising awareness on migration and asylum and for developing critical and reflective thinking.

In order to be influential, research should flow smoothly from grassroots to decision-making levels. Information should also be wisely managed by actors with a sharp political instinct. Unfortunately, the political dimension of social work is even more absent in academic curricula than contents regarding migration and asylum. Gal and Weiss-Gal (2017) note that 'Social work academics can be expected to play an active role in the policy process above and beyond academics' traditional role of disseminating knowledge' (Gal and Weiss Gal, 2017: 1). Both authors agree that the degree to which the transfer of knowledge relevant to policy formulation and involvement in this process actually occurs is still unclear.

The role of social work associations

Social work can influence politics through research made by individuals, think tanks and research networks, but also by the organisations that represent academics and professionals. The most well-known organisations are: the International Federation of Social Workers (IFSW), which represents social work practitioners; the International Association of Schools of Social Work (IASSW), which represents faculties and schools of social work; the Society for Social Work Research (SSWR), and the European Social Work Research Association (ESWRA). In this chapter, we focus primarily on associations.

IFSW as a political actor

IFSW defines itself as 'the global body for the profession'. On its website, it declares that 'the Federation and its national members strive for social justice, human rights and inclusive, sustainable social development through the promotion of social work best practices and engagement in international cooperation' (https://www.ifsw.org/about-ifsw/). Political activism is in the DNA of an institution that represents more than 3 million social work practitioners in 141 countries. IFSW is regionalised and has branches in Europe, Latin-America and the Caribbean, North America, Africa and Asia-Pacific, which operate with a large degree of autonomy and have representatives on the executive committee.

Since it was founded, the IFSW has had a remarkable trajectory in political activism through its presence at the United Nations (where it has consultative status since 1959), the Council of Europe (where it has participatory status since 1960) and the European Union Agency for Fundamental Rights (FRA) (the last two through its European branch IFSW-Europe).

IFSW at the United Nations

The consultative status at the United Nations Economic and Social Council (ECOSOC) enables IFSW to participate as a stakeholder in the Universal Periodic Reports and to submit numerous reports. This is clearly explained in the document titled: *IFSW Commission representation to the United Nations, objectives, structures, function and guidelines* (IFSW, 2019).

Social workers have an important function and, furthermore, should continue to endorse social work *as a human rights profession*. Also, to build networks that can provide support for the IFSW members working towards social change by imparting the *unique knowledge we have from community level to a national and international level*. The IFSW Representations to the United Nations (UN) Headquarters and offices foster a network with a wide range of UN Agencies (IFSW, 2019).

Imparting the unique knowledge gathered by social work from a community level to national and international levels is a key issue for the IFSW and relates to what the aforementioned pioneers called 'carefully collected information'.

For political purposes, the IFSW maintains a permanent office in Geneva from where it uses a number of approaches and procedures available to accredited NGOs at the United Nations. It submits reports, responses to consultations initiated by the UN and participates in alliance-building. As a result, it brings unique knowledge (based on research) to national and international levels. The office in Geneva comprises six people, each of whom is responsible for a certain area of interest, and migration is one of them. IFSW has a permanent representation to the UNHCR who participates in producing reports and statements.

IFSW at the Council of Europe

IFSW-Europe is present at the Council of Europe's Standing Committee (the ruling body) of the Conference of International Non-Governmental Organisations (INGOs) and, as such, coordinates the representation of the conference to all other bodies of the Council of Europe, prepares the meetings and meets on a regular basis. It also responds to acute situations of civil society organisations in distress in close cooperation with other bodies of the Council of Europe.

The membership of IFSW in the Council of Europe dates back to 1966. The IFSW participates actively in several committees, two of which are directly related to migration policies: The European Committee on Social Cohesion (which deals with migration, refugees, intercommunity relations and integration), and the UN Human Rights Committee that deals with the rights of minorities and human trafficking.

The Standing Committee issues periodic recommendations, some of which relate to migration, such as *The recommendation on climate change, migration and human rights in view of the United Nations Conference on Climate Change* (Council of Europe INGOs, 2019) *or the recommendation from the European Pillar of Social Rights* (Council of Europe, INGOs, 2018).

IFSW participation in other networks and platforms

IFSW-Europe is part of the following networks: European Social Platform, European Anti-Poverty Network, Eurochild, International Council of Social Welfare and the Platform for International Cooperation on Undocumented Migrants (PICUM), among others.

By participating in these networks and also by issuing reports, participating in common actions and/or consultation processes, IFSW is able to raise awareness on the issues it is concerned with, which most certainly include migration.

The European Union Agency for Fundamental Rights (FRA) has a specific website dedicated to migration and is particularly active in this field by issuing bulletins and reports dealing with fundamental rights (https://fra.europa.eu/en/themes/asylum-migration-and-borders).

The European Anti-Poverty Network (EAPN) comprises institutions that work directly on issues relating to migration such as the European Network Against Racism (ENAR) and PICUM. Both entities produce reports, issue recommendations and make contributions to different consultations. IFSW has been a member of EAPN since 2009 (https://www.eapn.eu/).

International Association of Schools of Social Work as a political actor

The IASSW was founded in 1928. As it explains on its website, its mission is to represent and promote social work education around the globe in partnership with national, regional and international associations. One of its aims is to 'support and facilitate participation in mutual exchanges of research and curriculum resources' and it does this not only by promoting the dissemination of knowledge and research, and celebrating biannual conferences, but also by developing a programme of small grants that promotes innovation in social work research.

One of the key features of IASSW is its commitment to 'encourage, promote and facilitate opportunities for Human Rights and Social Justice informed curricula' (www.iassw-aiets.org/concept-note-human-rights/) which is decisive in raising awareness and developing critical thinking. It achieves this through its regional branches in Asia-Pacific, Africa, North America, Latin-America and Caribbean, and Europe (there is also an association in Europe representing Nordic and Eastern European Countries).

IASSW has had consultative status as an NGO with ECOSOC since 1947 and advocates on human rights, equity, diversity and inclusion. It has a team of representatives at the UN headquarters in New York and Geneva. The team in New York regularly publishes a newsletter to explain its developments. In its role on migration and asylum, IASSW is represented by two members at the United Nations NGO Committee on Migration.

European Association of Schools of Social Work

As it states on its website (www.eassw.org/), 'EASSW brings together over 300 different schools, universities and tertiary education institutions supporting social work education'. EASSW forms part of IFSW and has representatives at its board.

EASSW has had participatory status in the Conference of INGOs of the Council of Europe since 2002 and is part of its committees for democracy, social cohesion and global challenges. It is also a member of the European Network for Social Action (ENSACT). With regard to social work research on migration, EASSW provides fora in order to disseminate research from the small projects it funds and also through its biannual conferences where migration is always on the agenda (see the Tallinn Conference held in June 2021 in which five reports relating to research on migration were presented).

Social work research associations as political actors
Society of Social Work Research

SSWR (https://secure.sswr.org/) was founded in 1994 and is based in Virginia (US). It defines itself 'as a free-standing organization dedicated to the advancement of social work research'. It represents universities, institutions and individual members and intends to raise awareness about and highlight the importance of social work research as well as promoting networking and, in its own words, 'encourages the design, implementation and dissemination of rigorous research that enhances knowledge about critical social work practice and social policy problems'.

Although some of its members are from outside the US, this organisation focuses its activism within the US, which is evidenced by reading its press releases, policy statements and sign-on letters – many of which are aimed at combating racist attitudes and white supremacism.

European Social Work Research Association

ESWRA (www.eswra.org) was founded in 2014 to create a hub for social work research development. Currently, there are 600 members in more than 33 countries. ESWRA's vision is 'to take forward the development, practice and utilization of social work research to enhance knowledge about individual and social problems, and to promote just and equitable societies'.

Consequently, ESWRA's mission is to give validity to knowledge and research to promote just and equitable societies, a very specific mission that is not shared by any of the other social work institutions with which

ESWRA expresses its willingness to cooperate – 'We will work in ways that respect and support the roles of existing European social work organizations and networks'.

In order to promote knowledge, ESWRA has developed several Special Interest Groups (SIG) that enable members to collaborate in different issues, one of which is the Special Interest Group on social work research on migration and asylum (SWIM) which aims to enhance the importance of social work research in this field.

ESWRA is registered as an association in the transparency register of the EU which allows it to interact with EU institutions and, in this regard, it has celebrated meetings with the Directorate-General for Research and Innovation. It is also a member of the European Alliance for Social Sciences and Humanities (EASSH) whose main aim is to promote learning and research in social sciences and humanities (SSH). EASSH performs efficient lobby work with policymakers and research funders at EU level in support of social sciences and humanities (https://eassh.eu/).

The impact of research on migration and asylum and the prospect of it influencing European policies is not only due to having presence on committees or issuing position papers that might have an impact; but also to the role of social work in the world of social sciences and humanities. SSH plays an important role within the whole concept of the sciences and the potential to influence.

The role of the individual, think tanks and informal research alliances

Social work organisations can be politically influential and transmit the principles and values of social work through different ways of participating in institutions, as previously mentioned. However, this is not the only way to influence policy, there also exists the possibility of prestigious social work researchers being appointed on the basis of their personal capacities to participate in expert advisory groups that exert political influence. Currently, there is not a single think tank on social work that produces research that could influence politics or transmits the views of social work.

At the EU level, informal research partnership alliances exist that consist of different universities coming together and joining other stakeholders to develop and implement projects under different funding schemes such as Horizon2020 and Horizon Europe, Erasmus+ and AMIF. While the first two schemes have a clear academic profile (Horizon, in particular, has a clear research profile), the Asylum, Migration and Integration Fund-Union Actions has a more open profile and a very specific objective, which is to strengthen EU priorities on migration and asylum policy.

Currently, it is difficult to determine to what extent the results of the projects funded under different schemes have influenced migration policy.

This is mainly because no research has been performed on the ultra-activity of projects once funding is finished and also because it is uncommon to make reference to funded projects that have served as a source of inspiration or knowledge in preparatory documents for or enacted EU legislation.

The presence of social work research in the European Commission expert advisory groups

In order to develop migration policies according to EU Treaty competences, the Commission can appoint expert groups defined as 'consultative bodies' to provide it with advice and expertise given that, 'Although the Commission has considerable in-house expertise, it needs specialist advice from outside experts as a basis for sound policy-making' (European Commission 2021). In these groups, social work could theoretically be represented by:

- Individuals appointed in a personal capacity, acting independently, and expressing their own personal views (called type A members), for example, a social work professor noted for his/her expertise in a particular topic.
- Individuals appointed to represent a common interest shared by stakeholder organisations in a particular policy area. They do not represent individual stakeholders, but a particular policy orientation common to different stakeholder organisations (type B members). For example, an individual that could be proposed by social work associations to provide the views of social work in a specific field.
- Organisations in the broad sense of the word, including companies, associations, NGOs, trade unions, universities, research institutes, law firms and consultancies (type C members). For example, FITS-Europe, EASSW, ESWRA.

There are many expert groups in the field of migration. However, in some of them the expertise comes directly from Member States and EU agencies with no representation from civil society entities or institutions. This is the case with the expert advisory groups on *Integration, Protection of Children in Migration, Search and Rescue, Reception Conditions Directive, Smuggling of Migrants* (although International Organization for Migration and United Nations High Commissioner for Refugees are also present in some of them), *Dublin III, Return Directive, Prevention and Countering Radicalisation, Right to Free Movement of Persons, Non-Discrimination,* and *Equality and Diversity*.

An analysis of the Commission's different expert advisory groups in the field of migration and asylum reveals the null presence of social work organisations and academics with a research profile in social work. Social work is only indirectly present in international platforms and networks though in a very limited way. This implies that the vision from social work research based on empathy and knowledge does not influence the orientation of migratory policy at the EU level and this may have an effect on the rights of millions of people and on how social work practitioners and academics develop their work. We will go through the different expert groups.

The contact group on legal migration

This group, whose mission is to exchange views with Member State experts on the application of EU Directives on legal migration, is formed *exclusively by representatives of the Member States.* It deals with relevant issues such as the situation of students and researchers, long-term residents and family reunification, among others. Although migration is a key issue for integration, no NGOs are members of the group. However, some stakeholders might be called punctually in cases of particular interest. So this is not a proper site where social work research exerts influence (https://ec.europa.eu/transparency/expert-groups-register/screen/expert-groups/consult?lang=en&groupID=2904).

The expert group on the views of migrants in the field of migration, asylum and integration

The mission of this expert group is to provide advice and expertise on policies in the field of migration, asylum and integration of migrants. The Commission considers that actively involving migrants, including asylum applicants and refugees, in the design and implementation of policies in this field is essential to make them more effective and better tailored to the needs on the ground. This group is much more diverse in its composition as there are nine individual experts appointed in their personal capacities (type A members), none of which are social workers, three individual experts appointed as representatives of a common interest (type B members) (none of which are social workers) and 12 NGOs (IFSW, EASSH and ESWRA are not represented). So, in this expert group that ideally would have lots to say on migration and asylum policies, social work research is also absent https://ec.europa.eu/transparency/expert-groups-register/screen/expert-groups/consult?lang=en&groupID=3734).

The expert group on economic migration

The aim of this group is also key in the drafting of migration policies as it intends to support the future policy development in the field of economic migration. This group comprises four individual experts appointed for their personal capacity, three of whom are researchers (but not in social work). There are also 14 organisations (trade unions, law firms, expert in human resources) and also research institutions (University of Oxford, Forum Internazionale ed

Europeo di Ricerche sull'Immigrazione and Migration Policy Institute Europe), none of which are directly related to social work, but to political science, anthropology and sociology (https://ec.europa.eu/transparency/expert-groups-register/screen/expert-groups/consult?lang=en&groupID=3253).

EU High Level Group on combating racism, xenophobia and other forms of intolerance

The aim of this group is to foster the further exchange and dissemination of good practices between national authorities and concrete discussions on how to fill existing gaps and better prevent and combat racism, xenophobia hate crime and hate speech.

The members comprise five organisations from the 27 Member States and three other public entities including the European Union Agency for Fundamental Rights of which the IFSW is a member. No social work organisation participates directly in this group (www.eumonitor.eu/9353000/1/j9vvik7m1c3gyxp/vk66hki61cxo).

A way forward

Perhaps the easiest and most intuitive conclusion to be extracted from reading this chapter would be that social work research has up to this point had little influence on EU migration policy and that this is not by chance. There are structural, cultural and academic elements that play against this and make the drive towards policy influence to seem more aspirational than actual. However, this inertia is not inevitable not irreversible. The following are five key elements of a critical framework and a corollary that can smooth the path towards more impact and influence of social work research

Critical thinking

For social work to be influential, social workers need to be aware of reality and possess a deeply entrenched critical consciousness and a strong commitment towards change and this does not come once and for all. It requires time, patience and context so that their critical framework can be developed.

Rediscovering social work values

Academia, public institutions and organisations can play a crucial role by promoting critical awareness based on empathy and knowledge in students and practitioners. To this end, many need to revise their academic and organisational cultures as well as the contents they teach so that they don't reproduce unquestioned hegemonic assumptions and managerial practices.

From residual to structural: migration contents in academia

Migration is a complex issue and, according to experts, is not sufficiently present in the content of academic curricula or in the skills and competences that are taught. In many cases, this means that social workers have to learn on the job and this has a clear impact on research. So it would be desirable that migration leaves residual spaces in academia and stop being placed in 'the corner of peculiarities'.

Leaving comfort zones and research bubbles: a true challenge

In order to stop migration research from becoming limited to academic bubbles, congresses, high impact factor journals and seminars, it is important that academic institutions balance the influence of research with the influence of practice and encourage the presence and participation of users (in this case immigrants) in an active and not tokenistic manner.

Social work is (always) political work

It is important to raise consciousness of the importance of social work in politics and the role of social workers as political actors. Although institutions like the IFSW are making important strides towards raising awareness about social work as a human rights profession and social workers as actors of social transformation, this information has little impact on academia and institutions. In much teaching, research and intervention environments, the image that prevails is one that focuses on child protection, casework or community work rather than the image of social workers as political actors. It is also imperative that the advocacy work undertaken by social work institutions such as the IASSW and IFSW becomes more visible and impactful. The increasing visibility of institutions such as ESWRA is helping to provide social work research in international environments. However, social work research is still missing at consultation and decision-making levels in migration policies.

As a corollary I would like to conclude by saying that the spirit that energised social work pioneers such as Jane Addams and Mary Richmond to act and challenge unjust narratives is still a prospect for social work research if the previous five key elements are implemented.

References

Addams, J. (1910, 2010) *Twenty Years at Hull House*, London: Signet Classics, Penguin.

Banks, S. (2012) *Ethics and Values in Social Work* (4th edn), Basingstoke: Palgrave Macmillan Education.

Beresford, P. and Boxall, K. (2012) 'Service users, social work education and knowledge for social work practice', *Social Work Education*, 31(2): 155–67.

Boccagni, P. and Righard, E. (2020) 'Social work with refugee and displaced populations in Europe: (Dis)continuities, dilemmas, developments', *European Journal of Social Work*, 239(3): 375–83.

Brick, J. (2009) *Academic Culture: A Student's Guide to Studying at University*, London: Bloomsbury.

Chen, G.M. and Starosta, W. (1996) 'Intercultural communication competence: A synthesis', *Annals of the International Communication Association*, 19(1): 353–83.

Council of Europe (2018) Recommendation relating to the proclamation of the European Pillar of Social Rights adopted by the Conference of INGOs on 24 January 2018, CONF/PLE(2018)REC1. https://rm.coe.int/recommendation-2018-1-european-pillar-social-rights-en/168077dcf7

Council of Europe (2019) Recommendation on climate change, migration and human rights in view of the United Nations Conference on Climate Change (COP25) to be held in Santiago de Chile from 2 to 13 December 2019. Adopted by the Conference of INGOs on 30 October 2019. CONF/PLE(2019)REC4. https://rm.coe.int/conf-ple-2019-rec4-climate-change-en/1680989f56

Cummins, I. (2018) *Poverty, Inequality and Social Work: The Impact of Neoliberalism and Austerity Policies on Welfare Provision*, Bristol: Policy Press.

Di Rosa, R.T., Mordeglia, S. and Argento, G. (2019) 'Social work and welfare system in Italy: Changes, critical issues and resiliencies', in A. López Peláez and E.J. Gómez-Ciriano (eds) *Austerity, Social Work and Welfare Policies: A Global Perspective*. Cizur Manor: Thomson-Reuters Aranzadi, pp 111–36.

European Union (2021) EU treaties. https://europa.eu/european-union/law/treaties_en

Fawcett, J.T. (1989) 'Networks, linkages, and migration systems', *The International Migration Review*, 23(3): 671–80.

Gal, J. and Weiss-Gal, I. (2017) *Where Academia and Policy Meet: A Cross National Perspective on the Involvement of Social Work Academics in Social Policy*, Bristol: Policy Press.

IFSW (International Federation of Social Workers) (2019) 'UN commission representation to the UN: Objective, structure, function and guidelines'. www.ifsw.org/wp-content/uploads/2019/11/2019_FINAL_UN-Commission_Guideline.pdf

Kolahowsky, L. (1975) 'Neutrality and academic values', in A. Montefiore (ed) *Neutrality and Impartiality: The University and Political Commitment*, Cambridge: Cambridge University Press, pp 49–71.

Levinas, E. (1985) *Ethics and Infinity: Conversations with Philippe Nemo*, Pittsburgh, PA: Duquesne University Press.

Limbery, M. and Butler, S. (2004) *Social Work Ideals and Practical Realities*, New York: Palgrave.
Marin, L. (1975) '"Le neuter" and philosophical discourse', in A. Montefiore (ed) *Neutrality and Impartiality: The University and Political Commitment*, Cambridge: Cambridge University Press, pp 72–85.
Masocha, S. (2015) 'Construction of the "other" in social workers' discourses of asylum seekers, *Journal of Social Work*, 15(6): 569–85.
McLaughlin, H. (2009) *Service User Research in Health and Social Care*, London: Sage.
McLaughlin, H. (2012) *Understanding Social Work Research* (2nd edn), London: Sage.
McLaughlin, H. and Teater, B. (2017) *Evidence- Informed Practice for Social Workers*, London: Open University Press.
McRoy, R., Flanzer, J.P. and Zlotnic, J.L. (2012) *Building Research Culture and Infrastructure*, New York: Oxford University Press.
Morley, C., Le, C. and Briksman, C. (2020) 'The role of critical social work education in improving ethical practice with refugees and asylum seekers', *Social Work Education*, 39(4): 103–16.
Palinkas, L.A. and Soydan, H. (2012) *Translation and Implementation of Evidence-based Practice*, Oxford: Oxford University Press.
Pawson, R., Boaz, A., Grayson, L., Long, A. and Barnes, C. (2003) *Types and Knowledge in Social Care*, London: SCIE.
Ravasi, D. and Schultz, M. (2006) 'Responding to organizational identity threats: Exploring the role of organizational culture', *Academy of Management Journal*, 49(3): 433–58.
Robinson, K. and Masocha, S. (2017) 'Divergent practices in statutory and voluntary-sector settings? Social work with asylum seekers', *British Journal of Social Work*, 47(5): 1517–33.
Schrodt, P. (2002) 'The relationship between organisational identification and organisational culture: Employee perceptions of culture and identification in a retail sales organisation', *Communication Studies*, 53(2): 189.
Teater, B. (2017) 'Social work research and its relevance to practice: "The gap between research and practice continues to be wide"', *Journal of Social Service Research*, 43(5): 547–65.
Tervalon, M. and Murray-Garcia, J. (1998) 'Cultural humility versus cultural competence: A critical distinction in defining physician training outcomes in multicultural education', *Journal of Health Care for the Poor and Underserved*, 9: 117–25.
Van Ewijk, H. (2010) *European Social Policy and Social Work: Citizenship Based Social Work*, London: Routledge.
Zaviršek, D. (2017) 'The humanitarian crisis of migration versus the crisis of humanitarianism: Current dimensions and challenges for social work practice', *Social Work Education*, 36(3): 231–44.

2

Participatory art in social work: from humanitarianism to humanisation of people on the move

Darja Zaviršek

Introduction

This chapter suggests that art, and participatory art in particular, can be used as an important perspective in social work education and practice to reach social work students and social workers in the context of the increasing invisibilisation and ghettoisation of migrant people.

Since the COVID-19 pandemic, we are confronted with a paradox: the issue of refugees has been marginalised, while wars and environmental disasters continue and millions of people who have migrated are held back on the Southeastern European periphery. Some countries have institutionalised push-back at their national borders.[1] At the same time, a number of artists, critical conceptual architects and cartoonists are addressing the issue of migration and depicting the lives of people who would otherwise remain unheard and dehumanised. They show how migration has become part of everyday life; many art projects involve in their performances and art work real migrants as the non-actors, aimed at demonstrating the increased degree of the conflicts related to migration and to bring the issue as close as possible to the viewers as a counter response to the increased anti-refugee sentiment.

The transdisciplinary approach aims to move beyond the discourse of 'humanitarian crises' towards the humanisation of people on the move.

Methodology

In the first part of the chapter, my autobiographical notes will alternate with interpretive guidelines to reflect on my own interest in writing about migration. A growing number of researchers studying migration have begun to use autobiography and autoethnography to 'stay in the text' and document the degrading conditions of people who migrate (Run, 2012; Holman et al, 2013). Their self-reflections highlight that researchers often experienced similar traumatic conditions to activists and people on the move themselves (Zorn, 2021). A social work educator told me, "I do not like going to fieldwork with the students, it's like being in a war zone" (personal communication, 2021). Refugees also said that crossing the border was similar to experiencing another war (Zaviršek, 2017). The language of war was repeated in the narratives of people situated in different places for monitoring and administration. Migrants referred to the resettlement centres as 'concentration camps', and the Italian reception centre on Lampedusa, where hundreds were housed in small rooms, was described as 'Italian Guantanamo' (Videmšek, 2016). Documenting the experiences of the 'undocumented' is also part of political social work, which has a marginal place among social workers in Southeast European countries.

The second part of the chapter presents selected examples of my original thematic and conceptual search for art projects, cartoons, documentaries and architectural projects on migration. I was particularly interested in the works of Slovenian artists working on the European periphery, whose works, with few exceptions, are hardly known to the international public. Various art formats and conceptual architecture could become important in social work education, especially in the field of migration. They are not only presentations of creative ideas, pieces of uniqueness and intellectual brilliance, but also of political thoughts that conceptually challenge the way people with a migration background are treated and thus transcend existing welfare state humanitarianism. They could additionally help social workers achieve epistemological flexibility in social work thinking and work with people on the run.

Conceptualising migration through embodied reflexivity

In Southeastern Europe, the humanitarian corridor (the so-called Balkan refugee route)[2] and the *Willkommenskultur*, as it was called by the then German Chancellor Merkel, created a unique window of time for migrants (Zorn, 2016; Buchanan and Kallinikaki, 2020) that soon came to an end. The countries of Southeastern Europe demonstrated high levels of racism and xenophobia (Zaviršek, 2017b, Zaviršek and Rajgelj, 2019; Berc, 2019; Bornarova, 2019). Since then, border security has increased by military patrols along the borders; walls and barbed wire fences erected; while the police and military practice violent push-backs. It is worth noting that in 2017, when the Slovenian Ministry of Interior attempted to institutionalise push-backs and actually erected new fences on the borders, the country had a Liberal Democrat government. During the same period the so-called 'reorganisation' of social care services was completed and social workers were in the worst situation since the 1980s–underfunded, bureaucratised, with no training opportunities or oversight and under constant attack from

Figure 2.1: Marko Kočevar, EU flag, 2015

Source: Reprinted with the permission of the author

the media (Rape et al, 2019). This situation only worsened in 2020, when a right-wing government came to power.

The institutionalisation and spatial segregation of refugees, the programmatic fomentation of racism and xenophobia among the local population by governments and state media have become daily practice. Political cartoonist Marko Kočevar published several cartoons in Slovenia's largest daily newspaper *Delo* in December 2015 that captured the transition from welcoming policies to treatment of refugees as a security threat.

The cartoons in Figures 2.1, 2.2 and 2.3 depict the European Union and its citizens surrounded by barbed wire as a symbol of the expansion of the security discourse. Shortly after the cartoons were published, the Slovenian government erected wired fences along parts of Slovenia's borders. In one of his cartoons, Kočevar used the slogan that has been used to promote Slovenian tourism, 'I feel Slovenia', to point out the ambivalence: the beautiful, open, and 'ecological' country for some, surrounded by fences for others. The cartoons broke the 'grand narrative' of the green landscape with friendly people and put the issue of migration at the centre of social interest.

With few exceptions, social workers in the public services remained silent, even when they were asked to take action when the unaccompanied children were encountered crossing the border (Bornarova, 2019; Zaviršek and Rajgelj, 2019). No wonder the government's strategy was to make migration a national security issue and make the stories of individuals

Figure 2.2: Marko Kočevar, Fences, 2015

Source: Reprinted with the permission of the author

Figure 2.3: Marko Kočevar, 'I feel Slovenia', 2015

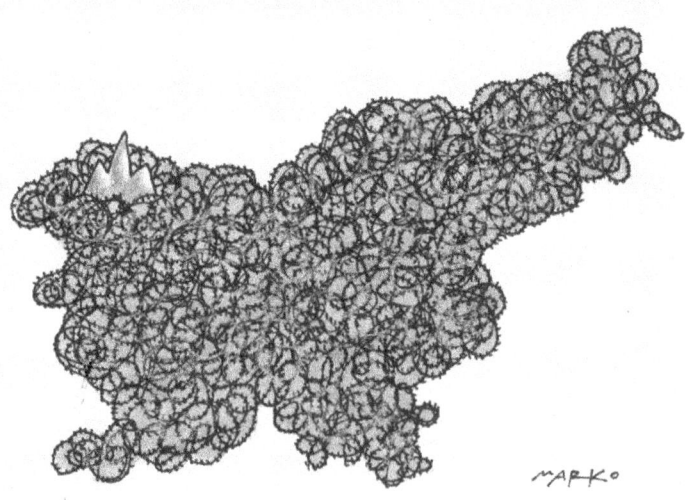

Source: Reprinted with the permission of the author

invisible. Social work generally has a weak political voice in the Southeast European post-socialist countries, and see themselves mainly as administrative and humanitarian workers. They are primarily dependent on government expectations of their work, and are based mainly in government services, but also partly in government-funded non-governmental social services. After 2017, when government discourse used anti-refugee rhetoric and countries such as Poland and Hungary rejected the EU refugee relocation system, Balkan countries also became more assertive about securing borders and common practices of forcible push-back (Zaviršek and Rajgelj, 2019).

It is during the height of the Balkan refugee route that I became interested in the phenomenon, which I initially perceived as a humanitarian crisis. I decided to document it from a safe academic place, and only later realised that what I was documenting was the crisis of humanitarianism; I was able to grasp some dimensions of what was officially called the 'migration crisis' based on my previous experiences of working with people labelled as disabled and people who had survived for a long time in socialist and post-socialist asylums.

As a Foucault scholar, I realised that I was facing another 'great confinement'. This time it was not the poor, disabled, and 'moral degenerates' who had been sent to prison-like administrative facilities since the late 18th century, but people on the run with no face and no personal history. I was used to researching, engaging with, befriending, and advocating for people with long-term disabilities who had been forcibly administered, incarcerated, and dehumanised since 1988 (Zaviršek, 2000, 2015, 2017a). In 2015 and 2016, temporary refugee camps and shelters set up at borders or on the periphery of major European cities, registration hotspots, resettlement centres, were mostly new facilities in Europe. The parallel between the great confinement and institutionalisation of people who migrated was almost self-evident. In both cases, they sang in spatially segregated, highly controlled, depersonalised, and silenced areas. I was reminded of the programmatic words of Foucault (1961/2006: 6): 'The game of exclusion would be played again, often in the same places, in a strangely similar way. ... The role of the leper would be played by the poor and the tramps, by the prisoners and the "alienated."'

From a Foucauldian perspective, I have followed how former hospitals for the incurable became military barracks, military barracks became asylums for the disabled and insane, and former psychiatric hospitals became centres for migrant registration and resettlement. They all must be simply invisible. People with social and physical disabilities have been forced to live in segregated places, excluded from society and taken in as 'people of no importance'[3] for a permanent period of time. For refugees, these places are presumably temporary ways of living that often-become the places of 'permanent temporaneity' (Hilal and Petti, 2021). Hilal and Petti (2021) raised the question of whether a camp has architecture and suggested that the Dheisheh refugee camp should be included in the World Heritage List of UNESCO. They claimed that one of the oldest camps (since 1949) meets the conditions for inclusion in the UNESCO heritage because it embodies the memory of the Nakba and at the same time is an expression of an exceptional spatial, social and political form.[4] People who live in the camp keep alive the belief in the right of return and are the memory-carriers.

I knew that the border regime, anti-refugee sentiment and violent humanism were wrong. But it was only when Franco 'Bifo' Berardi (2017), public intellectual, writer and media activist, addressed this – specifically referring to the situation in Eastern Europe – that I was able to place it in the temporal framework and understand the lost momentum:

> In the last twenty-five years (since a ship loaded with 26,000 Albanians entered the port of Brindisi in February 1991), we have known that the great migration had begun. At that point, two paths were possible. The opening of the borders, the beginning of a global distribution of resources, the investment of wealth in a lengthy process of reception and integration of the young people coming *en masse* across the sea. This was the first way. The second was to reject, discourage and make almost impossible the easy journey from Northern Africa to the shores of Spain, Italy and Greece. Europeans chose the second way, and every day countless children, women and men drown. Auschwitz on the beach.[5]

Berardi showed that the fragmentation of the social body was a long process that began almost invisibly before it became institutionalised and part of the new European normal. As Foucault (1988/2008) has shown that biopolitics, as a new technology of sovereign power, gradually created different 'populations' since the 17th century and took control of their lives, a new 'population' was created in the 21st century to manage and classify. Biological life and socio-political life are continually separated. Foucault's 'political culture of danger' (2008: 67) is no longer populated by madmen and cripples, but by migrants, asylum seekers, refugees and illegals. When I entered the asylum centre in Ljubljana, I was surrounded by numerous people who – as in the asylums for the disabled and the 'mentally ill' in Slovenia – told me at the same time that the food was bad, cold and insufficient, that the staff was abusive and that their movement was restricted. I visited the social workers' office; it was like entering another world, and different stories awaited me in a reserved and polite atmosphere. The social workers spoke in the language of power, while the 'subjects in exile' (Hilal and Petti, 2021: 35) used the language of 'people without importance'.

After the end of the humanitarian corridor, the situation worsened year by year both for the migrants and for those who offered support (volunteers, social workers, activists). In order to escape Eurodac fingerprints regulation[6] and push-backs, hundreds of migrants were accommodated in abandoned factories in the Balkans during the day and spent nights in the so-called jungle settlement in a forest even in winter (Završek and Rajgelj, 2019). The international NGO 'Moving Europe' and Human Rights Watch have been documenting violent push-backs of undocumented migrants at the Croatian and Serbian borders since 2016 (HRW, 2017; HRW, 2019; Gall, 2020).

The famous Chinese artist Ai Weiwei highlighted the brutality of border regimes with a series of installations in European metropolises such as London, Berlin and Vienna, where he displayed thousands of used life jackets from people who had crossed the Mediterranean Sea to reach European shores, many of whom died.[7] He used them to cover the concrete pillars of the countries' most important buildings and floated them like ribbon flowers on the surface of artificial lakes. His artwork showed how various practices of governmentality that are considered non-military (detention and asylum centres), pacifist (legal procedures for granting legal status), contractual (refugee status), and legal (deportation) are in fact part of the apparatuses of war, as Foucault wrote, 'We are always writing the history of the same war, even as we write the history of peace and its institutions' (Foucault, 1997: 16).

Ai Weiwei's conceptual installations are political critiques and a plea for the humanisation of people on the run. The life jackets shocked viewers by their large number of 14,000 pieces. The artist was able to use artificial material and paintings to create an aesthetic and visual effect. However, the emotional impact created by the dirty, used life jackets was potentially transformative, reminding viewers of real people.

In his short documentary 'Borders' (*Meje*), Damjan Kozole (2016) followed people crossing the Slovenian border from Croatia along the humanitarian corridor by documenting the dehumanising nature of the European asylum regime.[8] Escorted by police on horses, wrapped in clothes and blankets, with children and bags in hand, thousands struggled to reach one of their desired destinations in Western Europe. Exhausted from walking and waiting at various borders, they focused on the moment when the police would allow them to cross another border. They were a crowd without a history.

Erik Valenčič's film 'Seeing El Aaiun' (Videti Ai Aaiun, 2019)[9] addresses another 'permanent temporaneity' while capturing the lives of people in one of the largest refugee camps in Western Sahara (since 1975), a territory in northwest Africa, bordered by Morocco, Algeria, Mauritania and the Atlantic Ocean. Two-thirds of Sahrawi territory was occupied by Morocco, and the refugee camp was established by Sahrawi refugees fleeing the Moroccan military forces. Thousands of people were killed and many fled to Algeria; some fought by the Sahrawi Polisario Front until 1991. To this day there is no peace for the 174,000 people who live in the area.[10] The film shows how the refugee camp became a city and a state at the same time and so it became an educational tool to inform social workers and social work students about the existence of 'people of no importance', especially when international collaboration is not part of social work curriculum. Social work educators and social work students from the Carinthia University of Applied Science established an exceptional cooperation with the University of Tifariti, the first university located in a refugee camp (Höllmüller, 2021). Funded by the Austrian National Agency young Sahrawi academics met with social work students and educators from Austria in both places, in West Sahara and in Carinthia. The ongoing collaboration focuses on the common social work issues: children's wellbeing, disabled people, parental divorce and the issues of political engagement and democratic values (Höllmüller, 2021: 184).

Epistemological flexibility

There is no doubt that social work education and practice are caught up in nationalist discourses, as well as in being loyal government/local authority employees. Therefore, it is the biggest accomplishment during social work training that the students learn to 'humanize people on the run' instead of viewing them as people 'of no importance'.

The bureaucratic mandate to manage people at the borders, in the refugee camps, in the asylum and deportation centres has become so powerful that it turns people into non-persons in the first place, *the figures*, to recall Primo Levi (1986/2013). Levi showed that the successful administration of the concentration camps and the systematic extermination of the imprisoned was only possible through the ideological and actual systematic and total depersonalisation of human beings, who were de-humanised and had only what Agamben (2002) called biological life (bare life). How, then, can we achieve dialogic learning to enable students and social work practitioners to grasp the importance of epistemological flexibility in the field of migration?

One of the challenges which I call epistemological flexibility is to understand the border and border regimes and the different statuses of migrant people as both real and constructed. Moving back and forth along the line of dominant normativity towards awareness of its constructiveness is the precondition for humanising people who migrate. In the processes of granting people legal status instead of their bare lives, they acquire statuses, both real and constructed. These serve classificatory normativity (like the diagnosis of disability), while fragmenting the human field. They are real and construct a normatively accepted 'objectivity'.

As legitimate defenders of the constructed nation-state (Anderson, 1995) would argue, borders are both fictional and real when they restrict the movement of people. They are naturalised as they co-produce the refugees as a 'population'; people are divided into 'entitled' and 'unentitled', economic and political migrants, those who are granted asylum, have temporary status, or are illegal. Refugee camps, asylum centres, and detention centres are not neutral sites; rather, they are political sites of dehumanisation where the nation-state, with different administrative procedures, includes what should become part of the whole and excludes that which should remain outside it in order to preserve the ideal of national homogeneity. Can social workers imagine a political community beyond the idea of the nation-state, 'a state without a nation' (Žižek, 1993 in: Irwin, 2019: 21)?

The architecture of division and the biopolitical fragmentation of the social sphere (Foucault, 2015 [2004]) is repeated and reproduced in different times, contexts, and places. 'Injustice is a bodily experience: it stinks', as Hilal and Petti write in their Refugee Heritage Project (2021: 38). It is the smell that is remembered in these segregated places, the smell of bondage and dehumanisation. The smell becomes an oppressive sign that tells us we are in a place outside of everyday life, the non-place; 'I was constantly fighting the smell of the wards, which ate into my skin and soaked my clothes', I wrote in my ethnographic diary when I worked as a researcher in an institution for the mentally disabled in Slovenia (Zaviršek, 2015: 123). Being a refugee is an extreme physical experience: people run through forests, cross rivers and go by boat, swim, hide, get beaten up, suffer hunger and thirst, and have no shelter.

Humanising people on the move therefore involves going beyond the humanitarianism of social work and seeing people who migrate as subjects who have the universal right to live ordinary lives, which most countries of Southeast Europe rejected. The need of epistemological flexibility might be more easily achieved by using art, film, and architecture to reach students and expand their empathy.

Participatory art in social work

Participatory art can be useful for thinking about social work theory and practise. The use of art in social work offers a transdisciplinary approach in which professionals from different disciplines bring their knowledge together to find new responses to complex situations. Transdisciplinarity is not just about combining additional knowledge with existing knowledge, but rather about transforming knowledge from a particular professional field into more complex knowledge that provides a more holistic understanding of human problems. It brings together theories, research and practical knowledge from different disciplines and transcends the theoretical, epistemological and practical boundaries of a discipline; it generates new knowledge, creates synthesis, and goes beyond traditional problem solving and division of science into 'pure' disciplines. Self-evident hierarchies are challenged (for example, medical professionals who are said to have 'hard', that is, quantitative, data versus social workers who are said to have 'soft', that is, qualitative, data). This allows for more efficient problem solving and knowledge transfer from researchers to policy makers, and ultimately better translation of theory into practice. Participatory arts can help social work achieve a new reflexivity in thought and action. Both disciplines, I argue, have much in common and can provide a transdisciplinary basis for more in-depth understanding people with a migration background.

Participatory art involves the participation of a larger number of people (non-actors) who become the 'art material' and its central component; it focuses on the 'social' and sees the process as more important than the final image or object (Bishop, 2012). Participatory art depends on the direct experience of those who participate in it, and may have a long-lasting effect. Its beginning and end cannot be precisely determined.

The theatre director Žiga Divjak has staged two plays in which people with a migration background participated as non-actors and became part of the artistic documentation. One, entitled 'Six' (Šest) 2018, recalled real events in the small town of Kranj, where six unaccompanied minors were to be placed in a student dormitory. The racist reactions of the local population, Slovenian parents whose children lived in the same dormitory, and local politicians led to an orchestrated anti-refugees' reaction of rejection and hatred against the six minors.

The young unaccompanied refugees were partially involved in the process of creating the play and performed on stage, which was an encouraging event. For the theatre-goers, the play was an opportunity for identification; the six young people could be you or me, my children or someone in the neighbourhood. Aside from the emotional impact, which required raising awareness, the play also documented and critiqued a strong anti-refugee sentiment among locals in Slovenia. "This may be naïve, but I insist that the only way to connect with the community is to acknowledge the problems of others as our own," Divjak said (Butala, 2020).

In his last play, 'Gejm' (The Game) from 2020, he showed the brutality of push-backs at the borders of European Union (Bosnian-Croatian and Croatian-Slovenian borders). People on the move call the crossing of this territory 'the game' (colloquially 'gejm'), expressing the arbitrary procedures at the borders, where forcible push-back prevents people from applying for asylum; it also has the function of discouraging the next group of people to come. 'Everything depends on luck', it says, who is the policeman or the customer at the border that day. Many people have been pushed back several times; then they return to Bosnia or Croatia, only to try their 'luck' another day. Most of the people on the run are injured, beaten up, hungry and lacking clothes. The play is based on actual reports from the International Human Rights Organisation. Divjak himself visited the places where people are hiding and recorded their testimonies, which were incorporated into the play. On the theatre stage, the narratives of individual people are aestheticised through the artistic use of language and objects and become brutally real in their ethnographic factography. Tattered clothes, empty plastic bottles, shoes, first aid equipment, leftover food are the objects of survival and the only possessions of the people on the run. They become part of the art and theatre backdrop as well as a visible document of unjust treatment.

Participatory art is not moralising and does not seek to 'lecture' as social work education does. It is primarily an opportunity to have emotional experiences that students often lack and that can change attitudes about thinking and acting.

For participatory art, as for social work, 'invisible' processes such as group dynamics, transfer situations and awareness raising are important. The artist is understood as a 'collaborator and producer of situations', and the audience, once made up of spectators and observers, becomes co-creators and contributors (Bishop, 2012). The parallel development in postmodern principles of social work is reflected in the processes of co-creation, enhancing user perspective and power sharing and in postcolonial social work (Ramon, 2003; Dominelli, 2010; Luluquisen and Pettis, 2014; Ostrander et al, 2017; Kleibl et al, 2019).

The beginnings of participatory art date back to the early twentieth century, the period after the October Revolution, when the Bolsheviks restaged the Winter Palace storm, the Dadaist interventions and the Futurist serrates came into being (Bishop, 2012: 9). Within the student movement from the late 1960s, art projects engaged with dictatorships, military hunts and communism. 'Delegated performances' (where non-actors were staged to meet the needs of the artist) and educational projects that were part of educational activities and objectives became part of participatory art. In the 1990s, artists' interest in collaborating with audiences, society and collectives increased dramatically, and participatory artists were in constant dialogue with everyday life and real people, which is why performances were sometimes referred to as community art.

In 2000, the well-known German film director and artist Christoph Schlingensief (1960–2010) carried out a highly acclaimed project criticising xenophobia in Austria, which is one of the best examples of participatory art entitled 'Please Love Austria!' (Bishop, 2012: 333). The artist was invited to Vienna to create a work for the Vienna Day of Celebration. He decided to respond to the recent electoral successes of the far-right FPOe (Austrian right-wing party) led by Jorg Haider; party members used xenophobic and racist slogans such as the word *Überfremdung*, used by the Nazis to describe a country overrun by foreigners. Schlingensief set up a container in the middle of the city of Vienna with real asylum seekers (non-actors) who were watched by the audience at home on their TV screens. The audience could participate during the spectacle and vote via webfreetv.com who of the asylum seekers should not be granted asylum and deported, similar to a reality show. During the performance, Schliengensief shouted various contradictory slogans into the megaphone from the roof of the container. Some slogans had racist content, so much so that one far-right supporter even expressed satisfaction that the performance ended up speaking for himself. In contrast, some left-wing spectators were disgusted and even tried to destroy the container. The artist's provocation was a critique of xenophobia and institutional racism in Austria. Throughout the performance, Schliengensief divided the audience, angering some, fascinating others, and pointing out the many paradoxes of modern societies. One of them was that the container caused more excitement among some people than the actual existence of deportation centres. Its provocation aimed to divide people and stimulated reflection on how populist slogans work. Schliengersief's notion of 'undemocratic behaviour' actually pointed to modern virtual democracy, to democracy as a reality show.

Thus, participatory art constantly criticises unjust society, addresses consumer capitalism, totalitarianisms and military dictatorships that have led to the alienation and depoliticisation of people. Schliengersief's performance sought to address these processes by activating the audience and inviting the engagement of people, who responded differently and sometimes in ways they themselves did not expect; discomfort, shock and sometimes transformation were part of the experience.

Again, various themes of community and self-reflection are part of critical social work which also addresses the devastating consequences of global capitalism and, like participatory art, emphasises the importance of human relationships. Both social work and participatory art are about creating community (Pease and Fook, 1999; Roose et al, 2014). In participatory art, people are no longer passive observers who merely look at art objects, but are part of the artistic process and its practise. Just as social work is concerned with helping people who, for one reason or another, have lost social ties and support networks (Moreau, 1990; Healy, 2001), participatory art works to restore social ties. Just as an artist is no longer only interested in the passive process between the exhibited object and the viewer because it is a commercialised relationship determined by capital, critical social work is not only interested in the classic 'helping' of the individual, but in empowering and changing social inequalities (Ward and Mullender, 1991; Ramon, 2003; Dominelli, 2010; Kallinikaki, 2019; Karlsson and Jönsson, 2020). Consumer fragmentation, individualism, anomie, which create an ever-increasing social anaesthesia, reflected in part in the way social workers distance themselves from migration issues in Southeast Europe, are the focus of both participatory art and critical social work.

Feldman (1996) refers to 'cultural anaesthesia' as a state in which people do not want to hear, and cannot hear, the experiences of violence and suffering of others. Even at the collective level, people are unable to confront and endure the pain of others. Feldman bases his analysis on Adorno's theory when he shows that during the Holocaust, the objectification of the 'other' was the precondition for inflicting pain on another person (Horkheimer and Adorno, 1973). Today, the 'institutional anaesthesia' in relation to migration can be seen in the disinterest of social work in the topic of migration, which sees migration as a problem of nation-state protection and not as a human rights issue.

In 2016, Ai Weiwei brought a large piano to the Idomeni refugee centre on the border between Greece and Macedonia; Nour Al Khzam, a refugee from Syria, one of thousands waiting at the border to continue their journey to the West, played it. The presence of the artist, the white piano and the plastic sheet improvised because of the rain made the whole event a performance, an almost artistic moment with the non-actors and empowerment at the same time. Ai Weiwei himself said that it was not about the performance and not about the concert, but about life itself.[11]

The event was a political story in the language of art; Ai Weiwei wanted to draw attention to the inhumane events at the borders and in a large refugee camp, and the event fractured the stereotype of poor and uneducated refugees. The girl at the piano individualised and personified 'the refugee' and triggered empathy and compassion. The question is whether more similar events and images might encourage social work students and practitioners to become more involved in critical social work in the area of migration.

Social workers themselves sometimes use art techniques to engage and personify people 'with no importance' (Huss et al, 2021). Greek volunteers and social work activists used the method of memory work to engage with children in the Idomeni refugee camp in 2016. They encouraged children at the border to draw self-portraits, which were then plasticised and returned to the children (personal communication from Prof. Theano Kallinikaki, May 2016). The portraits were intended to be a stored memory of a child on the move at a time when they had no possessions, and their personal history of crossing borders and countries was at risk of being erased. The portraits could help the child connect the lived parts of chaotic events during an undocumented journey. Memory work helps children survive the monotony and horror of the overcrowded camp in Idomeni. It is also political and subversive to the politics of humanitarian aid in the crisis, as the children were asked not to write down names of cities, countries or borders they knew or had crossed, to ensure that the data could not be used as documentation in the dehumanising bureaucratic system.

The ongoing project The State in Time by the Slovenian artist group IRWIN, part of the larger art collective Neue Slowenische Kunst (NSK), addressed the issues of the state and statelessness as early as 1992. NSK was founded in the last years of socialist Yugoslavia and criticised the authoritarian system in a way that used the totalitarian symbolism of various authoritarian systems. The large posters (Figures 2.4 and 2.5), which were hung in various cities and countries around the world for several years, carried the text: 'Time for a new state. Some say you can find happiness there' (Irwin, 2019). The exhibitions in real places outside museums and galleries were a critique of the authoritarian socialist state, a critique of ethnic wars (primarily in former Yugoslavia) based on the original fantasy of an exclusive mono-ethnic place, and a critique of the exclusive concept of citizenship.

Figure 2.4: IRWIN, State in Time, Lagos, 2010

Source: Courtesy Galerija Gregor Podnar; reproduced with the permission of the artists

Figure 2.5: IRWIN, State in Time, London, 2012

Source: Photo: Wig Worland; courtesy Galerija Gregor Podnar; reproduced with the permission of the artists

The posters were accompanied by participatory art performances called 'NSK passport'. During the performance, the artists invited people to become NSK passport holders, citizens of a new imaginable state without geographical territory:[12] 'The passport holder thus finds himself a member of a virtual state whose tangible presence is a passport that looks like a real passport (and is even printed with official machinery and materials of the Slovenian state)' (Westerman, 2019: 110). Since 1992, NSK passport holders have been mostly artists, for whom the NSK passport was an art object (Figure 2.6). Yet, for some people it was more than just an art object; some described their experiences as NSK passport holders and events of actual border crossings; one man crossed the border from Slovenia to Croatia during the period of political chaos after the disintegration of Yugoslavia, another man entered Korea with it when he was without a visa (Westerman, 2019: 103).

In 2004, when the number of migrants from African countries to Europe began to increase, the NSK passport project was put into action by those who needed a valid passport and visa out of need and hope for a better future:

> Suddenly, thousands of NSK passport applications arrived at the NSK headquarters in Ljubljana from the African state of Nigeria, especially from the densely populated metropolitan region of Ibadan. For the Nigerian users, the NSK passport was not understood as an art object, but as a legitimising form of self-identification and self-registration.

Figure 2.6: NSK passport holders, London, 2007

Source: Photo: Haris Hararis; reproduced with the permission of the artists

Some of the NSK passport holders from Nigeria later said in an interview that they have 'heard' that NSK was a beautiful country and wanted to travel there. Slovenian embassies in the region were inundated with calls from these new NSK citizens asking questions about visas and their citizenship rights. Eventually, the situation went so far that the Slovenian Ministry of Foreign Affairs asked NSK members to draft a statement clearly stating that 'NSK is not a "real" state, but an "art" state' and that the NSK passport is not a valid document for crossing state borders or applying for visa. (Čufer, 2019: 144)

While the project criticised the state (either the authoritarian or the violent and exclusionary state) and emphasised the importance of the (new) state, the people who were actually deprived of movement, the non-actors, could not recognise the 'NSK state' as a critical participatory art project, but only as a hope and help to achieve the desired goal in the situation of their own lack of movement.

Conclusion

In recent years, several art projects have addressed the issue of migration, which is a relevant social work topic. Yet social workers are often part of the machinery of securitisation and bureaucratisation of the social field, even though they formulate their work primarily in the discourse of 'helping'. The question raised in this chapter is whether social workers, including social work students in countries with extreme refugee hostility, might become more engaged with the problems of migration through the use of critical art in social work. Participatory art does not moralise or lecture, but is a way of identification, of emotionally grasping what is very far from the experience of students and social workers, and can therefore sharpen their epistemological flexibility and strengthen their humanistic perspective despite mainstream nationalisms. In the post-socialist countries of Southeast Europe, social work and politics have become conflated, and social workers have very limited capacity to think critically and advocate for a 'new state'. The use of participatory art could connect critical social work with the engaged and action-oriented practice of social work in the field of migration in a transdisciplinary way.

Acknowledgements

This chapter is part of the Faculty of Social Work scientific research programme group 'Social work as the bearer of the processes of social justice and inclusion in Slovenia - theoretical, methodological and methodical perspectives and historical development', funded by the National Research Agency of Slovenia (project number: P5-0058). I would like to thank the artists' collective IRWIN; Damjan Kozole; Erik Valenčič, and the cartoonist Marko Kočevar, who gave me access to their work and permission to reproduce it here. I would like to thank Prof Shula Ramon and Dr Irena Šumi for their valuable comments while writing this chapter.

Notes

[1] In Slovenia, the Ministry of Interior wanted to institutionalise push-backs in 2017 by amending the Foreigners Act (2011), but the Slovenian Constitutional Court repealed the law in 2019 (see: Written decision of the Constitutional Court No. U-I-59/17, 18 September 2019; www.us-rs.si/odlocba-ustavnega-sodisca-st-u-i-59-17-z-dne-18-9-2019/). In 2021, the Ministry of Interior amended the law again (Official Gazette of the Republic of Slovenia 91/21), stating that in crisis situations the government has the right to close the borders completely and make individual asylum procedures impossible. The law was criticised by several non-governmental organisations. However, neither the Slovenian Ombudsman raise his voice; nor did social workers react (see Smajila, B. M., The Foreigners Act: Why is the Ombudsman Silent? N1 SLO, 26 July 2021 Zakon o tujcih: zakaj varuh človekovih pravic molči? N1 (n1info.si).
[2] The Humanitarian Corridor (July 2015–March 2016) existed temporarily as a route of relatively free movement of people, free from smugglers, pushbacks and other violent practices. It ran from Turkey, Greece, through Balkan countries including Slovenia to Austria and other Western countries. Over a million migrants from the Middle East, Asia and Africa took advantage of it.
[3] This was an expression of a refugee from DR of Congo two decades ago: 'We are victims of no importance' (Le Pape, 2004: 209).

4   The Dheisheh refugee camp (called *as Duheisha* by the Palestinian Authority) is located along the main street in Bethlehem in the West Bank after the Arab-Israeli war in 1948 when Palestinians were expelled from 44 villages (the event called *Nakba*, the 'disaster'). Hilal and Petti proposed that beside the Dheisheh refugee camp also the today's non-existent Palestinian villages should become part of the UNESCO heritage (2021: 119).

5   Using the memory of the Nazi extermination camp Auschwitz-Birkenau was starkly criticised; cf. Neuendorf (2017): Documenta 14 Cancels 'Auschwitz on the Beach' Performance Amid Intense Criticism. *Artnet News*, 22 August. https://news.artnet.com/art-world/documenta-performance-outrage-1058285

6   EURODAC is the EU regulation for comparing the fingerprints of asylum seekers to determine whether the person has previously applied for asylum in another country. See https://ec.europa.eu/home-affairs/what-we-do/policies/asylum/identification-of-applicants_en

7   His work has also attracted some criticism for example: Wayne, E. (2016) Ai Weiwei, Refugee Vests, and the Inarticulateness of Conceptual Art. Art Criticism. 20 February. https://artofericwayne.com/2016/02/20/ai-weiwei-refugee-vests-and-the-inarticulateness-of-conceptual-art/Sierzputowski; Kate (2016) Ai Weiwei wraps Berlin concert hall columns with 14,000 Salvaged Refugee Life Vests; 16 February. PD (2021) (Accessed 27 July 2021).

8   Eastern neighbours Film festival. Borders (Meje), 2016, 10 min. https://enff.nl/film/borders-2016/

9   The film (50 min) was shot between 2017 and 2018 in West Sahara. Then Years of Reality. Dokudoc. www.dokumentarci.si/portfolio-item/videti-el-aaiun/; and Videti El Aaiún – Mednarodni festival dokumentarnega filma DOKUDOC (dokumentarci.si); Slovenian film Database. Erik Valenčič. https://bsf.si/en/name/erik-valencic/. Štok, K. (2020) 'Should the Sahrawi people go to war, this film explains why' ['Če bodo šli Sahravijci v vojno, bo ta film pojasnil, zakaj']. RTV MMC, 16 September 2020. www.rtvslo.si/svet/afrika/ce-bodo-sli-sahravijci-v-vojno-bo-ta-film-pojasnil-zakaj/536042

10 In 1963 the United Nations asked Spain as the colonial power of Western Sahara, to decolonise the territory; instead Spain handed on the colony to the neighbouring countries of Morocco and Mauretania. In reaction, the Saharawi people proclaimed the Democratic Arab Republic of Western Sahara, DARS (Höllmüller, 2021).

11 Syrian refugee performs on piano for Ai Weiwei at Idomeni camp, *BBC News*, 12 March 2016. www.bbc.com/news/av/entertainment-arts-35795225; Wassenberg, A., 'Ai Weiwei brings white grand piano to muddy Greek refugee camp', *Inquisitr*, 13 March 2016. www.inquisitr.com/2882560/ai-weiwei-brings-white-grand-piano-to-muddy-greek-refugee-camp/; AFP, 'Ai Weiwei brings white grand piano to muddy refugee field', *Ahramonline*, 13. March 2016. https://english.ahram.org.eg/NewsContent/5/0/190825/Arts--Culture/0/Ai-Weiwei-brings-white-grand-piano-to-muddy-refuge.aspx; N.N., 'Piano in the mud of Idomeni shames EU over refugee haggling', DW, 13 March 2016. www.dw.com/en/piano-in-the-mud-of-idomeni-shames-eu-over-refugee-haggling/a-19113544

12 The NSK Passport Holders, NSK STATE: English.

References

Agamben, G. (2002) *Remnants of Auschwitz: The Witness and the Archive. Homo Sacer III*, New York: Zone Books.

Anderson, B. (1995) *Imagined Communities*, London: Verso.

Berc, G. (2019) 'Croatian experience with the refugee crisis on the Balkan Route and possible implications for social work practice and education', *Journal of Human Rights and Social Work*, 4(1): 63–73.

Bifo Berardi, F. (2017) 'Resignation letter from Franco Bifo Berardi to Yanis Varoufakis and DiEM25'. www.yanisvaroufakis.eu/2017/07/08/bifo-i-am-no-longer-a-european-given-europes-daily-crimes-thus-i-resign-from-diem25-and-my-response/

Bishop, C. (2012) *Umetni pekli*, Ljubljana: Maska.

Bornarova, S. (2019) 'Transit migration and human rights: Macedonian Policy and social work responses to transit migration crisis', *Journal of Human Rights and Social Work*, 4(1): 74–82.

Buchanan, A. and Kallinikakki, T. (2020) 'Meeting the needs of unaccompanied children in Greece', *International Social Work*, 63(2): 206–19.

Butala, G. (2020) 'Živa Divjak, theatre director: In the theatre you cannot look away' [Žiga Divjak, gledališki režiser: V gledališču ne moreš pogledati proč], *Dnevnik*, 8 June. www.dnevnik.si/1042931370

Čufer, E. (2019) 'It is time to rethink the state: On NSK state', in Irwin (ed) *State in Time*, Prishtina: National Gallery of Kosovo, pp 138–52.

Divjak, Ž. (2018) *Šest*. Slovensko mladinsko gledališče, Ljubljana.

Divjak, Ž. (2020) *Gejm*. Slovensko mladinsko gledališče, Ljubljana.

Dominelli, L. (2010) *Social Work in a Globalizing World*, Cambridge: Polity Press.

Feldman, A. (1996) 'On cultural anesthesia: From Desert Storm to Rodney King', in N. Seremetakis (ed) *The Senses Still: Memory and Perception as Material Culture*, Chicago: University of Chicago Press.

Foucault, M. (1997) 'Society must be defended', in M. Bertani, A. Fontana and A.I. Davidson (eds) *Lectures at the Collège de France, 1975–1976*, New York: Picador, pp 13–63.

Foucault, M. (2006/1961) *Madness and Civilization: A History of Insanity in the Age of Reason*, London: Routledge.

Foucault, M. (2008/1988) *The Birth of Biopolitics. Lectures at the College de France 1978–79*, ed M. Senellart, general eds F. Ewald and A. Fontana. London: Palgrave Macmillan.

Gall, L. (2020) 'Violent pushbacks on Croatia border require EU action: Human Rights Watch', 29 October. www.hrw.org/news/2020/10/29/violent-pushbacks-croatia-border-require-eu-action

Healy, K. (2001) 'Reinventing critical social work: Challenges from practice, context and postmodernism', *Critical Social Work*, 2(1). https://ojs.uwindsor.ca/index.php/csw/article/view/5618/4591

Hilal, D.S. and Petti, A. (2021) *Refugee Heritage. World Heritage Nomination Dossier*, Stockholm: Art and Theory Publishing.

Holman Jones, S., Adams, T.E. and Ellis, C. (2013) *Handbook of Autoethnography*, New York: Routledge.

Höllmüller, H. (2021) 'An Austrian social work project in Western Sahara', *Socialno delo*, 60(2): 181–6.

Horkheimer, M. and Adorno, T.W. (1973) *Dialectic of Enlightenment. Cultural Memory in the Present*, New York: Continuum.

HRW (2017) 'Croatia: Asylum seekers forced back to Serbia', 20 January. www.hrw.org/news/2017/01/20/croatia-asylum-seekers-forced-back-serbia

HRW (2019) 'EU: Address Croatia border pushbacks', Human Rights Watch, 8 November. www.hrw.org/news/2019/11/08/eu-address-croatia-border-pushbacks

Huss, E., Ben Asher, S., Walden, T. and Shahar, E. (2021) 'Towards a model for integrating informal and formal learning for children in refugee camps: The example of the Lesbos School for Peace', *Social Sciences*, 10(3): 11.

Irwin (2019) *State in Time*, Prishtina: National Gallery of Kosovo.

Kallinikaki, T. (2019) 'Social work education in uncertain times: Protecting the human rights of migrants', *Journal of Human Rights and Social Work*, 4(1): 28–35.

Karlsson, S.G. and Jönsson, J.H. (2020) 'Forced migration, older refugees and displacement: Implications for social work as a human rights profession', *Journal of Human Rights and Social Work*, 5(3): 212–22.

Kleibl, T., Lutz, R., Noyoo, N., Bunk, B., Dittmann, A. and Seepamore, B. (eds) (2019) *The Routledge Handbook of Postcolonial Social Work*, London: Routledge.

Kozole, D. (2016) *Meje*. Short documentary film, Slovenia.

Le Pape, M. (2004) 'Democratic Republic of Congo: Victims of no importance', in F. Weissman (ed) *In the Shadow of 'Just Wars': Violence, Politics and Humanitarian Action*, London: Hurst and Company, pp 209–27.

Levi, P. (2013/1986) *The Drowned and the Saved*, London: Abacus.

Luluquisen, M. and Pettis, L. (2014) 'Community engagement for policy and systems change', *Community Development*, 45(3): 252–62.

Moreau, M. (1990) 'Empowerment through advocacy and consciousness-raising: Implications for a structural approach to social work', *Journal of Sociology and Social Work*, 17(2): 53–67.

Neuendorf, H. (2017) 'Documenta 14 cancels 'Auschwitz on the Beach' performance amid intense criticism', *Artnet News*, 22 August. https://news.artnet.com/art-world/documenta-performance-outrage-1058285

Ostrander, J.A., Lane, S., McClendon, J., Hayes, C. and Rhodes Smith, T. (2017) 'Collective power to create political change: Increasing the political efficacy and engagement of social workers', *Journal of Policy Practice*, 16(3): 261–75.

Pease, B. and Fook, J. (eds) (1999) *Transforming Social Work Practice: Postmodern Critical Perspectives*, St Leonards: Allen and Unwin.

Rape Žiberna, T., Žnidar, A., Cafuta, J. and Flaker, V. (2019) 'Reorganizacija centrov za socialno delo –kaj se pravzaprav dogaja?' [Reorganisation of the centers of social work – What is actually going on?], *Socialno delo*, 58(2): 145–54.

Ramon, S. (2003) *Users Researching Health and Social Care: An Empowering Innovation*, London: British Association of Social Workers.

Roose, R., Roets, G. and Schiettecat, T. (2014) 'Implementing a strengths perspective in child welfare and protection: A challenge not to be taken lightly', *European Journal of Social Work*, 17(1): 3–17.

Run, P. (2012) '"Out of place": An auto-ethnography of refugee and postcolonial exile', *African Identities*, 10(4): 381–90.

Sierzputowski, K. (2016) 'Ai Weiwei wraps Berlin concert hall columns with 14,000 salvaged refugee life vests', 16 February.

Valenčič, E. (2020) Videti El Aaiún, *Baza slovenskih filmov*.

Videmšek, B. (2016) *Na begu. Moderni eksodus (2005–2016): z begunci in migranti na poti proti obljubljenim deželam*, Ljubljana: Umco.

Ward, D. and Mullender, A. (1991) 'Empowerment and oppression: An indissoluble pairing for contemporary social work', *Critical Social Policy*, 11(2): 21–30.

Wayne, E. (2016) 'Ai Weiwei, refugee vests, and the inarticulateness of conceptual art', *Art Criticism*, 20 February. https://artofericwayne.com/2016/02/20/ai-weiwei-refugee-vests-and-the-inarticulateness-of-conceptual-art/

Westerman, J. (2019) 'Contesting utopias: Individual collectivity and temporal hybridity in the NSK state in time', in Irwin (ed) *State in Time*, Prishtina: National Gallery of Kosovo, pp 94–120.

Zaviršek, D. (2000) *Disability as a Cultural Trauma*, Ljubljana: *Cf.

Zaviršek, D. (2015) 'Anthropology, social work and disability studies: Researching diversity in Eastern Europe', in M. Treiber, N. Grießmeier and C. Heider (eds) *Ethnologie und Soziale Arbeit: fremde Disziplinen, gemeinsame Fragen?* Opladen: Budrich UniPress, pp 107–30.

Zaviršek, D. (2017a) 'Delayed deinstitutionalisation in postsocialism', *European Journal of Social Work*, 20(6): 834–46.

Zaviršek, D. (2017b) 'The Humanitarian crisis of migration versus the crisis of humanitarianism: Current dimensions and challenges for social work practice', *Journal of Social Work Education*, 36(3): 231–44.

Zaviršek, D and Rajgelj, B. (2019) 'Anti-refugee sentiment without refugees: Human rights violations and social work in post-socialist countries of Southeastern Europe in their social contexts', *Journal of Human Rights and Social Work*, 4(1): 5–16.

Žižek, S. (1993) 'Es gibt keinen Staat in Europa', in Irwin (ed) *State in Time*, Prishtina: National Gallery of Kosovo, pp 20–1.

Zorn, J. (2016) 'Social work with refugees at the Schengen border: "… but they are the same people as we are"', *Critical and Radical Social Work*, 4(1): 121–5.

Zorn, J. (2021) 'The case of Ahmad Shamieh's campaign against Dublin Deportation: Embodiment of political violence and community care', *Social Sciences*, 10: 154.

3

Grasping at straws: social work in reception and identification centres in Greece

Marina Rota, Océane Uzureau, Malte Behrendt, Sarah Adeyinka, Ine Lietaert and Ilse Derluyn

Introduction

In May 2015, at the beginning of the so-called 'refugee crisis', the European Commission devised the 'hotspot approach' to help Member States at the Southern EU-borders manage increasing migratory pressure. Under this approach, European Union (EU) agencies (European Asylum Support Office [EASO]), European Border and Coast Guard Agency (EBCG, FRONTEX), and Europol started to work on the ground with Greece and Italy in the identification and registration processes of newly arrived migrants and asylum applicants.[1] The objective of this was to ensure that all new arriving persons were immediately registered and pointed, as soon as possible, to the correct direction (that is, application for asylum, return to their home country or relocation to another EU-country[2]), and as such to avoid so-called 'secondary movements' to other European countries.

Greek reception and identification centres (RICs) opened their doors in early 2016, together with the Greek government adjusting its asylum legislation (Law L4375/2016), formalising the existence of RICs. As an extension to the EU-Turkey agreement, which was finalised on 20 March 2016,[3] five new first reception centres were created on the Aegean islands of Lesvos, Kos, Chios, Leros and Samos, all in close proximity to the EU-Turkey border. The islands' geography posed an additional movement restriction for the arriving refugees, extra to the one created by the police and authorities on arrival. The initial examination of their asylum application could lead to relocation to the Greek mainland or abroad in case of proved vulnerability, or deportation to Turkey in case of rejection.

International organisations, NGOs and human rights observatories have repeatedly shed light on the living conditions in Greek RICs (see for example, ECRE, 2016; FRA, 2016; HRW 2016, 2018; Avocats Sans Frontières, 2019), and scholars have demonstrated the human rights abuses in these hotspots and the effects of the living conditions there on the refugees' physical and mental health (Rozakou, 2017; Jones, 2019; Boccagni and Righard, 2020).

Social work in Greek reception and identification centres

Professionals working in these centres include, among others, asylum authorities, security staff and social workers. The work of frontline social workers in providing services for refugees and asylum seekers is generally considered difficult and stressful (Robinson, 2014). Although the number of social workers working with newly arrived communities is increasing, there are only a few studies examining the day-to-day working conditions they face, specifically in the RICs (Jones, 2019; Witcher, 2021). Teloni et al (2020: 10) mention that 'social workers employed in refugee "crisis" are young graduates and/or with limited work experience with refugees' and stress in their conclusions the social workers' high work load, low pay and lack of supervision and training. Although their sample consisted of mainland centre personnel,[4] it can be assumed that conditions at the entry points are even worse because of the crowded conditions and documented subpar living conditions in the RICs.

This chapter aims to shed light on the working conditions of the social workers in the RIC of Samos, how they realise their 'discretionary space' (Lipsky, 2010: 17) how they use the 'freedom' that the specific context offers them to 'interpret' the rules in a way that allows them to combine their limited resources with their professional knowledge, in order to maximise the support to their beneficiaries. In order to do so, we will use Lipsky's street-level bureaucrats' theory (1969, 1980, 2010) as an overarching theoretical framework. Lipsky defined

> Street-level bureaucracy as public service employment of a certain sort, performed under certain conditions ... street-level bureaucrats interact with citizens in the course of the job and show discretion in exercising authority; in addition, they cannot do the job according to ideal conceptions of the practice because of the limitations of the work structure. (2010: 17)

As 'discretion', Lipsky (1980) and Evans (2010) define 'the extent of freedom a worker can exercise in a specific context and the factors that give rise to this freedom in that context' (quoted in Akosa and Asare, 2017: 1). The main idea of discretion in frontline social workers is that

> Complex services are designed (typically by those far removed from the front line) to ration services so that there are enough resources (in

simplistic terms) to go round. They are, however, operationalised and implemented by front line workers who have to redesign them in order to fit procedures with day to day realities, make them manageable and their own experience bearable. (Turbeit, 2020: 4)

Thus, professional independence and worker discretion when working with refugees and asylum seekers are critical and NGOs have been identified as a place to engage in innovative social work practice, where person-centred work predominates (Robinson, 2014).

In this sense, Lipsky's theory can include RIC's social workers (Witcher, 2021): although they are not public servants, they perform a vital part of RIC's functions, operate under the control of the Centre's Administration and work together with national and international organisations, including FRONTEX, EASO, Asylum Service and the Greek Police. Their beneficiaries and local societies also consider them as being part of the state apparatus. On the other hand, NGOs that assist refugees and asylum seekers face increasing demands and pressures. The focus on human rights and social justice frameworks risks being diminished due to the limited capacity imposed by financial constraints (Robinson, 2014: 10).

In this context we specifically address the following questions:

- How do social workers deal with the lack of resources, especially when compared to the huge needs in the specific settings?
- How do they position themselves in this context: are they contributing to their current work situation or do they oppose it?

Methods

This research is part of the ChildMove project funded by the European Research Council (ERC). The project's objective is to examine how transit/flight experiences affect unaccompanied refugee minors' (URMs) psychosocial wellbeing in relation to the past traumatic experiences in their home country and the daily stressors in their current living setting. Our aim is to provide unique insights into the diversity of – and evolution in – their experiences while fleeing from home, and its impact on their wellbeing, hereby combining both qualitative and quantitative data collection methods. This chapter reports on the research carried out at the reception and identification centre (RIC) of Vathi on the island of Samos from 3 October 2017 to 4 November 2017, mainly relying on participant observations.

At the time of the research, Lesvos and Samos received the largest number of sea arrivals.[5] Although we initially thought of asking permission to conduct research in the RIC of Moria in Lesvos, the situation there was also at that time already out of control and thus both practical and ethical constraints (Rozakou, 2017) made us to decide not to choose Moria as our research setting. In October 2017, the conditions for research in Samos were considered better, despite the fact that RIC employees and volunteers were already warning that 'a new Moria' was under creation in Samos, with hundreds of people living in makeshift camps around the RIC. The timing of the research was optimal, because the NGOs that were until then responsible for the psychosocial and medical support of the refugees in the RIC were about to vacate it, since the then-current government had decided to take over all humanitarian actions in the centres.[6] If we had operated after that 'change of guard', we would have been faced with more bureaucratic obstacles and controversy.

We chose to rely on participatory observations of the staff and residents of the centre, in combination with semi-structured interviews with unaccompanied refugee minors.

The method of participatory observation emphasises the importance of the researcher's integration in the social space, so that simple and distanced observation of events can be replaced by the researcher's participation in the construction of meanings through the process of interacting with respondents (Holy, 1984). As in most methodological approaches in this field, the researcher needs to be aware of his/her positionality and the ways the researcher's gender, ethnicity, class and theoretical approach may affect the processes of data collection, analysis and interpretation (Kawulich, 2005). An additional limitation in our study was the limited time we had, since the researcher had only one week to enter the RIC, to observe and to collect data. In any case, one main rule we set from the beginning was that the researcher's presence should in no way interfere with the normal operation of the centre.

Before starting our research in Greece, we received Ethical Clearance from the Committee of Ethics in Research of the University of West Attica and from the Ethics Committee of the Faculty of Psychology and Educational Sciences of Ghent University. We also obtained permission for the study from the First Reception Service as from the NGOs working in the RIC, who also expressed their willingness to cooperate in the study.

Upon entering the centre, we revealed our scientific identity and announced our research intentions to the centre's staff, and sought to participate as much as possible in the activities of the social workers. This practically meant trying to bond with team members and participate in their daily activities (Bogdan and Taylor, 1975), while constantly introducing ourselves as researcher. The main area of participatory observation was the medical and social services of the centre and the courtyard waiting area. During this period, two NGOs provided psychosocial services at the centre. One of the two was also responsible for the medical care of the residents of RIC, while a third NGO provided interpreters, and, in some cases, guardians for URMs. Additionally, we were able to observe other parts of the RIC, including the area where the URMs lived, the clothing distribution depots organised by volunteers, and the makeshift camp that was growing rapidly outside the official RIC.

On the first day of the research, participatory observation focused mainly on getting acquainted with the RIC area, mapping points of interest, and obtaining an overview of the space we wanted to observe: how it is organised, who is there, and who is responsible for the operation of the place. We also met the social workers and explained our presence. We gave them time and space to ask anything they wanted in relation to the study and the researcher, and they gave us information about their work. Throughout the research, we were going to the RIC at 8 am, and leaving by the time of closure of the clinic and the social service office. Observation time was divided between the social service, courtyard waiting area and the clinic. Because of the proximity of the spaces (containers next to each other, each being turned into two separate spaces), we were often present during informal discussions between beneficiaries and social workers.

At the end of each observation day, we wrote a detailed report on the events that took place, using Ad Libitum Sampling (Altmann, 1974). All observations were recorded through the note-taking method, combining descriptive and reflective information. Using thematic analysis (Braun and Clarke, 2006), the notes, which included observations, informal discussions with social workers and actions and incidents that took place in the RIC, were deconstructed and coded, with help of NVIVO-12, in order to identify the key themes relative to the chapter's focal research questions.

Research setting

On our first day in the centre, we were welcomed by an epidemic of scabies in the unaccompanied minors' sector. The medical personnel immediately stepped in, using interpreters to find the extent of the problem, treating the infected and putting the sector in an informal quarantine. The next day, the army came to disinfect the entire area. This led to us losing access to the minors for the first days of the research, which turned our focus towards participatory observations of the professionals. From our discussions with the social workers, and judging the state of the facilities, we understood that an epidemic, such as the one we witnessed, was not exceptional.

The RIC of Samos is located on a hill directly above the capital of Samos, Vathi, an area previously used by the Greek Army. It has two entrances/exits, the first located on the main road and leading to the town, and the second on a side road that leads to the various RIC services. Next to the second exit, the makeshift camp, where those live who fail to find a place in the RIC, extends. When we visited the reception and identification centre of

Samos in October 2017, its official capacity was 650 people. At that time, the estimated total number of people inside and outside the RIC was over 2,000, including 63 registered unaccompanied minors (45 boys and 18 girls) and dozens of families with young children. The RIC consisted of a mixture of containers and tents, and was divided into different sectors. At the time of the research, it also housed the administrative services, the First Reception Service, FRONTEX, EASO, UNHCR, IOM, the Greek Police, the Greek Army, and NGOs that provided medical and psychosocial assistance as well as interpreting services. Although the centre was open and residents could move freely in and out, the container areas were divided with iron fences into different sectors, while the centre's perimeter was enclosed by wire mesh and barbed wire fence, giving the impression of a closed structure.

Catering at the time of our visit was provided by the army, and consisted of three meals per day plus 1.5 litres of water per person. The average waiting time in the queue for food was 1.5 to 2 hours, while sometimes the number of portions fell short.

There were just enough toilets and bathrooms to serve the needs of 650 people, exclusively situated inside the RIC area. Clothes and bedsheets were hung out everywhere, either to dry from the rain and humidity or as partitions offering a basic form of privacy.

Unaccompanied girls lived in the sector housing the families, while unaccompanied boys were at a different place (level 2), near the administrative services. Although the minors were not sharing their containers with adults, there was no way of controlling who was entering the minors' level, especially at night.

The first thing one faced when entering from the second entrance were the medical and social services. These consisted of two containers forming an L-shape, each with its own entrance and sharing a small outdoor waiting area. In order to access the services, one had to pass through two controlled gates. This area would become our primary research setting for the duration of our visit.

Lack of resources

At the time of our visit, the clinic and the social service were run by the same NGO. The social service container was divided into two offices – one belonged to a psychologist and the other to the social workers. There was another office in a separate container where another NGO provided additional social services. Both offices were understaffed when compared to the number of cases they were called to help daily. In total, one psychologist and five social workers were the focus point for the 2,000 people living in the camp. Equally, the number of interpreters was insufficient. Priority was given to administrative and medical services, often leaving social services with little or no interpretation. Lack of resources in the RIC's social services can be found both in the organisational and personal level (Lipsky, 1969). Regarding the organisational level, the manpower/client ration was inadequate. This lack of professionals led to a gap in personal resources too, meaning insufficient 'time to make decisions (and act upon them), access to information, and information itself' (Lipsky, 1969: 5).

In most cases, the social workers were not able to allocate the necessary time and space to each person. Often, when the office was occupied and there was a large number of people waiting, social workers worked in the shared 'waiting room' outside, trying to administer help and giving a literal interpretation of the definition of 'street-level' frontline worker. On the second day of our observation, the office of the social services was visited by, among others, a rape victim, a teenager with serious self-injury behaviour and a teenager with panic attacks. The latter had a history of suicide attempts and was under medical treatment, while the application filled by the social workers asking for his relocation to a minors' hostel because of extreme vulnerability had been pending for 4.5 months.[7] All the while, out in the yard, other social workers were talking to people, trying to prioritise cases and resolve issues on the spot, while not forgetting to play with the children who were there with their parents.

Of course, under these circumstances, it was impossible to maintain confidentiality. To work in this way was imposed by the reality of the camp, the setup of the containers and the low proportion of workers versus people in need. An extensive absence of discretion was evident as it often happens in 'less structured or "strategic" decision situations, especially those characterized by fluidity, high uncertainty, interpersonal conflict, and environmental turbulence' (Murdach, 2009: 184), an approach not always successful. For example, social workers were often forced to talk to the beneficiaries using their friends or relatives as interpreters. This of course created a lot of problems for both the migrants and the staff:

> Today a woman who had visible bruises in the face and was carrying a one-year-old girl came to the social service. She looked very upset, and the social workers were not sure if she came for them or if she needed medical help. As there were no interpreters available, the social service tried to find someone who spoke her language in order to help her. Eventually they managed to find another woman from her country who, immediately after entering the container and seeing the young mother, started a heated conversation in their language. The woman was very upset, and the 'interpreter' left the container. The staff realized that something serious must have happened and immediately notified the police, while they urgently requested an interpreter in the language of the woman. After about 20 minutes, the interpreter

came. The woman explained to the social worker that she is a victim of domestic violence. She lived in a tent outside the RIC and her husband abused her physically and sexually on a daily basis. By the time she had finished her story, her husband appeared together with the woman who had offered to help with interpretation. Her husband tried to enter the social service. The social workers tried to stop him and called for the police once again. Her husband managed to enter the container. Without saying a word, he went straight to his wife, snatched the baby from her arms and left. The woman stood frozen for a few minutes and then got up to leave. The staff told her to wait there for the police who would arrive soon. She thanked them for trying to help, and left. When the police arrived, the social worker went with them to the makeshift tent camp outside and tried to find the woman again but failed. When she returned to the office, she told to her colleagues, almost in tears: 'Everything we did was wrong. She came to us for protection and we disappointed her. And the worst thing is that we cannot do anything to prevent this from happening again'. (Field notes, day 4)

The lack of basic resources, such as time, fixed work schedule, interpreters and a safe space to offer their beneficiaries, made the social workers spending their day chasing after emergencies. The complexity and the diversity of the needs the social workers were confronted with and their inability to address them in an organised manner created in turn feelings of powerlessness, frustration and anger.

Working conditions

As already described, lack of resources in combination with the huge caseload created a stressful and overwhelming working environment for the social workers. In addition to that, their responsibilities were anything but clear. During our observations, we noticed that the social workers had stopped trying to fulfil their role in the RIC and ended up trying to close gaps that fell outside their work curriculum. This led to an extensive use of discretion, undermining in some cases their own work (Evans and Harris, 2004).

> Sometimes I think that nobody really knows what we (the social workers) are here to do. When someone is sick, they call the doctor, and if they cause problems with their behaviour, they call the police. For everything else, the solution is the social service. At first, you are shocked by the demands coming from all sides. You try to set some limits, but in the end, you give up. You just accept the fact that you cannot organize your day. You start work with a full agenda, and

from the beginning you already know that there is no way you can pull it off. Sometimes it's ridiculous, for example they may ask you to go and tell their next tent neighbours not to have sex because the children are listening. But most of the time; things are serious. How can you convince them that you have no influence in the decision on who gets to leave the centre for the mainland? (Word-by-word note, day 3; discussion with a social worker in the context of the research)

One of the biggest misunderstandings had to do with the power of the social workers to declare someone as being 'in a vulnerable situation', offering him/her, as such, a 'get out of jail' card. All they could do was draft a report about a case and make a transfer suggestion on the grounds of vulnerability. In truth, the final decision for transfer to the mainland was made by the director of the centre, in consultation with the medical team who had the main role in identifying vulnerable individuals. The workers in social services were trying to explain this, but their explanations were met with mistrust by the beneficiaries who didn't want to believe that the social workers had no power. As a consequence, the social workers often found themselves under physical and psychological threats (Lipsky, 1969). At the time of our research, there was a rumour that the social workers were able to give a certificate of vulnerability on the spot, so a lot of incidents of self-harm happened in front of them. Apparently, only a week before our visit, a young man had slashed his veins open during the social intake (information from a social worker – field notes). At the end of the shift of the second day of research, we witnessed a similar event.

> A young man tried to set himself on fire while entering the container of the social service. He was having an appointment with the social worker and the psychologist, and he told them that if they don't give him a paper stating that he is vulnerable, he will come back with gasoline to kill himself as well as both of them. The social workers informed the police and the first reception authorities about the threat, but both took no action. After 30 minutes, he came back, douched himself with gasoline and tried to enter the social service container with the lighter in hand. One of the social workers was close to the door and managed to shut it and keep him out, while another young man who was waiting outside fell on him and took the lighter from his hand. It was a chaotic and fearful moment for everybody. From the yard, we could hear screams from the social services container, but because the windows and door were shut, we had no view and didn't know whether he had managed to set the container on fire. An interpreter broke one of the windows and helped the care workers get out, all of them scared but otherwise unharmed. After that incident,

the area had to be evacuated for the rest of the day. The two containers hosting medical and social services are next to each other and the area around them was full of people with small children and babies among them. 'People attempt to kill themselves because they believe that it's a win-win situation. Either they die or they get to leave this place. In either case they believe that they will go to a better place. (Word-by-word note, day 2; discussion with a social worker in the context of the research)

On the next day, social services was again functioning normally. With the broken window covered with a black tarpaulin to keep out rain and cold, the workers just re-entered the container and resumed their work.

During our research, we observed that care providers were trying to balance the reality of their surroundings with their idealised way of working, while being left to improvise. Because of the workload, they didn't even have the time to process serious incidents. They were trying to discuss them inside their team, but there was no external support or supervision available. In most cases, they were unprepared for the working conditions and lacked specific training to face the situation in the RIC (Gkionakis, 2016; Teloni et al, 2020). Despite working overtime regularly, most of the time they left work with the feeling that they hadn't accomplished anything.

> When I think about everything they taught us at school, I feel like laughing. None of us was prepared to work in a situation like this. Most of the colleagues have no work experience, and suddenly they find themselves having to work in the middle of a war zone. Because this is what it is like here. Things we only saw on TV, that we thought were happening elsewhere. As much as you love your job, you can't stand it for long. That's why most people come and go. You must either really desperately need the salary or you have made a mental bet with yourself to endure. … Every morning you wake up tired, and then go to work to return feeling empty and frustrated, feeling that everything is meaningless. (Field notes, day 3; discussion with a social worker in the context of the research)

When a person working in the humanitarian sector faces emotional exhaustion and a reduced sense of accomplishment, they meet the criteria for burnout. For the social workers, 'a significant piece of their sense of purpose and identity is associated with their work, which means the consequences of burnout, vicarious trauma and secondary stress can be very high' (Guskovict and Potocky, 2018: 3). This was often the case with the social workers at the Samos RIC.

On the third day of observations and while we were at the clinic, a young man brought his unconscious 23-years-old wife. She had various health problems and suffered from a diagnosed posttraumatic stress disorder for which she was on medication. Doctors immediately called an ambulance to transport her to the hospital. She was carried off unconscious, with her husband accompanying her. As they were leaving the clinic, one of the social workers present recognized the couple. The ambulance left before she could intervene, and she entered the office upset, saying 'the girl who left now with the ambulance has two babies. Her husband went with her. We have to find the children'. Immediately the social service mobilised and requested the assistance of the First Reception Service. When later we asked the social worker how she could remember one person among the hundreds of people who passed through the social service every day, she replied that she was trying to remember all the people she had met at work. 'It is difficult, I hardly remember any names, but when they greet me in the camp, I want to know who they are, to remember their story. Our work is with people, with their lives. It's part of our job to remember. (Word-by-word note, day 3; discussion with a social worker in the context of the research)

Literature has shown that professionals who work with traumatised children may experience vicarious and secondary trauma themselves (Berrick, 2018: 182), and aid workers in similar contexts employ numerous positive and negative coping skills (Guskovict and Potocky, 2018). The social worker in the example displayed positive coping by regaining her professional purpose through displaying humanity. On the other hand, the impact of psychological distress may elicit negative coping, such as emotional dysregulation and cynicism (Guskovict and Potocky, 2018).

On the afternoon of the third day of observation, a fight started in the lower part of the centre near the entrance to the city. The fight turned into a widespread conflict between groups of different nationalities, made even more chaotic by the intervention of the Greek riot police unit. Tear gas was fired inside the centre with the air becoming suffocating, while the doors leading to the section of the clinic and social services were closed, isolating us from the rest of the centre. The fight lasted about 40 minutes. As soon as it stopped, many injured people were allowed through the door in order to approach the clinic and receive first aid. We were standing at the front door together with a social worker and asking the police officers on the other side of the door questions, trying to figure out what had just happened. At that moment, a man approached us and said in French that his pregnant wife wasn't well and was crying, but was not allowed to approach the doctor because she didn't appear to be injured. The social worker did not speak French, so we helped with the translation since we judged the situation to be urgent and there was no official interpreter available. As soon as the social worker heard our translation, she called for the nurse and asked the police to let them pass, so that they could examine what exactly was happening. At the beginning, the police was reluctant to do so, but one of the officers offered to accompany them. After a while, they returned supporting a young woman who was carried to the doctor's office, while the police officer who was with them told us that he had already called for an ambulance. When the social worker returned to the social service container, she said 'it's another miscarriage', and her colleagues shook their heads condescendingly. All in all, another 'normal' working day at the RIC of Samos. (Field notes, day 3)

Working environments afflicted by uncertainty and scarcity like Samos RIC were placed at the centre of Lipsky's theory on the dilemmas and tensions that impact on the exercise of professional discretion. He saw the problem of scarce resources as compounded by 'ill-defined organisational goals and unrealistically high expectations of public agencies and their staff' (Evans and Harris, 2004: 877). In this sense, the professional behaviour of the social workers can be explained by 'the work-related pressures, stemming from this context, with which they constantly had to cope' (Halwey and Lipsky, 1976: 209).

Discussion

In this chapter, we tried to examine the daily work of the Samos RIC's frontline social workers through the prism of Lipsky's theory of street-level bureaucrats. Although the results discussed here are specific to the period the research took place, there are many fundamental similarities between the working conditions of Lipsky's bureaucrats and those of the social workers at the Samos RIC. Unfortunately, while our observations are still indicative of the challenges faced by social workers at the Samos RIC, the situation there has further deteriorated. When the ChildMove project team visited the centre for a follow-up in February 2019, we found that the adjacent informal camp had grown to host an estimated number of 6,000 people, while the provision of medical and social services had been significantly reduced after the responsibility of medical and psychosocial support was transferred directly to the state. According to the report of Advocats sans Frontières:

> In the Samos camp only two doctors are in practice, only one of whom is competent to sign medical certificates, giving them value with the

Greek administration and the asylum services. The medical team is also composed of five nurses, a midwife, two cultural mediators, a military doctor (who does not have the competence to sign vulnerability certificates), two social workers and normally a psychologist who has not been present for several months. If asylum seekers have, once registered, the right to access the island's hospital, they must first go through the camp doctor's container to obtain an appointment. With more than 7,000 people in November 2019, access to the camp's medical services and to the only doctor qualified to identify people with special needs means queues of several hours. People sleep in front of the container hoping to get a date. (Advocats sans Frontières, 2019: 17)

This report is not the only one highlighting these problems. International organisations and NGOs have been reporting similar issues in recent years, as they tried to help improving conditions in the RICs. In response, the Greek government announced in August 2020 that it had received EU-funding for the creation of closed camps in Samos, Kos and Leros[8] in anticipation of the new EU Pact on Migration and Asylum.[9] In November 2020, the Ministerial Decision no 23/13532[10] on the function of the new RICs was signed. Article 8 of this decision – among other things – criminalises, under the pretext of privacy, any registration and disclosure of information concerning the centres' operation by employees or volunteers working in them. Even if they witness or learn about criminal activities in the camp, they may not make it public and are only allowed to inform the centre's director about it. The same decision renders access to the camps by external observers almost impossible, while, even if access is granted, those entering the site are also subject to Article 8 and may therefore not make any information they collect public. In this light, and at the time of writing this chapter, further independent scientific research on the working conditions of employees – and living conditions of residents – in Greek RICs is needed, but appears to be extremely unlikely to take place at the moment. It is nevertheless obvious by examining more current information gathered from a variety of sources (HRW, 2018; Avocats Sans Frontières, 2019; Jones, 2019) that the conclusions we reached during our own participant observations are still relevant, and possibly reinforced.

First-line social field work means acting as a professional but also as a human being. Throughout the participatory observations, we watched the social workers managing their discretionary space as if between a rock and a hard place, while trying to maintain a professional normality in an abnormal situation. The social workers we met at the Samos RIC were extremely fatigued due to the huge workload and lack of resources in material and personnel. Faced with the needs of the overwhelming number of beneficiaries they catered for, they felt disappointed and frustrated by their inability to make a difference. Far from being powerful representatives of the state as their beneficiaries imagined, they felt powerless and perplexed by the lack of resources, lack of support and supervision/guidance and the lack of clearly defined responsibilities. This resulted in them being called upon to resolve impossible situations that required the help of another specialist or a combination thereof. In this manner, their role is less that of one who contributes to the situation at hand, and more of one who is trying to negotiate the everyday challenges arising by it.

In order to improve the working conditions of the first-line personnel at the Samos RIC and similar structures, as well as the lives of the residents there, first of all, a large increase in funds is needed. Without this, it's impossible to address the problem of the disproportionate numbers of beneficiaries and social workers in the camp, or to ensure better living conditions of the residents, including housing, food catering and hygienic facilities. Social workers should receive special training specific to the target group they are faced with, and to situations they might encounter in the specific setting, including threatening or aggressive behaviour. Guidance and supervision by experienced field workers should be made available to them in order to resolve especially demanding cases. Special care is needed to guard the social workers from secondary trauma, psychological distress and burnout. Their workspace and surroundings should be amended to provide security against threats or violent attacks, and help should be readily available in these situations. The presence of interpreters in the social services is of utmost importance, as the use of community members presents many dangers, and requesting interpreters from administrative or other services takes too much time in a setting where situations can evolve very rapidly. Crucially, conditions in first reception camps in Europe's periphery must be made public reinforcing the discussion for open, small-scale structures, with humane conditions and for a short period of staying, while obscuring them from the public eye can only exacerbate problems and lead to an explosion similar or worse to the burning of the Moria camp in 2020.[11]

Acknowledgements

The authors would like to thank all social workers and participants for sharing their stories with us, as well as all colleagues who contributed to this work with their valuable comments.

This work was supported by the European Research Council under grant ChildMove project Number 71422.

Disclosure statement

We have no known conflict of interest to disclose.

Notes

1. According to Art. 2(h) of Directive 2011/95/EU (Recast Qualification Directive), an asylum application is defined as an application for international protection: 'A request made by a third-country national or a stateless person for protection from a EU Member State, who can be understood to seek refugee status or subsidiary protection status, and who does not explicitly request another kind of protection, outside the scope of Directive 2011/95/EU (Recast Qualification Directive), that can be applied for separately.'
2. FRA (2016), Opinion of the European Union Agency for Fundamental Rights on the Fundamental Rights in the 'Hotspots' Set Up in Greece and Italy, FRA Opinion 5/2016 [Hotspots], Vienna, 29 November 2016. https://fra.europa.eu/sites/default/files/fra_uploads/fra-2019-opinion-hotspots-update-03-2019_en.pdf
3. European Council EU-Turkey Statement. Brussels, 18 March 2016. http://www.consilium.europa.eu/en/press/press-releases/2016/03/18/eu-turkey-statement
4. In Greece there are RICs close to the borders with Turkey as well as in the main land. For more information see: https://migration.gov.gr/en/ris/ https://migration.gov.gr/chartis-ypiresion/
5. UNHCR Greece sea arrival dashboard, November 2017. https://reliefweb.int/sites/reliefweb.int/files/resources/61395.pdf
6. Joint agency briefing paper – transitioning to a government run refugee and migrant response in Greece. https://oxfamilibrary.openrepository.com/bitstream/handle/10546/620397/bp-roadmap-greece-refugees-migrants-131217-en.pdf;jsessionid=9C150B4181A5133968867E2063D7BE4F?sequence=1
7. The medical service was responsible for the identification of people in vulnerable situations. Social workers could only make an internal report as a suggestion to the medical service. For more information see https://asylumineurope.org/reports/country/greece/asylum-procedure/guarantees-vulnerable-groups/identification/#III_AP_D_3MedicalReports
8. https://migration.gov.gr/en/egkrithike-chrimatodotisi/
9. Ministerial Decision 23/13532, FEK 5272/B/30-11-2020. https://www.e-nomothesia.gr/kat-allodapoi/upourgike-apophase-23-13532-phek-5272b-30-11-2020.html (in Greek).
10. https://www.e-nomothesia.gr/kat-allodapoi/upourgike-apophase-23-13532-phek-5272b-30-11-2020.html
11. https://www.nytimes.com/2020/09/09/world/europe/fire-refugee-camp-lesbos-moria.html

References

Akosa, F. and Asare, B.E. (2017) Street-level bureaucrats and the exercise of discretion, in A. Farazmand (ed) *Global Encyclopedia of Public Administration, Public Policy, and Governance*, Cham: Springer.

Altmann, J. (1974) Observational study of behavior: Sampling methods, *Behaviour*, 49(3/4): 227–67.

Avocats Sans Frontières France (2019) 'The hotspot approach at the service of the geographical containment of migrants. Study on violations of migrants' rights on the island of Samos. Observation report', Mission carried out for Migreurop and by Mathilde ALBERT from 7 May–6 October 2019. www.migreurop.org/IMG/pdf/fiche_hotspot_-_m._albert_-_en.pdf

Berrick, J.D. (2018) *The Impossible Imperative: Navigating the Competing Principles of Child Protection*, New York: Oxford University Press.

Boccagni, P. and Righard, E. (2020) 'Social work with refugee and displaced populations in Europe: (dis)continuities, dilemmas, developments', *European Journal of Social Work*, 23(3): 375–83.

Bogdan, R. and Taylor, S.J. (1975) *Introduction to Qualitative Research Methods: A Phenomenological Approach to the Social Sciences*, New York: Wiley.

Braun, V. and Clarke, V. (2006) 'Using thematic analysis in psychology', *Qualitative Research in Psychology*, 3(2): 77–101.

ECRE (2016) 'The implementation of the hotspots in Italy and Greece – a study'. www.ecre.org/wp-content/uploads/2016/12/HOTSPOTS-Report-5.12.2016.pdf

Evans, T. and Harris, J. (2004) 'Street-level bureaucracy, social work and the (exaggerated) death of discretion', *British Journal of Social Work*, 34(6): 871–95.

FRA (2016) 'Opinion of the European Union Agency for Fundamental Rights on the fundamental rights in the "hotspots" set up in Greece and Italy'. https://fra.europa.eu/sites/default/files/fra_uploads/fra-2019-opinion-hotspots-update-03-2019_en.pdf

Gkionakis, N. (2016) 'The refugee crisis in Greece: Training border security, police, volunteers and aid workers in psychological first aid', *Intervention*, 14 (1): 73–9.

Greece: Law No. 4375 of 2016 on the organization and operation of the Asylum Service, the Appeals Authority, the Reception and Identification Service, the establishment of the General Secretariat for Reception, the transposition into Greek legislation of the provisions of Directive 2013/32/EC [Greece], 3 April. www.refworld.org/docid/573ad4cb4.html

Gustovict, K. and Potocky, M. (2018) 'Mitigating psychological distress among humanitarian staff working with migrants and refugees: A case example', *Special Issue Immigrants and Refugees*, 18(3).

Holy, L. (1984) 'Theory, methodology and the research process', in R.F. Ellen (ed) *Ethnographic Research: A Guide to General Conduct*, Oxford: Oxford University Press, pp 13–34.

Human Rights Watch (2016) 'Greece refugee "hotspots" unsafe, unsanitary. Women, children fearful, unprotected; lack basic shelter'. www.hrw.org/news/2016/05/19/greece-refugee-hotspots-unsafe-unsanitary

Human Rights Watch (2018) 'Greece: 13,000 still trapped on islands'. www.hrw.org/news/2018/03/06/greece-13000-still-trapped-islands

Jones, C. (2019) 'Social work and the refugee crisis: reflections from Samos in Greece', in M. Lavalette (ed) *What Is the Future of Social Work*, Bristol: Policy Press, pp 143–60.

Kawulich, B. (2005) 'Participant observation as a data collection method', *Forum: Qualitative Social Research*, 6(2): Art. 43.

Lipsky, M. (1969) *Toward a Theory of Street-level Bureaucracy*, Madison, WI: University of Wisconsin.

Lipsky, M. (1976) 'Toward a theory of street-level bureaucracy', in W. Hawley and M. Lipsky (eds) *Theoretical Perspectives on Urban Politics*, New York: Prentice-Hall.

Lipsky, M. (2010) *Street-Level Bureaucracy: Dilemmas of the Individual in Public Services*, New York: Russell Sage Foundation.

Murdach, A. (2009) 'Discretion in direct practice: New perspectives', *Social Work*, 54(2): 183–86.

Robinson, K. (2014) 'Voices from the front line: Social work with refugees and asylum seekers in Australia and the UK', *British Journal of Social Work*, 44(6): 1602–20.

Rozakou, K. (2017) 'Access to a hot field: A self-reflexive account of research in the Moria Camp, Lesvos'. www.law.ox.ac.uk/research-subject-groups/centre-criminology/centreborder-criminologies/blog/2017/11/access-hot-field

Teloni, D.-D., Dedotsi, S. and Telonis, A. (2020) 'Refugee "crisis" and social services in Greece: Social workers' profile and working conditions', *European Journal of Social Work*, 23(6): 1005–18.

Turbett, C. (2020) 'Radical social work in the real world', in L. Wroe, R. Larkin and R.A. Maglajlic (eds) *Social Work with Refugees, Asylum Seekers and Migrants: Theories and Skills for Practice*, London: Jessica Kingsley.

Witcher, A. (2021) 'Greece's discriminatory migrant regime: Volunteers, informal street-level bureaucrats, and moral rationalities', *Journal of Refugee Studies*, 3482: 1540–59.

4

Migrant girls' experiences of integration and social care in Sweden

Elin Ekström

Introduction

This chapter aims to illuminate a discord between the general integration discourse in Sweden, the way it is materialised in social work practice, and how young refugees view their own situation in relation to integration and resettlement.

Based on a study with 11 so-called 'unaccompanied female minors', the chapter illuminates alternative perspectives on what challenges these girls face as they seek to integrate into a new society post transit.

Integration (also the Swedish definition of the term) has been criticised for being vague and shifting in meaning, depending on the context in which it is used (Lalander and Raoof, 2017; Schierup and Ålund, 2011). Nonetheless, it is a recurring concept in social work with refugees, often in terms of aim or objectives (Wernesjö, 2019); consequently, it shapes the approach used by social workers with their clients (Vitus and Jarlby, 2021). In general discourse, structural challenges related to integration tend to be reframed as questions of problematic identities (Korteweg, 2017). Lalander and Raoof (2017) argue that individuals whose identities diverge from the majority are perceived in social work as 'unprocessed raw material' that are to be moulded through social interventions. Therefore, efforts made to promote integration are designed in ways that reinforce the individuals' sense of non-belonging (Eliassi, 2015; Lalander and Raoof, 2017).

This chapter is based on a study done with teenage girls having arrived in Sweden seeking refuge. The chapter begins by briefly introducing the study. It then proceeds by outlining and problematising a general discourse of integration and its application to social work in Sweden, with a focus on unaccompanied minors. Thereafter, it turns to the voices of the girls and analyses how their accounts regarding integration compare to the general discourse.

In the conclusion, I argue that the discord between the two perspectives of integration has a very concrete impact on the girls' reality, impeding on their ability to resettle as equal members of the Swedish society.

Outline of the study

This chapter is based on a study, conducted between 2017–2019, in which 11 girls who had arrived in Sweden as unaccompanied refugee minors were interviewed, seven of them were interviewed on two separate occasions. They were between 13 and 18 years old and came from Afghanistan, Ethiopia, Iraq, Syria and Somalia and had been in Sweden for between six months to two and a half years. Though they came from different backgrounds, they became part of the same system of reception in Sweden and, therefore, also faced common challenges. At the time of the first interviews, only three of them had received a residence permit, while the others had pending applications at the migration board. At the time of the second interviews, all of them had received residence permits, and two of them had also reunited with family members in Sweden.

The interviews were semi-structured around the girls' experiences of resettlement and their time in Sweden, rather than what had led to their migration or their experiences during transit. However, the conversations flowed between different time and spaces, as the girls referred to their past as well as considered their future.

What became apparent during the interviews was that while the girls went along with the integration process as it was expected of them, their own understanding of integration focused on more existential concerns. Most of them lived their first year(s) in Sweden in a continuum of deportability, as their asylum applications were pending. Furthermore, as forced migrants, they were in a particularly difficult situation since they had little, or nothing, to return to should their asylum application be denied. During the interviews, their challenges revolved around two main themes: (1) fundamental questions about the right to life and (2) how to understand their place in their new society. The chapter will focus on outlining these two themes and, in doing so, discuss how the girls' own perception of integration represent an alternative logic compared to the general discourse on integration in social work practice.

All names in this chapter are pseudonyms to protect the identity of the participants.

Integration discourses in Swedish social work practice

In Swedish social work practice, the concept of integration is often used but rarely defined (Lalander and Raoof, 2017; Wernesjö, 2019). Yet, social workers' interpretation of the concept impinges on individual migrants' efforts to resettle in a new country and their access to equal rights (Eliassi, 2015; Gustafsson and Johansson, 2018; Vitus and Jarlby, 2021).

Scholars have argued that discourses on migrant integration in receiving countries, contrary to the word's lexical meaning, construct a divide between normal identities and cultural Others (Anthias, 2013; Eliassi, 2015; Korteweg, 2017). Moreover, integration is often perceived as a binary and/ or linear process that focuses on the non-belonging of the Other, instead of structural challenges contributing to exclusion (for example, racism or economic and social inequality). In this sense, the process of integration is framed as a struggle for the individual migrant, who is perceived as not being integrated, rather than as a shared societal endeavour (Emejulu and Bassel, 2015; Korteweg, 2017). This inclination is further concretised at the frontlines of social work practice, as traditional social work is dependent on categorisation (Eriksson and Appel Nissen, 2017). In addition, social work with migrants, as it is carried out through public authorities, is often based on the needs of the host society, rather than on the needs of the individual (Gustafsson and Johansson, 2018).

In Sweden, it falls upon social workers to navigate the legal frameworks and provide guidance on this individual struggle by means of framing migrant identities, conceptualise challenges, and decide upon suitable interventions (Eliassi, 2015). Studies on social work with migrants in Sweden show that, in this process, social workers are ambivalent in their understanding of integration (Gustafsson and Johansson, 2018; Lalander and Raoof, 2017; Wernesjö, 2019). Nevertheless, integration is perceived as an individual, rather than a collective societal, struggle (Eliassi, 2015; Lalander and Raoof, 2017).

Difficulties in defining and concretising the meaning of integration in social work might stem from it being a second-order concept. Our understanding of integration is based on how we understand other (equally vague) constructs, such as 'society', 'culture' and 'identity'(Anthias, 2013). These first-order constructs, which, in themselves, also demarcate between inclusion and exclusion, are continuously framed and reframed in political and public discourse. Hence, the meaning ascribed to the concept of integration is likely to sway along with changing, broader political discourses (see for example Emejulu and Bassel, 2015; Gustafsson and Johansson, 2018; Schierup and Ålund, 2011; Vitus and Jarlby, 2021; Wernesjö, 2019).

In Swedish political discourse, as well as in social work practice, integration is generally approached as labour market integration (Sager and Öberg, 2017; Wernesjö, 2019). Even more so since 2016 when the Swedish government passed an interim legislation that drastically infringed upon Swedish migration law (Lag (2016: 752) 'om tillfälliga begränsningar av möjligheten att få uppehållstillstånd i Sverige', 2019). According to the interim legislation, permanent residence and family reunification can only be granted if the applicant has secured employment. As argued by Sager and Öberg (2017), this political and legal turn represented a further shift in an ongoing development away from a human rights perspective, contributing instead to a continuum of deportability for those seeking protection for themselves and/or their families.

Recent studies have shown how the interim legislation echoed in social work practice as stricter attitudes towards migrants (Gustafsson and Johansson, 2018). However, Wernesjö (2019) also demonstrate how social workers assigned to unaccompanied minors choose to approach integration in a way they believe can actually have an impact on their chances of staying in Sweden. Often, this means complying with a discourse of labour market integration by emphasising education, language courses and learning about 'Swedish norms and customs' (Lalander and Raoof, 2017; Wernesjö, 2019). This approach to integration aligns with what Anthias (2013) describes as a distinction between structural and cultural integration. Structural integration encompasses integration in the public space, for example, the labour market or educational institutions, while cultural integration refers to a more vague sense of belonging in a community. It is generally assumed that these forms of integration do not affect each other, that they can be separated, and that what is perceived as cultural is not involved in structural integration (Anthias, 2013). The problem with this divide is that it risks limiting the scope of social work interventions to what is perceived as strictly needed in order to be employable. This has been touched upon in a study by Gustafsson and Johansson (2018), where social workers explain that they do not see, for example, the existential needs of their clients as their responsibility. It is also visible in how efforts to support young migrants in their integration process is scaled down to focus on education, while leisure-time activities are perceived as something that can be used as a reward or withheld as punishment (Lalander and Raoof, 2017).

Since 2006, the reception of unaccompanied minors falls on the municipalities in Sweden. The municipalities are responsible for the minors, both during and after the asylum application process. It lies within their responsibility to investigate the minor's need for care and support, decide on interventions and continuously follow up on their situation (Socialstyrelsen, 2013). The responsibility falls on the social workers, as the intermediary between the welfare state and the minor, to safeguard the minor's best interest. In this endeavour, it is important how the minor's identity, interests and challenges are framed and conceptualised as it will have an impact on their integration processes and their access to equal rights (Eliassi, 2015). Yet, a study by Herz and Lalander (2019) illustrates how case workers often are detached from their clients, possibly due to increased bureaucratisation.

An alternative perspective

The girls who partook in this study described unique challenges when talking about integration. While education and employment were part of how they envisioned their future in Sweden, their primary concerns were of another character. To begin with, being forced to seek refuge in a new country brought about existential questions of rights, worth and identity. Second, they seemed to find no support in these questions, as they did not fall within the scope of the social services, and it was hard finding someone who would take time to listen to their concerns.

The right to life and being worthy of protection

During the first round of interviews, the girls who had not yet received their residential permits (9) kept circling back to the liminality of their situation. From these interviews, it was evident that the fear of being forced to leave Sweden had a continuous impact on their lives. Whenever they spoke about the future, it was conditional upon their asylum application. For most of them, there were no alternative plans; either they would be allowed to stay, or they would not. Some of the girls had careful aspirations for a future in Sweden, involving education and employment; however, when asked about these aspirations, they soon steered the conversation back to their pending asylum application. The awaited decision from the migration board seemed almost like a ghostly veil obscuring their future, an abstract obstacle that they could not lift themselves. The uncertainty and the insecurity of their situation are well illustrated by the following quote from Beydaan. She was 17 at the time of the first interview and was enrolled in high school, where she divided her time between ordinary classes and Swedish language courses. She was committed to making the best out of her new opportunities in Sweden and insisted on doing the interview in Swedish, which she spoke almost fluently. When asked about her plans for the future, she carefully talked about taking up voluntary work, to pay back what she said the Swedish society had given her. Yet, when asked about her outlook on the future, Beydaan described her situation as:

> 'You know, I don't know … because everything depends on, because now at this time, I don't know if I can stay in Sweden or not. So, it's a problem that you don't know if you can stay or not. But I do know there are many refugees who shall go back. … Many want to do good things, want a good future, want to study, go to school, everything. But it is different when you don't know; you can't do anything. So, you must just wait. And I've waited for so long now, almost two years. … So, I don't want to think about that anymore, but it's like they tell you that you're going to die. There is no life for me in my home country.'

What Beydaan described was the very present threat of deportation and how it affected her. She had arrived in Sweden just before the interim legislation was passed and had been told that this meant that a lot of people seeking asylum would be turned away. Even in this brief quote, she kept returning to the uncertainty of her situation, saying 'don't know'. It highlights how every part of her life was affected, both practically and emotionally. Not knowing whether she would be sent back, she could neither make plans for the future nor invest emotionally in her hopes and dreams. In this situation, her life was put on hold. She existed in a state of liminality, where she, for the last one and a half years, had been rendered powerless in front of her own possible death.

While she tried, as well as she could, to study and learn how to conform to the expectations that were placed on her, she pointed to the relativity of those efforts. Being denied residence permit was for her the same as being told that she would die, and in that case, her struggles would be pointless. The quote points to the discrepancy between official discourses, which locate integration efforts at the individual level, and the perspective of the girls, as their individual efforts would mean nothing if their asylum applications were denied.

Yasmiin, an 18-year-old young woman, expressed similar thoughts. Like Beydaan, she feared deportation. However, she also admitted that, sometimes, she did not know what to do if she were to stay in Sweden either. She was alone, without her family, in a foreign country where she did not know the people, or the culture. Worrying about her future had caused her to have physical symptoms, like severe headaches, and she had trouble sleeping at night. During the first interview, she revealed that she occasionally had been having destructive thoughts about her own worth. When asked about the content of these thoughts, she stated: "If I cannot stay in Sweden, then I can't live, so why should I keep living?"

Her words conveyed a double meaning regarding what would happen if her asylum application was denied. She had fled from extreme poverty as well as armed conflicts and, like Beydaan, she did not believe she would survive being sent back. Apart from this, in the same sentence, she also expressed a deeper existential concern. If she would be denied the safety of asylum, then what was her life worth? The awaited decision from the migration board was, for Yasmiin and Beydaan, not a question of what alternatives they had in the future; rather, it was a question of whether they had a future at all. It was also a question about the right to life. They belonged, as Beydaan framed it, to a category (that is, refugees) for whom the right to life and security in a peaceful country are conditional. For them, contributing to society becomes a prerequisite for the right to life, exceeding what is usually understood as the inherent worth of every human being. For Yasmiin, the reality of her deportability transformed into a questioning of her own existence as she worried whether she could live up to the demands of her new society.

This sense of conditional equality was reflected in most of the interviews, though it manifested differently depending on the girls' individual situation.

Kaela was one of the girls who, at the time of our first interview, had received a temporary residence permit. She was among the youngest of the interviewed girls and one of the few who had clear and ambitious plans for the future. Kaela jokingly described Swedes as 'all work and no play', but she admitted that living in Sweden had inspired her to see opportunities for her own life. She was thrilled to learn about the system of free education in Sweden, as it was not something that had been available to her in her home country. Seeing it as an opportunity, she was committed to study and to becoming 'something good', both in terms of a career and as a citizen of her new country. However, the temporary residence permit put her dreams just out of reach. Talking about her future, she expressed herself with both frustration and anger:

> 'I want to know why I can't stay … because I want to become something good in the future. But why can't they give me a … you know … with a picture and my name and social security number … ID! Why can't I have an ID? Eh, look, I will explain. I have this [residence permit], eh, only for two years. Why can't I get it for my whole life? To stay in Sweden … they told me that we shall see if the city where I lived, if it goes well there, we shall see if we have to go back or if we shall stay in Sweden. But I want to continue living in Sweden! Because [slapping her hand against the table] it's better! It feels really hard, because in my country I won't be able to do everything [that I want]. For example, I won't be able to learn lots of languages. I won't be able to become a good something in the future.'

It is interesting here how Kaela connects having an ID with having opportunities for the future. In Sweden, the use of social security numbers is common when dealing with different public authorities, health and educational institutions. The ID-card, a piece of plastic, was infused with possibilities, both abstract and concrete, and became yet another border, excluding her from fully entering the Swedish society. Kaela's description of what she wants links her own person, represented by the name and picture, to the possibilities and the proof of belonging that is represented by the social security number. Her frustration stems partly from why the link itself, so easily put together on a piece of plastic, is withheld from her but also from why there seems to be no valid reason for this. She is denied the opportunities of her new society based, not on her own ambitions and competences, but on a future evaluation, done by strangers, of a context she has left behind and that she has no control over.

Together, the way Beydaan, Yasmiin and Kaela frame challenges at the threshold of a new society represents an alternative logic within the integration context. Their perspectives illuminate what the integration concept seldom captures, namely that for the individual, it is sometimes less a matter of education and employment; rather, it is a matter of life and death.

Understanding identity in a new context

Among those girls who had received their residence permits or those who, regardless, could visualise a future in Sweden, integration was approached as a manner of understanding their own place and who they could become in their new society. It was evident that they had taken note of what path they were expected to follow to become recognised members of the Swedish society. To 'always think about the future' (Amber, 17), in terms of education and future employment was described as a Swedish mindset that they had to adopt if they were to have a good life in Sweden. Yet, when asked about their own priorities, their focus tended to be on more complex subjects relating to identity, rights and belonging.

Tahli, aged 17, was one of the girls who had been granted permanent residence, as her asylum application had passed just before the interim legislation was introduced. She now divided her time between high school and a part-time job as a cleaner. It had eased her mind to know that she was now going to stay in Sweden. Her new priority was to master Swedish, as language was 'key to integration'. However, she added, 'But right now, I'm also a part of [this]society. We [who live here] work together, together with Swedes also. So, I am [integrated].'

The statement that language is 'key to integration' has been a mantra in Swedish integration discourse for some time, both at the political level and in social work practice. While Tahli, on the one hand, recognises the benefits of conforming to the expectations conveyed through this notion of language as key to integration, she resists the idea that she is not yet integrated. In line with Korteweg's argumentation, she emphasises her own belonging, her living and interacting in Sweden, rather than her non-belonging. Later in our conversation, she revisited the subject of integration, but now from another angle.

> 'I have thought, eh, very much about this. Have you, you know, what duties do you have? … Yes, that was very much what I was thinking about … I haven't received any answer to that … yet. I've asked. … It's a lot of things, but I don't know exactly, rights and duties. What is the difference between rights and duties?'

The way she struggled to formulate her meaning suggests that the topic she tried to frame was itself something fluid and hard to grasp. However, her vague formulations become clearer against an integration discourse where that which is usually labelled as a right, free education, for example, instead becomes emphasised as a duty. She has asked for guidance in this matter, but no one has been able to help her navigate, or perhaps even formulate, what her ruminations are about. These kinds of thoughts around what the migration would mean for them, in terms of freedom, possibilities and obligations, were recurring in most of the interviews.

In particular, gender roles were mentioned as a question of interest. The majority of the girls described their previous societal contexts as more patriarchal and restrictive, in terms of women's rights, compared to Sweden. Some of them described a decline in women's rights and freedoms, often in the wake of war and conflict, as contributing in part to why they had fled. Naturally, they were curious about what it meant to be a (young) woman in Sweden. Azita did not know whether she could stay in Sweden at the time of the first interview. When she talked about what had so far been most important to her, she explained:

> 'The most important was safety, and then to learn the identity of a woman, of a girl in the society. What rights and obligations a woman or a girl has? So far, I'm new here, but I've understood what it can mean to be a woman. Being a woman, rights. That a woman can be like a man; that I've understood, but I'm still missing things that I need, that I want to learn for the future.'

Her quote can be read as a rather straightforward question about the status of women in Sweden. Where Azita came from, many things that are taken for granted in Sweden were forbidden or controversial for women. Thus, it is easy to see how she wanted to explore what new rights and opportunities she could now have. At a closer look, however, she located her exploration, not at a societal level, but with herself. She spoke about rights, which can be understood to be nation bound, but she also talked about capacities, 'that a woman can be like a man', which rather speaks about something innate. What she truly explores then, is not the conditions for women in Sweden; rather, she takes the opportunity, in this uncertain situation, to learn about aspects of her own identity that had previously been discouraged. She uses the new context to discover who and what she could be. In the last sentence of the quote, we can sense an urgency in how she still needs to learn more 'for the future'. At this point, she turns the liminality of her situation into a window of opportunity. Not knowing yet whether she would be able to stay in Sweden, her new insights also affected how she perceived the consequences of going back. When talking about the possibility of deportation, she pointed to recent events in Sweden where a young refugee had committed suicide (Backman, 2017a, 2017b), rather than face being sent back. She explained that even if she would survive in her former country, the way she would have to live her life would effectively be as if a part of her would die.

Both Tahli and Azita reflect the girls' struggle to navigate the structures governing their new social context. Tahli demonstrated that she already saw herself as part of the community, although she struggled to grasp the deeper implications of what that meant for her. Azita explored her own capacity, rather than society's expectations.

Finding someone who can listen

Gustafsson and Johansson (2018) have discussed how social workers do not see existential issues as lying within the scope of their responsibility. Additionally, Herz and Lalander's study (2019) illustrates how social workers who are responsible for unaccompanied minors in Sweden often have a distanced relationship with their clients. The girls who partook in this study confirmed these findings. Though most of them described their case workers in positive terms as kind and caring persons, some of them were critical of how and what kind of support they had received. In general, the girls met with their social workers once every three months. During these meetings, the social workers asked the girls about their wellbeing and if they had encountered any difficulties. However, there seemed to be little opportunity for the girls to elaborate on anything outside of the social workers' agenda. Azita commented that: "They just gave a lot of information. And spoke [in a] very complicated [manner], so it made you forget your own questions."

Despite the social workers', sometimes, complicated manner of speaking, the girls all seemed well informed about what they could and could not expect, in terms of aid and support from the social services. They were, for example, very aware of how the social services held no power, in regard to their asylum application. It seemed, however, as if the efforts made to properly inform the girls of the division of responsibility in the reception structure resulted in an emptiness between these seemingly clear-cut borders of bureaucratic and legal systems, where the bigger questions could not resonate. In the first interview, Mari described how she had trouble dealing with her anxiety about the future. She had a difficult relationship with her foster care guardians and felt isolated in their home. She sometimes talked to friends about the residence permit but seemed reluctant to do so. We talked about where else she could turn to get support:

> 'When you talk to the migration board, they just tell you that there are many people in line, you have to wait. And that yeah, that's the only answer you get. And now I have waited for one and a half years. … They [the social services] can't help me that much because they say that they have nothing to do with the migration board and they can't influence anything. But they can help me with other things,

like living arrangements and economy and such. But otherwise, they can't help me.'

In Mari's quote, we can see how not having to do with the migration board translated as not having to do with the uncertainty of their status. Still, the uncertainty of their situation was the most immediate concern for the girls and the root of far bigger questions that severely impacted on their everyday lives. While concrete matters such as housing and economy lay within the scope of the social services, Mari stood alone when it came to more complex and difficult worries.

Some of the girls reflected on how inner turmoil, causing great emotional pain, is sometimes obscured by the way it manifests itself physically. It was common during the interviews to hear the girls talk about having headaches or stomach aches, trouble sleeping or otherwise not feeling well physically. They often linked these physical symptoms to their emotional state, but not always right away. Ester was 14 years old when she arrived in Sweden with her older brother. She had been shocked to learn that her brother would have to stay in accommodation provided by the migration board in another town, while she was turned over to foster care. During their first two years, while they lived separately, she had felt incredibly lonely and confused as time passed. The separation that had been explained to her as being only temporary drew out. She often cried herself to sleep, thinking about her absent family. The crying, she said, was actually helpful since she could not possibly contain all her sad feelings inside. Sometimes the feelings of loneliness became too much and then she got sick. When she complained to the social workers responsible for her about not feeling well, she was told that as she did not appear to be suffering anything (physically) serious, she was probably fine.

> 'So, sometimes … for example, when I'm ill, I don't feel well. Then they say that 'you don't look ill. You don't seem to be sick'. … So, they think … they think mostly about … [they] look at your face, how your face is. They don't think about what's inside your heart.'

Ester revisited this discussion in our second interview. She had then been granted a residence permit together with her brother, and they had been able to move in together, in their own apartment. When looking back, she frustratingly commented that "It's them [the social workers] that need to understand, they need to understand that you are lonely". The first quote by Ester encourages us to look beyond the surface and try to understand where the sensations (physical or emotional) come from. Her second quote is a call for a deeper listening and a deeper understanding of her spoken words, words that cannot always properly convey her complex emotional state. To her, it was evident that as a young individual, separated from her family in a foreign country facing an uncertain future, she would struggle with loneliness. To her, her feelings were both natural and valid and no matter how she expressed her feelings, they should have been taken seriously. A parallel can be drawn to when Yasmiin, whose case was mentioned earlier, sought help from her social worker when her overall condition had become unbearable to her. She had then been offered to see a physician who could prescribe stronger painkillers for her headaches as well as sleeping pills to help her sleep. Both Yasmiin and Ester described how the underlying causes of their symptoms were not investigated or even recognised. Their experiences confirm Maris' conclusion that the support available to them is restricted to concrete matters that can be solved by equally concrete interventions.

The girls, of course, had coping strategies of their own. For example, as discussed in a previous article based on the same study (see Ekström et al, 2020), several girls turned to their faith and used religion as a support structure. Religion provided them with both comfort and hope for the future as well as guidance in finding their place in the new society. However, for the Muslim girls, especially those wearing a veil, religion also became a source of differentiation and othering. Several girls found an outlet in physical activities and, of course, receiving a residence permit transformed their situation, as did reuniting with family members.

Among the different ways the girls found to deal with the ambiguity of existing in liminality, there was one story that stood out. Beydaan, the girl who feared that she would die, had found a sounding board for her thoughts and feelings. A bit farther into the conversation during the first interview, she talked about a woman, a social worker, who was doing fieldwork. She had come to Beydaan's school to inform them about opportunities for leisure-time activities. Without having the specific task to offer counselling, this woman had listened to Beydaan when she had brought up her fear of deportation. Beydaan visibly lightened up during the interview when she explained that this woman had *just listened* to her. There were no timeframes for their meetings; once they had talked for more than two hours, which was more than double the time Beydaan had with her social worker every third month. This person never required or expected Beydaan to account for her situation. Nor did she seem to shy away from, or dismiss, the complex and sometimes difficult feelings Beydaan had.

> 'She told me to only think of good things uhm, you can do much in the future. You can make a difference between … bad times and the future. So, she is the best. [laughs] She gave me her card. She said that "if you need to talk, you can talk to me".'

The quote here stands in stark contrast to the first quote by Beydaan. Here, hope is visible in the way Beydaan is given both concrete advice on how to tackle her anxiety by focusing on possibilities and 'good things'. She describes being encouraged to look forward, and it seems like the advice given offers a break between the 'bad times' in the past and her uncertain future, regardless of what it might hold. Most importantly, it presents a lifeline. "If you need to talk, you can talk to me" becomes the opposite of the restricted support usually offered by the social services. It also signifies an understanding of what became important in a situation, where little else could be done: at least someone could listen.

Conclusion

This chapter has presented two perspectives on the challenges and expectations relating to the concept of integration. On the one hand, a general discourse on integration, as it is often framed in social work, which emphasises labour market integration, locates challenges with the individual and in that frame their non-belonging (Eliassi, 2015; Korteweg, 2017; Sager and Öberg, 2017). On the other hand, an alternative perspective represented by the narratives of young girls seeking refuge in Sweden. This perspective problematises how labour market integration is emphasised in general discourse and instead highlights issues of rights, worth, identity and equality.

It becomes clear that the general discourse of integration allows little room for the challenges which, according to the girls themselves, prevent them from becoming equal members of their new society. The demands placed upon them, regarding education and employment, stand in stark contrast to the fundamental questions about the right to life, and whether one is worthy of protection, which influences how the girls look upon their future prospects. In addition, while the general discourse focuses on the individual's ability to contribute to the host society, the girls focused on how to belong. Thus, they explored questions about rights and duties and identity.

For some girls, struggling on their own with these questions could be a challenge in itself. Here, it becomes clear that there was no apparent way for them to find support in dealing with their thoughts and feelings even though these sometimes had a very concrete impact on their everyday life as well as their plans and aspirations for the future.

Looking forward, a possible outcome of this neglect, as we have already seen in the stories narrated here, might be that individuals in need of support see no point in voicing their concerns. This might, in turn, lead to a gradual silencing among young refugees facing difficult challenges (see also, Ekström et al 2021; Kohli 2006).

Another risk is that the disregard for how young refugees' more existential concerns impede on their resettlement process creates a vicious circle, where a more and more strict focus on labour market integration instigates more existential doubts. In a way, contributing to the process described by

Korteweg, whereby constructs of individual identities as problematic obscure the structural challenges and discrimination faced by these individuals.

For social workers having to apply or adhere to the concept of integration in their work, it is important to reflect upon whose perspective is accounted for, from which viewpoint challenges are conceptualised and what meaning the concept of integration is given in social work interventions. A too narrow understanding of what integration means and how it is achieved might fail to address fundamental issues of rights, equality and belonging. I might also disregard what Tahli points out in her quote; that in her everyday life she is already part of her new society, she is already, in some ways, integrated. It is also important to remember that the girls in this chapter found their own ways of coping. By recognising their perspective, their coping strategies can be encouraged and supported instead of questioned or hindered. Returning to Anthias description of integration as a second-order concept it could be wise to acknowledge, in this case the girls', interpretation of underlying concepts such as society, culture and identity. Social workers might want to deliberate on these vague but often used concepts, together with their clients, and perhaps open up for a broader perspective on integration and its meaning in the context of social care.

On a final note, this chapter has argued that the perspectives represented here highlight a conditional equality that the girls are very aware of and that affects how they think about themselves and their belonging. Returning briefly to the concept of equality, it can be problematic from a social work perspective when, by treating everybody equally, individual preconditions and experiences are not considered. Anthias (2013) suggests 'solidarity' as an operational term, as it emphasises individual subjects as holders of rights. Listening has been argued to be an act of solidarity (Back, 2007; Bassel, 2017). On that note, the stories of the girls represented in this chapter can be interpreted as a call for solidarity. That was indeed what many of the girls were asking for, namely that someone took the time to listen.

References

Anthias, F. (2013) 'Moving beyond the Janus face of integration and diversity discourses: Towards an intersectional framing', *Sociological Review*, 61(2): 323–43.

Back, L. (2007) *The Art of Listening*, Oxford: Berg.

Backman, M. (2017a) 'Detta är slutet på mitt liv – jag har inget att förlora', *Svenska Dagbladet*, 5 March. https://www.svd.se/a/4aBg9/detta-ar-slutet-pa-mitt-liv-jag-har-inget-att-forlora

Backman, M. (2017b) 'Utvisningshotade ungdomar överväger självmord i grupp', *Svenska Dagbladet*, 5 March. https://www.svd.se/a/8aqo2/utvisningshotade-ungdomar-overvager-sjalvmord-i-grupp

Bassel, L. (2017) *The Politics of Listening: Possibilities and Challenges for Democratic Life*, London: Palgrave Macmillan.

Ekström, E., H Bülow, P. and Wilinska, M. (2020) '"I don't think you will understand me because really, I believe": Unaccompanied female minors re-negotiating religion', *Qualitative Social Work: QSW: Research and Practice*, 19(4): 719–35.

Ekström, E., Andersson, A.-C. and Börjesson, U. (2021) '"I've got many stories you know": Problematizing silence among unaccompanied migrant girls', *Journal of International Migration and Integration*, 23(2): 797–814.

Eliassi, B. (2015) 'Constructing cultural otherness within the Swedish welfare state: The cases of social workers in Sweden', *Qualitative Social Work: QSW: Research and Practice*, 14(4): 554–71.

Emejulu, A. and Bassel, L. (2015) 'Minority women, austerity and activism', *Race & Class*, 57(2): 86–95.

Eriksson, M. and Appel Nissen, M. (2017) 'Categorization and changing service user positions', *Nordic Social Work Research*, 7(3): 183–7.

Gustafsson, K. and Johansson, J. (2018) 'A worthy reception? Ambivalences in social work with refugees and migrants in Sweden', *Advances in Social Work*, 18(3): 983–1004.

Herz, M. and Lalander, P. (2019) 'An abstract and nameless, but powerful, bystander – "Unaccompanied Children" talking about their social workers in Sweden', *Nordic Social Work Research*, 9(1): 18–28.

Kohli, R. (2006) 'The sound of silence: Listening to what unaccompanied asylum-seeking children say and do not say', *British Journal of Social Work*, 36(5): 707–21.

Korteweg, A.C. (2017) 'The failures of "immigrant integration": The gendered racialized production of non-belonging', *Migration Studies*, 5(3): 428–44.

Lag (2016: 752) om tillfälliga begränsningar av möjligheten att få uppehållstillstånd i Sverige. https://www.riksdagen.se/sv/dokument-lagar/dokument/svensk-forfattningssamling/lag-2016752-om-tillfalliga-begransningar-av_sfs-2016-752

Lalander, P. and Raoof, D. (2017) '"Vi vet vad du behöver" Konstruktion och motstånd av "ensamkommande" på HVB', *Socialvetenskaplig tidskrift*, 23(3–4).

Sager, M. and Öberg, K. (2017) 'Articulations of deportability: Changing migration policies in Sweden 2015/2016', *Refugee Review*, 3, 2–14.

Schierup, C.-U. and Ålund, A. (2011) 'The end of Swedish exceptionalism? Citizenship, neoliberalism and the politics of exclusion', *Race & Class*, 53(1): 45–64.

Socialstyrelsen. (2013). 'Barn och ungas hälsa, vård och omsorg 2013', *Artikelnr*. https://www.socialstyrelsen.se/globalassets/sharepoint-dokument/artikelkatalog/ovrigt/2013-3-15

Vitus, K. and Jarlby, F. (2021) 'Between integration and repatriation: Frontline Experiences of how conflicting immigrant integration policies hamper the integration of young refugees in Denmark', *Journal of Ethnic and Migration Studies*, 1–19.

Wernesjö, U. (2019) 'Integration i ett tillfälligt undantagstillstånd?' in M. Darvishpour and N. Månsson (eds) *Ensamkommandes upplevelser & professionellas erfarenheter: integration, inkludering och jämställdhet*, Stockholm: Liber.

5

"Come to my house!": Homing practices of children in Swiss asylum camps

Clara Bombach

Introduction

In her essay 'We Refugees', Hannah Arendt wrote, 'We have lost our home which means the familiarity of daily life. We lost our occupation, which means the confidence that we are of some use in this world' (2007 (1943): 264). What does 'home' mean for children and their parent(s) who live for months and years in transitional situations and the improvised community of a camp? Studies discussing camp life describe the structural conditions as gruelling for residents and staff. Jaji (2012) calls refugee camps 'a form of human warehousing' (p. 227). UNICEF (2017) describes growing up in German camps as 'childhood in waiting'. A study by World Vision and the Hoffnungsträger Foundation (2016) showed that because of unregulated structures, cramped living conditions and restrictions of privacy, camps were 'unsuitable places for children to stay' (p. 49). In Switzerland, infants, toddlers, children and young adults, together with their parent(s) or adult siblings, live from several months to several years in communal accommodations/camps before they may rent apartments. Waiting and uncertainty are the main structural and emotional elements of everyday life for thousands of people in Swiss cantonal camps.

In recent years, studies in the field of forced migration/refugee studies have demonstrated a growing interest in documenting the living conditions in camps (Fozdar and Hartley, 2013; Dilger and Dohrn, 2016; Hartmann, 2017; Fichtner and Trân, 2020). Ethnographical studies of refugee camps in the global South offer solid comparative evidence (see for example Inhetveen, 2010; Lutz, 2017). While certainly not all, some of the results are transferable to camp life in Europe. A commonality between these studies is that for refugees housed in camps, stagnation prevails for an indefinite period of time and provisional accommodation settings become permanent:

> Refugee camps are places where one can live, but they are not a real home. The arrival is limited in its perspectives; the situation remains tense and uncertain, even after many years. Camps are planned only

temporarily, for a certain period of crises and conflicts. If these persist, camps become vulnerable places of uncertainty. (Lutz, 2017: 376)

Werdermann (2016) demonstrated that German camp accommodation was a central element of the deterrence policy of the 1980s (p. 89f). Berthold (2014) examined camps as a 'sanctioning device', when, for example, families, because they do not want to cooperate in their deportation, live for many years in precarious circumstances. 'For the children, this means that they are partly born in the facility and grow up here. They know no life outside the shelter' (p. 40).

Until now, in Switzerland, research has been focused on unaccompanied minors and their living conditions and experiences (see for example Bitzi and Landolt, 2017; Keller et al, 2017). This narrow focus is also true for other European countries. Studies regarding accompanied minors in Europe reveal similar attention to the arrival experiences of unaccompanied minors. Studies have found discrimination and violation of rights of refugee children (Berthold, 2014; Eisenhuth, 2015; UNICEF, 2016; Fichtner and Trần, 2020; Schmitt, 2020), a lack of opportunities for play and retreat (Johansson and Schiefer, 2016; Rehklau, 2017), and barriers in the education system (Berthold, 2014). A growing number of studies highlight the health burdens and inadequate medical and psychological care of refugee children (Reavell and Fazil, 2017).

This chapter examines the ways in which homing strategies – all attempts and efforts to feel at home and belong to a place – of children in Swiss cantonal camps are compromised by the structural conditions of daily life. The chapter will weave together a situated ethnography with Augé's (1995/ 2019) concept of non-places. By using Winther´s (2009) definitions of 'home' and 'homing' to outline the challenges facing the children and their families, I will interrogate the reasons why these strategies are typically unsuccessful. The starting point for this chapter was the continuous invitation of children asking me to 'Come to my house'. For this article, as part of my dissertation, which takes a much broader look at the everyday lives of children in camps, I have delved deeper into the questions of what home means to children and to which places in camp they can and cannot feel a sense of belonging. This article, then, is a small glimpse into my dissertation and shares initial findings on the path toward an ethnography of children's lives in a Swiss cantonal camp. For the focus of this book, the final discussion also pointedly addresses challenges for social workers in this field.

The coercive community of an asylum shelter

Studies of the everyday practices in camps often connect to Foucault's (1994) disciplinary institutional framework to describe the particularities of structure, rules, and surveillance mechanisms (Täubig, 2009; Schmitt,

2020). This perspective provides insight into the structural conditions of those forced to live in a camp. Although recently, studies focus more and more on the agency of refugees, asylum regimes create dependencies, control and limit individual decision-making processes, which is linked to individual homing practices of inhabitants of camps, as will be shown in the following chapters after initially outlining the Swiss asylum procedure and statistics.

Asylum procedure and residency of asylum seekers in Switzerland

Since March 2019, an 'accelerated asylum procedure' has been in effect in Switzerland. This procedure requires that decisions about whether an asylum seeker may stay or has to leave the country be delivered within 140 days. During this time asylum seekers live in a federal 'reception and procedure center'. If there is a 'prospect to stay' they will be transferred to the cantonal level. If until then their refugee status is not approved, they will either be provided with an F-permit (when their application is still in process and the decision about whether to stay or to leave the country has not been taken yet) or an N-permit (if the application was rejected, but the 'removal' isn't possible, permitted or reasonable). Adults holding an F-permit are allowed to work in Switzerland and have the right to rent an apartment. They may be granted with a settlement-permit (C-permit) after ten years (Asylum Act Art. 74 2-3), provided that the Federal Council has not yet revoked the temporary protection.

All information about camp life in this chapter refers to the cantonal level, where the study presented took place. Swiss cantons are responsible for accommodation, medical care, education for school-aged children, and integration measures (SODK et al, 2018 (10): 1f). They offer different types of accommodation for asylum seekers: houses with shared kitchens and bathrooms, small studios or private flats.

According to UNHCR (2021), 82.4 million people worldwide were forcibly displaced in 2020, 42 per cent of them children, that is, under 18 years of age, and 1 million children were born as refugees (p. 3). In 2019, 14,269 asylum applications were filed in Switzerland; in 2020 it were 11,041 applications in total (Staatssekretariat für Migration SEM, 2021). In 2019, 45 per cent of asylum seekers in Switzerland were minors: 42 per cent applied for asylum together with their adult family members (n=5,924), 3 per cent were registered as unaccompanied minors (n=441). In 2020, 41 per cent of the applicants were minors applying for asylum together with adult family members (n=4,498) and 5 per cent were unaccompanied minors (n=535) (Staatssekretariat für Migration SEM, 24.03.2021). In 2020, 2,435 children were born into their asylum process in Switzerland (Staatssekretariat für Migration SEM, 2021a: 5).

Unfortunately, there are no valid data on the number of accompanied children in cantonal centres available in Switzerland. Figures provided by the State Secretariat for Migration are not comparable with the figures recorded separately at the cantonal level. It is unclear what is recorded as a cantonal centre in the statistics and what is not. It is also important to note that children listed as not being placed in a camp may nevertheless have lived, or may still be living or soon be living there.

Since the start of the study in July 2019, some of the participants were still being processed under the old, not 'accelerated asylum procedure', and some of the families had already been living in the camp for many months to years and their perspective was unclear. Lida, a 9-year-old girl, whose family was required to leave the country but didn't, was living in the camp since she was 3 years old without clarified residence. She was tired of her life in the camp and just wanted to leave: "I hate it here!" she kept saying.

Methods and terminology

The field research of this ethnographic study was conducted between July 2019 and July 2020 in a Swiss cantonal camp. Up to 90 people can live in the camp where the field research took place. Usually, one family has one room available to stay in. Bathrooms and kitchens are shared. There is a community room in the camp and also a courtyard and garden outside the camp. The children speak of the 'camp' when referring to the asylum shelter and call the family room their 'house'. This naming practice is adopted in this article.

Research took place during 42 days and eight nights and a total of 365 hours over a 12-month period. The research covered four seasons, days and nights, weekdays and weekends, school and public vacations. Over 700 pages of protocols from participant observation, over 160 children's drawings, and numerous notes from ero-epic interviews (Girtler, 2001) with children were transcribed. Some of the families and children stayed in touch with the researcher after they had left the camp respectively when data collection on site ended. They were visited afterwards and interviewed again. Data analysis was through sequential deconstruction and abductive analysis (Rosenthal, 2015).

Twenty families and 44 children participated in the study. They lived in the camp between a few months up to 6 years during the time of data collection. The age range of the children was between a few weeks up to 18 years old.

Ethics

The Ethics Committee of the University of Zurich approved this study. In refugee and forced migration studies, the extent to which voluntary participation in research activities can be ensured is intensely debated and the boundaries increasingly clear. In this context, Clark-Kazak (2017) and the Refugee Studies Centre (2007) formulated standards and demands that critically reflect the conditions of refugee studies and research. This development is co-emergent with critiques of ethics committees, which primarily ensure 'informed consent' through signed documents. A comprehensive literature discusses these issues (Block et al, 2013; Krause and Williams, 2021). Reflection about the researcher´s role and voluntary participation of study participants in a coercive context involves constant dialogue with all stakeholders.

During the preparatory phase of the study, I assumed that because of the cramped living conditions, I would not conduct my participatory observations in the 'houses', so as not to further limit the little privacy of families in the camps. However, the urgent invitation to "come to my house" was issued at day one of the study and I was invited to start fieldwork inside the houses, too.

Non-places

Marc Augé's (1995/2019) non-places serve as the theoretical framework when researching the everyday lives of children in Swiss camps and houses. Augé distinguishes non-places from anthropological places. Anthropological places are those where people feel they belong, a place 'occupied by the indigenous inhabitants who live in it, cultivate it, defend it, mark its strong points and keep its frontiers under surveillance' (1995: 42) Augé identifies a 'character' at home 'when he is at ease in the rhetoric of the people with whom he shares life. The sign of being at home is the ability to make oneself understood without too much difficulty, and to follow the reasoning of others without any need for long explanations' (Augé, 1995: 108).

The non-place is not an anthropological place, nor is it home. These can be airports, shopping malls, and asylum camps, where 'a person entering the space of non-place is relieved of his usual determinants. … What he is confronted with, finally, is an image of himself, but in truth it is a pretty strange image. … The space of non-place creates neither singular identity nor relations; only solitude, and similitude' (p. 103). Following this logic, camps cannot provide a sense of home for those who live there. Residents cannot feel a sense of belonging, the place is not freely chosen. Camps are transitory places characterised by a deficit of enduring social relationships. Individuality won't play a major role here.

Dimensions of home

In a later publication, Augé (2019) calls into question strict divisions between non-places and anthropological places by explaining that there are neither places nor non-places in the absolute sense: 'The place/non-place pair serves as a measure of the social or symbolic character of a space. Of course, places (those of encounter and exchange) can also form where others continue to see only a non-place' (p. 124). Consequently, not all homes are also anthropological places, or rather, a home can be a place for some, while others experience a non-place.

Winther (2006, 2009) and Petersen et al (2010) elaborated dimensions of 'home' when studying the lives of 'extremely mobile people'. Winther has described homing practices that serve to make one feel more at home in transitory or difficult circumstances. Winther's reflections emerge from studies with people, who live and are at home in different places for different reasons, for example, expats, international business (wo)men, or children growing up in different places because of their parents separation. This case study connects these dimensions of 'home' with the children's perspective on their lives in a cantonal camp.

Home as a place

In the spatial understanding of home that Winther and colleagues outline, access is granted to selected individuals only. Home is where everyday practices and the domestic life take place: 'The home (as place) is often understood as a cave, a place reserved for certain (included) people. The home is the concrete material and tactile space. It is the inhabited space. … At home in a house everyday practices take place' (Petersen et al, 2010: 2). Winther (2009) also states that this understanding refers to a 'protective shelter' or 'cave', that can also be a 'dangerous place' or 'prison' (p. 61f).

How do children in camps characterise the non-place as home? What strategies do they deploy to build a sense of connection and permanence to their surroundings?

The camp buildings are characterised by long corridors with numerous doors opening into the houses. Kitchen and toilets are shared and accessible from the corridors, too. The adults of the families have keys to houses which are assigned upon arrival. The house is a room a family lives in. For example, family Khan has one room for its six family members: 8-year-old boy Sami, 6-year-old girl Camen, 3-year-old girl Sada, new born boy Shahzad and their parents Mister and Misses Khan. To call the room 'house' by the children is well applicable for the everyday practices taking place there in a very confined space: The house is a place where the family members sleep, eat, feed, play, pray, dream, talk, clean, prepare meals, cuddle, fight and do much more. If there is a sink in the house it's not only used for brushing teeth and washing hands, it is also a bathtub for the youngest family members, and used for washing clothes and dishes. The house is where the family members receive visitors, where they store their belongings. There is never enough space: shoes rest on the windowsill or cooking pots wait underneath the beds. Almost every aspect of family life takes place inside the house. The bedroom is the living room, is the children's room, is the dining room, is the kitchen, is partly the bathroom, is the storage room, is the retreat and reception area at the same time. It is cramped, every corner and every possible storage space is used. The most visible reminder of the unexpected arrival and equally uncertain departure are the suitcases, which are usually visibly placed on top of the metal lockers or pushed under the beds and used as children's storage space for clothes or toys.

Furniture is moved around until the best use of space is achieved. There are low levels of intimacy and privacy. Children sleep while visitors are entertained, and family members pray or prepare their meals.

In the camp in which the study took place, all the rooms were furnished the same way: metal bunk beds, mattresses covered with plastic protectors, scratchy wool blankets, pillows, sheets, narrow metal lockers, chairs and a table. For every family member there is one cup, one knife, one plate and so on. There are associations with a prison atmosphere here and yet one doesn't even know how long one will have to stay. The equipment available is 'practical', rigorously monitored, and does not create a welcoming atmosphere for residents.

Home as an idea and feeling at home

Following Petersen et al (2010), home does not only exist spatially, but also as a complex set of ideas and conceptions linked to the cultural understanding of domesticity: 'Home (as an idea) is strong and complex. Home is not one idea but multiple ideas with a number of normative demands attached to them. Home is the abstract idea connected to the cultural ways of understanding the domestic' (p. 2). The authors also describe the need of feeling at home as a 'necessity of our modern world' (Petersen et al, 2010: 2) Whether and why one feels at home is the result of a wide range of feelings and experiences. The feeling is not always connected with a place, but one can also feel at home in an idea or a language: 'It is not a feeling you obtain once and for all, but a complex feeling, bound in a mixture of restlessness, homelessness and homeliness' (Petersen et al, 2010: 2).

The children in the camp all have vivid ideas of home, ideas and wishes that are often quite contradictory to their experiences on a daily basis in the camp. Exceptions are the desire to live together with family members and enjoying the company of other children and friends. In many respects, the children's idea or concept of home contradicts with their lived reality. Thus, children express their hope for a lot of space for themselves but also for their family members. Connected to this vision of the future is the urgent desire to no longer have to share 'smelly toilets' and 'ugly showers'. They also dream about a place of peace and quiet. The children express their hope that everything will be better after leaving the camp. Fifteen-year-old Ayden expressed one great wish for his future: "I only wish for a private apartment!"

For some, dreams come true. When looking back, what is it they remember about the camp? Would they go back for a visit one day? Children shake their heads, when being asked that question, "No way!" They remember the annoying noise all day and night, the disgust of toilets and bathrooms, dirty rooms and corridors. They also remember friendly teachers and good friends, too. But this does not change the fact that this life is finally over, that the real life has finally begun and one may finally go to 'normal', not 'camp school'.

For many children, their dreams and hopes are disappointed again, when moving from one camp to the next camp to the next camp. There are children who are not able to disentangle all the stays in different camps, who are not able to think back and talk about how it was where. How could this surprise anyone, when there are 7-year-old children who have lived in eight different camps (on federal, cantonal and community level) in the past two years?

To the children in the camp, 9-year-old Lida was the embodiment of a miracle, when after six years of waiting she was allowed to move out and move to a 'private house'. She was visited by the researcher in the flat the family now lived in. Lida was particularly proud when showing her room. She emphasised that the furniture was her own: "My own desk, my own bed!" Was there anything left from the things she had during her stay in the camp? She thought about it and looked around, then said: "No, nothing."

Lida's parents were also very proud about their own room, their comfortable bed with many pillows and soft blankets. All those years in the camp, they shared a typical metal camp-bed with Lida. The only thing Lida enjoys thinking about when looking back is that nobody cared about the noise in the camp and the children were "allowed to run around and be loud until late at night". Now it can be sometimes a bit too quiet, she says. She is worried about the kids who are still in the camp, because she knows that the COVID-19 pandemic forces them to stay even longer in a place they don't want to be.

When still living in the camp, children think about their lives before and share their thoughts: 6-year-old Madihah is disappointed when looking at the small Swiss birds and remembers fondly the "beautiful, big, colourful birds" in her country of origin. She remembers playing in the yellow sand, much more fun than the dusty soil of the camp garden. There are children who express their worries about their family members and talk about their fathers, hoping that they will come to Switzerland soon.

Those who have photos from their 'lives before' are interested in sharing them with the researcher: former houses, beautiful furnishing, party pictures, smiling faces of friends and family members, and repeatedly, injured people and war scenes. The TV plays sad love songs about the lost homeland. The 'home before' can be a vivid reminder that home is now a past memory.

The children who took part in the study do not feel at home in the camp or like they belong there. School vacations and weekends were described as especially boring, also because children can't 'escape' the place as often, they are forcibly connected to a place that is difficult to connect with. Young adults, mostly boys, leave the camp as much as possible; they go to the train station, window-shopping, or join sports clubs. When coming back 'home', the feeling of return is not joyful, and plans are made to leave again. Nobody wants to be here. No one is here by choice. But everyone is bound to stay until it is decided by 'them' – the states administrative bodies – that one can leave. A 'transfer' (the term used by staff, children and adults living in the camp to describe a move to the next place) – if the dream comes true, to a 'private house' – is not a well-planned shift from one place to another. Often, the families only get a few hours' notice about their transfer and they start hastily packing. The asylum regime moves bodies from space to space, and people are controlled through the room(s) they are provided with. People leave, people come, they are in motion between camps and houses. Everything is in flux and standstill at the same time.

'Homing'

According to Petersen et al (2010), homing strategies are activities with the goal of feeling more at home. '"Homing" is a way to relate oneself to everyday life and to obtain the necessary impression of "coping". Homing activities are done in order to feel more at home' (p. 2).

Although there are hardly any possibilities on the part of the families to feel at home or to arrive at the non-place camp, homing practices can nevertheless be observed. They have the goal of making the enforced stay more bearable. As much as the camp and the houses as places to live in are rejected by the residents, it is and remains a formative place to live. During their six years' stay, Lida's family got rid of the impractical metal lockers and friends helped them getting a wooden wardrobe and a sofa they were very proud of. Again and again, Lida mentioned the special pieces of furniture in her 'house' and specifically asked me to sit on the sofa and invited me to drink a latte macchiato from the families' coffee machine.

A family that was hopeful that with the birth of a third child they would be allowed to move to a 'private house' were badly disappointed when they were moved to another camp. Before the transfer, in their house they had two colourful birds in a cage. When the researcher visited the family after the 'transfer' they had gotten rid of the birds, claiming that it didn't make sense to keep them, now that they lived in an even smaller room.

When a family leaves or arrives at a camp, they bring/take suitcases and plastic bags as well as large carpets. The carpet is an important element of home-making. It is especially important for trying to feel a little more comfortable in a non-place, as (a little) comfort is a key element of homing practices in the camp. The carpet muffles the noise, makes the house cosier and the floor warmer. This is where children crawl, learn how to walk and play. This is where families sit and eat; this is where visitors are welcomed. Sitting in a circle, facing each other, food is shared, and conversations revolve around memories and events of the country of origin while children play and fall asleep in their parents' laps.

The entrance doors from the camp corridor to the families' houses mark a border or shield to keep the inner shelter from the outside and hence to keep the important things inside and delimit the house from other residents or staff. The doors to the families' houses are usually closed, not always by key, but they are rarely open. Whoever knocks must wait for a reaction from the inside. Children and adult residents know that if there is no answer one must leave or keep waiting.

Many rules structure camp life. Formal, institutional rules are there for orientation and may lead to punishment if they are not followed. There are also unwritten rules. For instance, only residents are allowed to open the door to their house. The doorstep is an important boundary between the camp and the house. Here the movement slows down, the preparation to enter follows: knocking, waiting in silence for the response, listening, the door opens, being recognised, greeted and invited in, taking off shoes, crossing the border, being inside and accepted into the circle of those present, talking and laughing, gossiping about the camp, playing and eating together. Eventually there will be a farewell and the door closes behind the visitor.

The children look for places of retreat in their houses. They hide under blankets, behind curtains made of sheets, or slip under beds. They create little caves or small tents that sit on top of the bunk beds. Up there, they have set up a kind of playroom for the children. There the children play with toys and dolls, watch video clips or draw pictures, escaping parental supervision.

One of the typical camp noises is a constant knocking on doors. Knocks are often ignored, for example when children know that the friend they want to play with is already in the house, or if a family wants peace and quiet. Residents respect this rule as they know it is an important strategy to feel a little more at home, allowing oneself to not to be disturbed, to having the right to choose who is welcome when 'inside my home'.

De-homing

At camp, children are working towards a sense of home in a place they cannot withdraw from and cannot leave as they wish. Young adults withdraw themselves from the camp by leaving it as often as possible or stay busy with everyday practices so that time passes faster. One of the strategies is also to sleep as long as possible.

But what needs to be added to Petersen et al's (2010) and Winther's (2006, 2009) concept in order to make it applicable for this particular context is the practice that I would like to call de-homing. De-homing in this particular field of camp life includes all rules, regulations and behaviour of the asylum regime that undermines the continuous attempts of homing strategies of children and their family members. De-homing powerfully underlines and reminds residents that the camp is a non-place. The following examples show that de-homing practices are putting into question attempts to home oneself:

- The residents respect signs to take off shoes when entering a house. Their carpets are well treated, meaningful and sometimes the only family possession (besides cloths, toiletries and toys). Still, security and staff enter the houses with heavy boots and cannot be asked to leave.
- Knocking is often ignored when a visitor is not welcome. This rule does not apply to staff. Even if the timing is not good, the door must be opened. Residents call the staff 'boss' and in a submissive tone: 'Yes boss, yes boss!' and often present themselves as being grateful and obedient.
- Keys to houses are held by adult family members, but staff and security also have access to every room in the camp, including the children's playroom. Residents understand that staff can use the master key to gain access to doors at any time.
- Children talk about disturbances during the night: babies cry, adults argue in other rooms, doors bang, fire alarms beep, cars honk. Six-year-old Madihah talked agitatedly about how she was asleep when all of a sudden, the police were there.
- The staff may remove personal items if they do not meet guidelines. Inspections of homes may be conducted at any time.
- When there are visits by the cantonal officials, residents are urged to be especially clean and asked to provide access to their houses.

Discussion

The children only invite selected people to visit their house; adults ask chosen visitors to eat or drink food with them on their carpets in the house. They do not ask the staff to come for a visit, because they come without invitation. 'Come to my house!' is both a personal invitation and a homing practice. The goal is for the person being addressed to respond to the invitation, and to respect and acknowledge what the children and their family members are trying to live in and make as their home.

The discrepancies 'between what is professionally and ethically required and what is legally and practically suggested' (Müller et al, 2016: 2) in the context of social work in camps are increasingly discussed (Muy, 2016). In consequence, in the past years, position papers, minimum standards and protection concepts emerged (Scherr, 2016; Rehklau, 2017). Until today, in Switzerland it is not even common for social workers to be employed in 'cantonal camps'. The idea that children accompanied by their parent(s) are sufficiently protected by them seems to be still widespread. Thus, volunteers and teachers become particularly important attachment figures for children outside the family. But these relationships can also easily break down, which the children regret very much. 'Transfers' are announced on such short notice that children often cannot say goodbye to teachers or friends from school or from inside the camp. Volunteer programs were interrupted during the COVID-19 pandemic and they often do not take place at times where children are particularly bored and frustrated: weekends and school holidays.

A consistent cycle of homing strategies and de-homing activities is the lived reality. It can only be broken by moving away to one's 'own private house'. The study by Aumüller and Aumüller and Bretl (2008) show that moving away from a camp to a 'private house' always leads to a better wellbeing. If centralised accommodation of refugees for a short and defined period of time is unavoidable, separate units with private bathrooms and cooking facilities enable homing strategies, as privacy and retreat opportunities within the family would be available (cf. Berthold, 2014: 40).

Social workers try to remain capable of acting in this coercive context and the in-between. But what does social work mean in a place where people don't want to be, where they don't feel they belong, where they can't/aren't allowed to relate even if they try to, and where the development of life perspectives is limited to a maximum? Social work discusses its necessary work in this context under massively aggravated conditions. Life in the camp is characterised by contradictions, which can also become a daily test for social workers (Pieper, 2011; Muy, 2016; Scherr, 2016: 20), often leading to quitting the job or burnout.

Refugee families in cantonal camps live in a permanent temporary transition in an in-between and have a challenging time making or feeling at home. They are asked to integrate while there is a lack of offers for doing so. Täubig (2009) calls this 'organized disintegration'. Refugees do not want to live in a camp, but they must stay there. They are forced into immobility (Etzold, 2019), while yet everything remains in motion.

The camp spaces, rules and conditions complicate the practice of homing for asylum seekers. The desire to make a difficult situation comfortable is met with varying strategies and informal rules. The power dynamics are highly unbalanced, and the authoritarian nature of the camps creates frustrations, particularly for children who shake their heads and say "it's not good here".

Eight-year-old Karima says that her favourite place in the camp is the compound wall that separates the property of the camp from the outside, where she sits and looks outside, dreaming about the home she might find one day. She sits there, the camp to her back, looking at the cars passing by as if everything was already behind her and as if she was moving away, too.

References
Arendt, H. (2007) 'We refugees', in H. Arendt, J. Kohn and R. H. Feldman (eds) *The Jewish Writings*, New York: Schocken Books, pp 264–74.
Augé, M. (1995) *Non-Places: Introduction to an Anthropology of Supermodernity*, London: Verso.
Augé, M. (2019) *Nicht-Orte*, Munich: Beck.
Aumüller, J. and Bretl, C. (2008) *Lokale Gesellschaften und Flüchtlinge. Förderung von sozialer Integration*, Berlin: Die kommunale Integration von Flüchtlingen.
Berthold, T. (2014) 'In erster Linie Kinder. Flüchtlingskinder in Deutschland', in *Auftrag gegeben beim Bundesfachverband Unbegleitete*, Köln: Minderjährige Flüchtlinge e.V.
Bitzi, B. and Landolt, S. (2017) 'Unaccompanied minor asylum seekers: Processes of subject formation and feelings of belonging in the context of educational experiences in Switzerland', *Geographica Helvetica*, 72: 217–26.
Block, K., Warr, D., Gibbs, L. and Riggs, E. (2013) 'Addressing ethical and methodological challenges in research with refugee-background young people: Reflections from the field', *Journal of Refugee Studies*, 26(1): 69–87.
Clark-Kazak, C. (2017) 'Ethical considerations: Research with people in situations of forced migration', *Refuge: Canadas Journal on Refugees*, 33(2): 11–17.
Dilger, H. and Dohrn, K. (eds). (2016) *Living in Refugee Camps in Berlin: Women's Perspectives and Experiences*. Berlin: Weissensee Verlag.
Eisenhuth, F. (2015) *Strukturelle Diskriminierung von Kindern mit unsicheren Aufenthaltsstatus. Subjekte der Gerechtigkeit zwischen Fremd- und Selbstpositionierungen* (Vol. 14). Wiesbaden: Springer VS.
Etzold, B. (2019) *Auf der Flucht – (Im)Mobilisierung und (Im)Mobilität von Schutzsuchenden*. Bonn International Center for Conversation. Bonn: Institut für Migrationsforschung und Interkulturelle Studien.
Fichtner, S. and Trần, H.M. (2020) 'Lived citizenship between the sandpit and deportation: Young children's spaces for agency, play and belonging in collective accommodation for refugees', *Childhood*, 27(2): 158–72.
Foucault, M. (1994) *Überwachen und Strafen. Die Geburt des Gefängnisses* (15. Auflage). Frankfurt am Main: Suhrkamp Verlag.
Fozdar, F. and Hartley, L. (2013) 'Housing and the creation of home for refugees in Western Australia', *Housing, Theory and Society*, 31(2): 148–73.
Girtler, R. (2001) *Methoden der Feldforschung*. Vienna: Böhlau Verlag.

Hartmann, M. (2017) 'Contested boundaries: Refugee centers as spaces of the political', *Zeitschrift Für Flüchtlingsforschung*, 1(2): 218–43.

Inhetveen, K. (2010) *Die politische Ordnung des Flüchtlingslagers: Akteure – Macht – Organisation. Eine Ethnographie im Südlichen Afrika*, Berlin: Verlag.

Jaji, R. (2012) 'Social technology and refugee encampment', *Journal of Refugee Studies*, 25(2): 221–38

Johansson, S. and Schiefer, D. (2016) 'Die Lebenssituation von Flüchtlingen in Deutschland – Überblick über ein (bisheriges) Randgebiet der Migrationsforschung', *Neue Praxis. Zeitschrift Für Sozialarbeit, Sozialpädagogik Und Sozialpolitik, Sonderheft*, 13: 73–85.

Keller, S., Mey, E. and Gabriel, T. (2017) 'Unaccompanied minor asylum-seekers in Switzerland: A critical appraisal of procedures, conditions and recent changes', *Social Work & Society*, 15(1): 1–18.

Krause, U. and Williams, T. (2021) 'Flexible Ethikgremien. Impulse zur Institutionalisierung ethisch verantwortlicher Feldforschung in der Konflikt- und Fluchtforschung', *Soziale Probleme*, 32: 97–113.

Lutz, R. (2017) 'Der Flüchtling woanders. Verletzliche Orte des Ungewissen: ein Leben in Lagern', in C. Ghaderi and T. Eppenstein (eds) *Flüchtlinge. Multiperspektivische Zugänge*, Wiesbaden: Springer Fachmedien, pp 367–80.

Müller, A., Prasad, N., Riede, M., Sauer, S., Schäuble, B., Jungk, S., Kubisch, S., Scherr, A., Scherschel, K., Schneider, A., Strassburger, G., Völter, B., Velho, A. and Wagner, L. (2016) 'Position paper: Social work with refugees in refugee accommodation centers', *Professional Standards and Socio-political Basis (Initiative of Professors on Social Work in Refugee Accommodation Centres)*. Berlin: Alice Salomon Hochschule.

Muy, S. (2016) 'Interessenskonflikte Sozialer Arbeit in Sammelunterkünften gewerblicher Träger', *Neue Praxis. Zeitschrift Für Sozialarbeit, Sozialpädagogik Und Sozialpolitik, Sonderheft*, 13: 157–66.

Petersen, M.G., Lynggaard, A.B., Krogh, P.G. and Winther, I.W. (2010) 'Tactics for homing in mobile life: A fieldwalk study of extremely mobile people', Paper presented at Mobile HCI 2010, Lisbon, pp 1–10.

Pieper, T. (2011) 'Soziale Arbeit im Ausnahmezustand', *Migration & Soziale Arbeit*, 2: 124–28.

Reavell, J. and Fazil, Q. (2017) 'The epidemiology of PTSD and depression in refugee minors who have resettled in developed countries', *Journal of Mental Health*, 26(1): 74–83.

Refugee Studies Centre, Queen Elizabeth House University of Oxford. (2007) 'Ethical guidelines', *Refugee Survey Quarterly*, 26(3): 162–72.

Rehklau, C. (2017) 'Flüchtlinge als Adressat_innen Sozialer Arbeit? Sozialarbeitswissenschaftlicher Zugang', in C. Ghaderi and T. Eppenstein (eds) *Flüchtlinge. Multiperspektivische Zugänge*. Wiesbaden: Springer Fachmedien, pp 305–22.

Rosenthal, G. (2015) *Interpretative Sozialforschung. Eine Einführung* (5., aktualisierte und ergänzte Auflage). Weinheim: Beltz Juventa.

Scherr, A. (2016) 'Sozialstaat, Soziale Arbeit und die Grenzen der Hilfe. Neue Praxis', *Zeitschrift Für Sozialarbeit, Sozialpädagogik Und Sozialpolitik, Sonderheft*, 13: 9–20.

Schmitt, C. (2020) 'Vermessen, Klassifizieren, Zuweisen. Das AnKER-Zentrum als machtvolle Organisation der Asylverwaltung', *Soziale Passagen*, 12(1): 135–54.

SODK, KKJPD and SEM (eds) (2018) 'Themen- und Kantonsfaktenblätter'. www.sem.admin.ch/sem/de/home/asyl/asylverfahren/asylregionen-baz/faktenblaetter.html

Staatssekretariat für Migration SEM. (2021a). *Asylstatistik 4. Quartal 2020*. Bern-Wabern: SEM, 1 February.

Staatssekretariat für Migration SEM. (2021b). 'Bestand Minderjährige im Asylprozess am Jahresende – ZEMIS', Bern, 24 March.

Täubig, V. (2009) *Totale Institution Asyl, Empirische Befunde zu alltäglichen Lebensführungen in der organisierten Desintegration*. Weinheim: Juventa.

UNHCR (2021) *Global Trends Forced Displacement in 2020*, Geneva: United Nations High Commissioner for Refugees.

UNICEF (2016) *Globaler UNICEF Bericht mit neuen Daten zu Flucht und Migration von Kindern. Executive Summary and Key Findings*, Zurich: UNICEF Schweiz.

UNICEF (2017) 'Kindheit im Wartezustand. Studie zur Situation von Kindern und Jugendlichen in Flüchtlingsunterkünften in Deutschland'. www.unicef.de/blob/137024/ecc6a2cfed1abe041d261b489d2ae6cf/kindheit-im-wartezustand-unicef-fluechtlingskinderstudie-2017-data.pdf

Werdermann, D. (2016) 'Rechtliche Grundlagen der Teilhabe und Ausgrenzung von Flüchtlingen. Neue Praxis', *Zeitschrift Für Sozialarbeit, Sozialpädagogik Und Sozialpolitik, Sonderheft*, 13: 86–95.

Winther, I.W. (2006) 'Kids' rooms as plus territory', *Interacções*, 2: 9–26.

Winther, I.W. (2009) '"Homing oneself": Home as a practice', *Home and Space*, 4(2): 49–83.

World Vision Deutschland and Hoffnungsträger Stiftung (2016) *Angekommen in Deutschland*. Friedrichsdorf: Wenn geflüchtete Kinder erzählen.

6

Transnational dynamics of family reunification: reassembling social work with refugees in Belgium

Pascal Debruyne, Kaat Van Acker, Dirk Geldof and Mieke Schrooten

Introduction

Belgium – as most other Western European countries – has become an immigration country in the last decades. One in five Belgian citizens has or was born with a non-Belgian nationality. On a yearly basis, around 140,000 immigrants arrive in Belgium (Myria, 2020). Refugees granted international protection represent about 10 per cent of these immigrants. The increasing numbers of refugees Belgium has been confronted with from 2015 onwards – due to wars in the Middle East and the persecution of people by authoritarian states – have mainly led to policy initiatives aimed at asylum reception and integration, while support for maintaining family ties across borders and support during the process of family reunification has received far less political attention. Family reunification is for refugees and other migrants, however, the most important legal ground for migration to Belgium: 42 per cent of migrants from non-EU countries and 27 per cent of EU citizens migrating to Belgium obtained their first residence permit on the basis of family reunification. In total this concerned 35,169 people in 2018 (Myria, 2019). Within the group of non-Europeans, 2,722 people had received an approval for family reunification with someone with refugee status (Myria, 2018).

Family reunification is a unique process within the migration processes, as it concerns 'not only "outsiders knocking at a state's doors and requesting entry" but also the "moral claim of insiders", people living within state borders who ask to be united with their family' (Block, 2012: 37). Notwithstanding the right to family life inscribed in Article 16 of the Universal Declaration of Human Rights, in Article 8 of the European Convention on Human Rights and in Article 22 of the Belgian Constitution, family reunification is subject to a policy of problematisation and suspicion. The association with 'fraudulent marriages' and possible fraud involving papers, ages or relational ties has become standard. Wray (2006: 303) calls this 'moral gatekeeping', which contributes to the image of 'the undesirable family migrant'.

In general, the political discourse on migration is often very negative. Migration is framed by some as a danger; a threat from the outside for the 'body of the nation' (Schrooten et al, 2016). Numbers are thereby enlarged and exaggerated to create an image of massive influx. Moreover, refugee immigration is coupled with unprecedented problematisations of Islam – including an association with terrorism – and widespread populism (Lucassen, 2018). 'The refugee' and 'the newcomer' have become the emblems of politically produced boundary work to determine who belongs to 'us' and who is 'the other'. This political culture of suspicion has pushed an array of legal and administrative changes that have been implemented in Belgian family reunification policy during the last decade.

The policy changes that were implemented in Belgium in 2011 are illustrative in this sense, as they further tightened the conditions for family reunification. The European directive on family reunification (2003/86/EC), which Belgium already partly took over in 2006, became fully transposed into Belgian law in 2011, setting up new barriers for family reunification. One example is the requirement to dispose of sufficient financial means – 120 per cent of the social benefit norm – before family members are allowed to come over. Another example is the prerequisite to have housing that matches the family size. These conditions were introduced for third-country nationals (non-EU citizens), including Turkish and Moroccan family reunifiers (Bonjour and Block, 2016; Mascia, 2020).

Until today, family reunification has slightly more flexible rules for refugees compared to other third-country nationals. After being granted refugee status or subsidiary protection, there is an exception period of one year during which the conditions of income, suitable residence and health insurance are released. However, despite this concession, the actual process of family reunification is still extremely complex for refugees within this one-year period, due to a lack of guidance and support, but also due to administrative, legal and financial obstacles (Brummel-Ahlaloum et al, 2018; Caritas International, 2018). Time pressure, costs for obtaining documents and other material conditions (for example, income and housing), but also the requirement for family reunifiers to file a demand in the closest embassy to the country they have fled from, put a strong pressure on the applying/first-arrived family members, and on the relationships with their relatives abroad. Negotiating expectations about the reunification process and rebuilding family lives after reunification are complex processes with a strong impact on family dynamics (Brummel-Ahlaloum et al, 2018).

In this chapter, we bring attention to the complex story of family reunification from a social work perspective. Social workers, as human rights professionals (Gibens et al, 2019; Healy, 2008), play an important role in supporting refugee families throughout reunification processes, not only by providing legal support, but also by supporting transnational family relations and negotiations, or enabling and supporting the rebuilding of family relations after reunification. Another – more political – role of social work is to take position in the politics of family reunification, and asylum and migration at large, even if only by providing insights into the everyday politics on the nexus of transnational migration law and the national welfare state.

Working with refugee families requires a 'transnational awareness', challenging social workers to work across borders and to become familiar with the challenges of transnational lifestyles (Withaeckx et al, 2017). To gain insights into the possibilities of transnational social work in the context of family reunification, this chapter presents the results of a research project on family reunification of refugees conducted in Belgium between 2019 and 2022. Our findings are based on 35 in-depth interviews with social workers, academics and volunteers at civil society organisations and semi-state institutions, as well as semi-structured interviews with 30 families who are currently in the process of family reunification or have already completed the process. These families are of Somalian, Eritrean, Afghan, Iraqi, Syrian and Palestinian descent. Before discussing our research findings, we first problematise the methodological nationalism present in social work. State power, we argue, is located in a transnational assemblage of power. We end our article by outlining the building blocks for transnational social work in the context of family reunification and migration at large.

Beyond methodological nationalism

In order for social workers to be able to work with family reunifiers, the practical and political practice of social work needs to be reassembled within the transnational dynamics of family reunification. This challenges social work professionals to act beyond the boundaries of the nation-state, which is not self-evident

> Given the methodological nationalism at work in the theory and practice of social work, meaning that the nation-state remains firmly embedded in social work concepts, policies and practices as a naturalised and unquestioned frame of reference. Problem definitions, categories of analysis and methods of social work are still mostly situated within the context of the nation-state and its organisations and institutions. (Schrooten, 2021: 1166)

Notwithstanding the continuing relevance of state power, two problems arise with methodological nationalism. One is the reification of the state as 'a thing in itself', an institutional spatial container of power. In practice, however, there is no such thing as 'the state' since state power is performative and arises from the many practices and places from where its power is exercised, and constantly reproduced. As Yael Navaro-Yashin (2002: 2) observed, the state is not a fixed or static entity: rather, 'like a phantom, it haunts a multitude of sites, appears in many guises and constantly transfigures itself'. This is key for family reunification processes of refugees, that are more than often embroiled in a range of mandatory conflicts between different state agencies (and private agencies) on multiple scales of government, and that are crafted and transformed through regimes and technologies of power (DNA-test and documents). To grasp this complexity of state power, we find it more appropriate to talk about '(state) assemblages of power' (Ong and Collier, 2005; Allen and Cochrane, 2007; Anderson and McFarlane 2011; Debruyne and Parker, 2015). This concept fits a more complex ontology of state power and allows us to better detect the (emergent) practices of state power and the many 'faces of the state' (Navaro-Yashin, 2022). What is attractive in assemblage geography is its reading of power as multiple co-existences whereby bits and pieces can be assembled together (McFarlane, 2009: 562).

The second problem with methodological nationalism in social work theory and practice is its local focus and the lack of a border crossing perspective. Family reunification confronts social workers with the transnational dimensions of refugees' lives: the spatial distance between family members as well as the layered realities of politically produced boundaries in migration. As relationships between refugee family members transcend state boundaries, social work theory and practice need to be reassembled to fit the everyday transnational realities of refugee families. Notwithstanding the importance of state agencies in processes of family reunification, we also need to look at the production of state power and the actual whereabout of its power beyond state boundaries. A transnational perspective on working with refugees 'facilitates better understandings of how localities in different countries can be interlinked in multidirectional processes in everyday life and how these interlinkages impact on social problems and, in the best of cases, on the practice of social work' (Righard and Boccagni, 2015: 313). We will argue that social work needs to rearrange itself to fit a multi-scalar reality. Family reunification makes social work 'glocal' welfare work, whereby transnational dynamics beyond state boundaries craft the everyday social issues at hand.

The transnational lives of refugee families

In the following we present insights into the transnational lives of refugee families in different stadia of the process of family reunification. Insights are grouped into three themes. First, we discuss how refugee families 'do family' at a distance. Doing family in the context of refugee families refers to the strategies families develop in order to deal with the distance and everyday realities of transnational migration (Strasser, Kraler, Bonjour and Bilger, 2009; Madianou, 2017, 2019). Second, we discuss conflicting roles, fractious loyalties and alternated positions of parents and children during and after reunification has taken place. Finally, we turn to how working with family reunifiers implies working on the nexus of transnational migration law and the welfare state.

Doing family at a distance

Conceptually, family can be thought of as a set of practices that can take place in a range of contexts, including mediated (Morgan, 1996). Processes of family separation and reunification have a profound impact on the practices of 'doing family'. One young Syrian woman, whose father migrated first, told us about the importance of keeping in touch with family members while being separated, and about the impact of a lack of contact on her sense of being a family. Her father never attained refugee status and after 13 years of separation she decided to flee herself, in order to try to obtain the refugee status and make family reunification possible.

> 'It's just really hard, because I lived with my mom for 13 years and it wasn't fun leaving her. It was just the last hug and then 4.5 years. ... I had to wait a long time until I could hug her again. She's here now, but if I remember ... I've forgotten a lot of things, but the bad things remained for a long time. It was difficult. In the beginning we couldn't really contact her. It was very difficult. No internet ... we tried many things but there was no contact. After a long time, we were able to reach her and talked to her. But she was also not always available. It was difficult.' (Syrian woman, with refugee status)

She also told us how the long separation from her father at an early age made it hard for her to still experience him as a father:

> 'I was 5 years old when he left. I also lived here with him [after I arrived in Belgium], but it was a strange feeling inside. I know that he's my father, but I didn't have that feeling inside. I thought "he is family but rather like an aunt, not a father". I had to do a lot of things on my own and he couldn't do much.' (Syrian woman, with refugee status)

This quote illustrates that an important factor in how family relationships evolve over time and distance is whether and how families manage to stay connected. People can be near, in touch and together, even when great distances tear them physically apart (Elliott and Urry, 2010: 100). Some authors refer to 'care circulation' for all day-to-day attempts to socially and emotionally bridge the distance and re-establish proximity (Baldassar and Merla, 2013; Bonizzoni and Boccagni, 2013).

In diverse interviews parents and youngsters testified about how, notwithstanding the distance, family relationships remain very active. They are involved in the daily activities of their children and they comfort them at difficult moments of missing each other, sadness and insecurity (see also Madianou and Miller, 2002; Schrooten, 2012). A Syrian woman, whose husband migrated first, testifies how he remained present while separated:

> 'He was calling us on Skype or WhatsApp each hour at work and he asked me to turn the video on, when he called me on Skype for example at 2 o'clock after midnight and he told me: "Leave it open. I want to watch you while you are sleeping. If something happens because you are tired, so I can watch you while you are sleeping with the kids. Sleep together in one room so that I can see you all." As a father, normally at night you have to wake up at least two times to check on the kids. The oldest still remembers [his father's absence]. He was only like 9 or 10 years old. It affects him until today. Honestly, he forgets that his father is here now. He shouts at his brothers "don't do that." He's still the ... dad number 2.' (Syrian woman, reunified family)

While the refugee families we interviewed generally conveyed a high degree of togetherness, this was not necessarily expressed in the sharing of difficult or painful experiences. Family members sometimes withhold information from their relatives in order not to frighten or worry them. An Afghan-Pakistani youngster told us:

> 'I talk to my parents (who live abroad) about my school, that I was learning a language, etc. I have always had support from my parents to go for it, to study. If I was doing well, I expressed my feelings, then they were a bit more at ease. If it didn't go well ... I never shared that. When I had bad times, I didn't tell. ... Afterwards I said, "Look, I was in trouble, this and that, that was the complexity of the matter" and they understood why I didn't tell that. Once the problem was solved, then there was nothing to argue, no worries. I am a family person. I am very concerned about my mom, dad, brothers and sisters. I wish them the best; I hope they can live happily.' (Afghani-Pakistani youngster, recently reunited)

The importance of such disclosure for a family's wellbeing is somewhat contested in the literature. While the dominant Western notion of disclosure holds that the sharing of sensitive information and the expression of feelings within a family fosters wellbeing (Walsh, 2003), some authors have suggested that 'narration must be understood as a complex transaction of disclosure and silencing, rooted in family members' experiences in sharing pain', and that this complex balancing between remembering and forgetting may be vital for families' wellbeing (De Haene et al, 2012: 394). Rooted in cultural coping strategies, refugee families often share patterns of silencing in an attempt to protect oneself and family members from worrying or experiencing pain (De Haene et al, 2012; Vindevogel et al, 2015; Sleijpen et al, 2016; Groeninck et al, 2019, 2020).

Conflicting roles, frictious loyalties and altered positions

Throughout the interviews, we regularly witnessed conflicting roles and loyalties between the family members involved in family reunification processes, particularly between those family members that came first and those that joined or are to join later. In certain cases, there may even be a conflict about the family reunification itself. Young people in particular may have a mandate to pursue family reunification while after having spent some years in Belgium they may personally doubt that they want to. One social worker testifies to this:

> 'Many young people come [to inquire about family reunification], even though they don't want to be reunited after so many years because they are integrated and actually have an okay life here. I think the most important thing is, that we also talk that through, "What if they [your parents] are here? What's that going to do to you? How are you going to change?" There are young people who also indicate that they are afraid their parents will find them too westernized. I think that by starting the conversation, we will continue to ask whether this family reunification is really something that the young person wants or whether it is just a mandate.' (Social worker, welfare organisation for unaccompanied minors)

Some unaccompanied minors are so caught up in relations of loyalty that they have no mental space to really consider what kind of effect of impact the family reunification will have on their lives. Another social worker told us in this regard:

> 'I also often have the feeling that young people have not thoroughly thought through what it will look like in reality when they start that process. Because I see that they often get lost when you say: "if they come, it means that you will also live together, that is one of the conditions". And then it's like "oops, that's going to have a serious impact on what I do here, on my trajectory and on the freedom that has been acquired" … that is like turning back time.' (Social worker, welfare organisation for minors)

In a limited number of cases, children or youngsters reported feeling loyal to their distant family members to such an extent that it prevented them from functioning. In such cases feelings of loyalty may become dysfunctional. A guardian testifies about the case of a 16-year-old Afghan boy.

> 'I accompanied one, that situation was incredible. He didn't even go to school anymore. He said: "My brothers and sisters can't go to school; so, I don't go either." He was completely blocked. He had problems with his ears and had to go to the doctor. "My brothers and sisters can't go to the doctor, so I don't go either." He refused to take medication. … That was really extreme, he just kept. … Everything his brothers and sisters were denied, he denied himself. He no longer wanted to take care of himself. Yes, that was really extreme.' (Volunteer guardian for unaccompanied minors)

Family reunification almost inevitably implies changing family dynamics. In a range of interviews, social workers described the relationships between (un)accompanied minors and parents after reunification as rather difficult, with issues such as asymmetric dependency or parentification. As one social worker testifies:

> 'The parents don't know anything yet and their child doesn't know everything but sure knows a lot more than they do. He or she can pay, has to do the school registration, has to do everything actually because they can't do anything yet. And then often, it is the son, who is usually the one who has to pay everything. So, there is also a financial imbalance. So, I have already seen a few times that the son feels responsible and in charge.' (Social worker, welfare organisation)

But others narrate how family relationships may be restored after reunification:

> 'A number of them simply restore the family relationship as it was before. Daddy is Daddy, really the way it used to be. Of course, the dad is partly dependent on who is here, for everything. But the respect and listening to and so on that yes … recovers. Despite the fact that they have been apart for a long time.' (Volunteer guardian for unaccompanied minors)

Working on the nexus of (trans)national migration law and the welfare state

Working with refugee families on family reunification demands a social intervention strategy that picks in on transnational realities of migration. It obliges social workers to think and act beyond the borders and boundaries of the national state, as the relevant legal and administrative procedures are embedded in transnational spaces. Working in a transnational way is not self-evident, because one works with people at a distance, in situations that are often unknown territory. Not only social workers, but also lawyers have to work across borders. One migration lawyer phrased it as follows:

> 'That is not an easy task and that is very difficult for us as lawyers, I think, to gain insight because you often … I need those documents; I need them all. But how to get to them? … I don't know how it is in Afghanistan or in Eritrea or in Ethiopia. Because you often have people from Eritrea who are in refugee camps in Uganda. So how do you get there? Which competent Belgian embassy is nearby? It also costs a lot of money to travel with a whole family. So, people who say that family reunification is easy, I think … they don't really have much knowledge of the family reunification procedure.' (Migration lawyer)

Working with refugee families on family reunification also requires an understanding of the ways in which the rights of refugees and their families are politically fabricated through everyday social institutions that reassemble the boundaries of possible rights and reproduce state power through administrative regimes and instruments of power. One social worker of a welfare organisation in Brussels mentions the following about dealing with the federal Immigration Department (DVZ):

> 'They are also politically driven, so I think they will receive instructions. There is also not always benevolence on the part of all Immigration Department employees. For example, if I call them and the head of department asks me "if I am someone who falls within the 12-month period", I try to discuss the file, and they say, "Is Mister already working?" … Do you know it? … While it does not have to be asked. Because that person at DVZ finds it important that someone is willing to work. But we do know which people you can contact within the Immigration Department that you can talk to and with whom you can put forward decent arguments about how the law is applied. We prefer to call those people. But there are other people who are very unwilling within the Immigration Department. We say, "an Immigration Department (DVZ) mentality".' (Social worker, welfare organisation)

Another social worker tells us about the legal and administrative impact of the way names are written down:

> 'What is also sometimes difficult are mundane spelling mistakes in their birth and marriage certificates. This is often very frustrating because

you have to deal with translations of documents. In Afghanistan they have the Arabic script, in Armenia they also have their own alphabet … with, for example, a mister "Hovanissian" in one word. His birth certificate said it was 2 n's and his identity card only had only 1 "n". That is just a translation from Armenian so it is not clear, you can translate it in 1 or 2 ways, there is no right or wrong translation. Then you have to go to the municipality, go to the public prosecutor's office again to have it certified. This is a time-consuming and unnecessary procedure because these are clearly elements that should not involve bad faith. These are factors that often make people despondent.' (Social worker, welfare organisation)

This generates conflict with state agencies that obstruct the rights of reuniting families and forces social workers to act politically.

'It is not because the Immigration Department says "no" that they are right. I think as long as they are not right then we will continue until we are right. And that works, because we have had successes with the "Ombudsman" (this is the Commission for Administrative Complaint) before. … Myria too. I think that we as an organisation may have to take the lead at that level ourselves, but we do work together with Myria, who actually has the mandate to do so. So … they always ask us if there are things to report when they have a meeting with the Immigration Department. If we really have things that we think are not acceptable, then we signal that to Myria and they then act upon it.' (Social worker, welfare organisation)

This citation illustrates that in order to secure refugee families' rights, social workers have to deal with the complex assemblage of state power and plural 'faces of the state' (Navaro-Yashin, 2002). Thus, they have to work on the nexus of transnational migration law and social rights.

'Our guidance consists of actually guiding from A to Z, so from the beginning … that starts with an intake interview. … So that means that they start collecting their documents, that we check them, that we say that is not good, you should do it differently, that we often also make agreements, fill in visa forms online. And then afterwards, once it has been submitted, also communicate with the Immigration Department, with embassies if certain things are not progressing or are difficult. … Plus, of course, what I also said earlier; it differs from country to country. In some countries the visa offices or embassies are very helpful and in others they are not. And in one country they are very knowledgeable about what that is and is not needed and in other countries they ask for documents that are not needed, but that blocks a file because they say, "we cannot take it" and the people cannot actually submit their file.' (Social worker, welfare organisation)

Not only formal social workers, but also informal volunteer social workers have developed ways of playing into the transnational assemblages of power, in order to secure families' rights. One family testifies about the social interventions of a volunteer towards a Red Cross professional. Her story illustrates that informal social workers can act transnationally in a proactive way.

> 'It was J. (a volunteer social worker) who said, "why haven't you sent an email to Tanzania UNHCR yet? Why haven't you yet? Three days. Why? What are you waiting for? What are you doing here? What are you doing here?". The lady of the Red Cross who called quickly the next day "tell your family tomorrow at 10 am they have to go to UNHCR". … And J. who is looking for an address, she is looking for a telephone and she calls UNHCR directly to arrange everything.' (Volunteer social worker, platform volunteer organisations for newcomers)

Building an infrastructure for transnational social work

Critical perspectives of transnational social work allow to de- and reconstruct the relationships with transnational populations, because they allow for more cross-boundary complexity, and challenge social work in relational terms. Transnational social work is described by Furman, Negi and Salvador (2010: 8) as

> an emerging field of practice that (a) is designed to serve transnational populations; (b) operates across nation-state boundaries, whether physically or through new technologies; and (c) is informed by and addresses complex transnational problems and dilemmas. Transnational perspectives are instrumental in developing a powerful critique of the shortcomings of social work and welfare provisions of nation-states. (An et al, 2016)

But how do social workers build an infrastructure for transnational work, and reassemble social work within the transnational dynamics of family reunification of refugees? We discuss two levels at which possible social interventions may take place: the level of family relations and the political level of intervention.

The level of family relations

Central to transnational social work with 'families at a distance' is dealing with relations of care that take place at a distance, wherein parental presence does not necessarily imply face-to-face proximity. It is key to gain insights in the performative and enacting practices of migrants to establish their family relations from afar. In a range of interviews, social workers working with refugees contend that they should give more attention to the impact of the 'distant' (and still nearby) family. Working with absent family members is important to support refugees in all the challenges that come with settling in a new country and eventually in preparing for family reunification, particularly so for unaccompanied minors. Plugging into new technologies of communication used by refugee families is definitely part of the way forward (Madianou, 2016). Working with family members does not end when the procedure is completed but continues after reunification has taken place. Many of the social workers we talked to agree that accompanying families throughout this process often involves long-term family counselling.

Establishing transnational relationships is not always self-evident. There is an 'added layer of geography', which confronts family members with differential access to the resources necessary to their livelihoods and care relations (Dreby and Adkins, 2010: 684). Foremost it is important to explore the depth and realities of these family ties and try to understand the relations of loyalty that play a role. In multiple interviews, social workers told us about the importance of building relations of trust in order to achieve this. Social workers focusing on family reunification are not only dealing with precarious loyalties between family members at a distance but are also regularly confronted with the observation that apparent administrative procedures such as DNA tests turn out to be very emotional.

To protect this relation of trust, social workers should be reflexive about their own positionality and relation towards the state. Social workers often stand and act 'in between' citizens and the state. In relation to family reunification, the many boundaries in the process of family reunification impact the ways refugee families perceive and deal with the state. Research by Strasser et al (2009: 175) finds that migrant and bi-national families are repelled by the series of state interventions in their family life. They strive to shape their lives and their families according to their own wishes: 'living together, getting married, divorced, working and having and raising children, as and when they want to'. 'Those who experience that the laws and actors of the state prohibit them from having a "normal family life" inevitably take a different attitude towards that state: their sense of belonging and citizenship has been profoundly affected' (Strasser et al, 2009: 175). Or, as Schmidt

(2011: 272) argues about reunification through marriage, 'who you marry … has also become a practice that defines who you are as a citizen', which brings us to the political level of social interventions.

The political level

Building an 'infrastructure for transnational social work' does not stop at the level of family relations. It also means dealing with the multiple faces of the state within the context of transnational migration law and acting within this transnational assemblage of power. As a human rights profession, social work should reassemble itself to fit the present transnational reality. This implies integrating and combining a range of competences. Transnational social work first has to gain insights into 'transnational migration law' and integrate transnational migration law into practice. Transnational migration law is a juridical assemblage of practices, subjects and relations that become visible through particular analytics that refract questions of legal authority and lawful relations through the concept of the 'transnational'. Transnational migration law is the outcome of contested sites, forms and practices of legality that state agencies have come to create and use in the regulation of human mobility (Dehm, 2020).

Critical social work, dealing with transnational migration, thus has to take the political production, enactment and maintenance of particular sets of structural relations and the enactment of an assemblage of legal practices that shape how people move in the contemporary world into account. Transnational law making and other state practices of border policing and immigration law enforcement can lead to the illegalisation of the rights, claims and juridical status of minoritised citizens such as refugees and family reunifiers (De Genova and Roy, 2020). De Genova calls it 'the legal production of illegality' (De Genova, 2004). Consequently, dealing with transnational migration law inevitably implies a critical awareness of the whereabouts of state power in the complex state assemblage of power (Navaro-Yashin, 2002).

Foremost, this means that 'doing politics' is inevitable. Many of the civil society agencies deal with family reunification in different ways. Some limit their social work practice to a form of service delivery. Others also stress their political task, even if that means dealing with dissensus in relation to state agencies or leveraging 'within' the state institutions by using their so-called 'discretionary space'. Next to taking up a political role, there is also a need to build up actual transnational networks. Including transnational dynamics into social work practices, implies taking position in this political boundary work, enacted with the (trans)national state assemblage.

Conclusion

The right to family reunification in Belgium and other EU countries is far from self-evident, due to the political climate that leads to a range of restrictions and thresholds that undermine human rights and – in its extreme consequences – to the legalisation of illegalisation. The increasing conditionality for family reunification leads to an enormous differentiation of rules and differences in access to a certain residence status. Instead of the universal right to family life, a practice of unequal citizenship or 'civic stratification' (Morris, 2003: 75) is emerging. What's more, state agencies have installed (trans)national administrative regimes and legal techniques of power that define the boundaries of inclusion. Although there are some exceptions in place for refugees, the terms and conditions that are applied in practice lead to a range of difficulties undermining the rights and the everyday desires to reunite as a family.

As a human rights profession, social work has a political and social duty to take up the needs of reuniting refugee families. Family reunification defies the boundaries of social work practice and its intellectual canon. The realities of transnationalism and practices of cross-border relations, politics and law, working through a state assemblage of power, challenge the everyday practice of social work. In what we described, we are convinced that this challenge is inevitable, as transnational realities already define the actual needs on the ground (Schrooten, 2021). In the coming years the need to deal with transnational phenomena in social work will only increase, as European societies are becoming more and more diverse.

The assignment we ascribe to social work is twofold. First, at the level of family relations, social workers have to work with families at a distance and support transnational family life. Second, the task ahead is also political. Legal frameworks of transnational migration law, and its administrative and legal practices, are (re-)produced by political agencies. Social workers' political task implies breaking out of the post-war national container of sovereign state power to think through the transnational assemblages of power that shape the practices of family reunification and other migratory dynamics.

Acknowledgements

This project is financially supported by a PWO-grant of Odisee University of Applied Sciences, provided by the Flemish Government.

References

Allen, J. and Cochrane, A. (2007) 'Beyond the territorial fix: Regional assemblages, politics and power', *Regional Studies*, 41(9): 1161–75.

An, S., Chambon, A. and Köngeter, S. (2016) 'Transnational histories of social work and social welfare: An introduction', *Transnational Social Review*, 6(3): 236–41.

Anderson, B. and McFarlane, C. (2011) 'Assemblage and geography', *Area*, 43(2): 124–7.

Baldassar, L. and Merla, L. (eds) (2013) *Transnational Families, Migration and the Circulation of Care: Understanding Mobility and Absence in Family Life*, New York: Routledge.

Block, L. (2012). *Regulating social membership and family ties: Policy frames on spousal migration in Germany*, Unpublished doctoral dissertation. Department of Political and Social Sciences, European University Institute.

Bonizzoni, P. and Boccagni, P. (2013) 'Care (and) circulation revisited: A conceptual map of diversity in transnational parenting', in L. Baldassar and L. Merla (eds) *Transnational Families, Migration and the Circulation of Care: Understanding Mobility and Absence in Family Life*, New York: Routledge, pp 78–93.

Bonjour, S. and Block, L. (2016) 'Ethnicizing citizenship, questioning membership: Explaining the decreasing family migration rights of citizens in Europe', *Citizenship Studies*, 20(6–7): 779–94.

Brummel-Ahlaloum, J., Andreissen, T., Smal, E. and Kawou, R. (2018) *Welzijn en gezondheid van gezinsherenigers: Een verkenning*, Utrecht: Pharos Expertisecentrum Gezondheidsverschillen.

Caritas International (2018) 'The power of the people. Year report 2018'. www.caritasinternational.be/wp-content/uploads/2019/06/2019-06-27-CARITAS-ANNUAL-REPORT-2018-EN-finish-web.pdf

De Genova, N. (2004) 'The legal production of Mexican/migrant "illegality"', *Latino Studies*, 2(1): 160–85.

De Genova, N. and Roy, A. (2020) 'Practices of illegalisation', *Antipode*, 52(2): 352–64.

De Haene, L., Rober, P., Adriaenssens, P. and Verschueren, K. (2012) 'Voices of dialogue and directivity in family therapy with refugees: Evolving ideas about dialogical refugee care', *Family Process*, 51(3): 391–404.

Debruyne, P. and Parker, C. (2015) 'Reassembling the political: Placing contentious politics in Jordan', in F.A. Gerges (ed) *Contentious Politics in the Middle East*, London: Palgrave Macmillan, pp 437–65.

Dehm, S. (2020) 'Transnational migration law: Authority, contestation, decolonization' in P. Zumbansen (ed) *Oxford Handbook on Transnational Law*, Oxford: Oxford University Press.

Dreby, J. and Adkins, T. (2010) 'Inequalities in transnational families', *Sociology Compass*, 4(8): 673–89.

Elliott, A. and Urry, J. (2010) *Mobile Lives*, London: Routledge.

Furman, R., Negi, N.J. and Salvador, R. (2010) 'An introduction to transnational social work', in N. Negi and R. Furman (eds) *Transnational Social Work Practice*, New York: Columbia University Press, pp 11–27.

Gibens, S., Hubeau, B. and Berkvens, L. (2019) 'Mensenrechten en sociaal werk', in M. Tirions, P. Raeymaeckers, A. Cornille, S. Gibens, J. Boxstaens and Y. Postma (eds) *#Sociaal Werk*, Leuven: Acco, pp 311–32.

Groeninck, M., Meurs, P., Geldof, D., Wiewauters, C., Van Acker, K., De Boe, W. and Emmery, K. (2019) *Veerkracht in beweging. Dynamieken van vluchtelingengezinnen versterken*, Leuven: Garant.

Groeninck, M., Meurs, P., Geldof, D., Van Acker, K. and Wiewauters, C. (2020) 'Resilience in liminality: How resilient moves are being negotiated by asylum seeking families in the liminal context of asylum procedures', *Journal of Refugee Studies*, 33(2): 358–70.

Healy, L. M. (2008) 'Exploring the history of social work as a human rights profession', *International Social Work*, 51(6): 735–48.

Lucassen, L. (2018) 'Peeling an onion: The "refugee crisis" from a historical perspective', *Ethnic and Racial Studies*, 41(3): 383–410.

Madianou, M. (2016) 'Polymedia communication among transnational families: What are the long-term consequences for migration?', in E. Palenga and M. Kilkey (eds) *Family Life in an Age of Migration and Mobility: Global Perspectives through the Life Course*, London: Palgrave Macmillan, pp 71–93.

Madianou, M. (2017). '"Doing family" at a distance', in L. Hjorth, H. Horst, A. Galloway and G. Bell (eds) *The Routledge Companion to Digital Ethnography*, New York: Routledge, pp 102–11.

Madianou, M. (2019) 'Migration, transnational families, and new communication technologies', in J. Retis and R. Tsagarousianou (eds) *The Handbook of Diasporas, Media, and Culture*, Hoboken, MJ: Wiley, pp 577–90.

Madianou, M. and Miller, D. (2012) *Migration and New Media: Transnational Families and Polymedia*, London: Routledge.

Mascia, C. (2020) 'How bureaucracies shape access to rights: The implementation of family reunification in Belgium', *Journal of Ethnic and Migration Studies*, 47(9): 2127–43.

McFarlane, C. (2009) 'Translocal assemblages: Space, power and social movements', *Geoforum*, 40(4): 561–7.

Morgan, D.H.J. (1996) *Family Connections*, Cambridge: Polity Press.

Morris, L. (2003) 'Managing contradiction: Civic stratification and migrants' rights', *International Migration Review*, 37(1): 74–100.

Myria (2018) 'Recht op een gezinsleven'. www.myria.be/files/NL2018-5.pdf

Myria (2019) 'Hoorzitting over wetsvoorstel 574 Gezinshereniging. Kamercommissie Binnenlandse Zaken 26 November 2019'. www.myria.be/files/Myria_Kamercommissie_Binnenlandse_Zaken_Gezinsherenig ingDEF_(1).pdf

Myria (2020) 'Migratie in cijfers en in rechten: Recht op een gezinsleven'. www.myria.be/files/2020_Recht_op_een_gezinsleven.pdf

Navaro-Yashin, Y. (2002) *Faces of the State: Secularism and Public Life in Turkey*, Princeton, NJ: Princeton University Press.

Ong, A. and Collier, S. (eds) (2005) *Global Assemblages: Technology, Politics, and Ethics as Anthropological Problems*, Hoboken, NJ: Wiley.

Righard, E. and Boccagni, P. (2015) 'Mapping the theoretical foundations of the social work–migration nexus', *Journal of Immigrant and Refugee Studies*, 13(3): 229–44.

Schmidt, G. (2011) 'Law and identity: Transnational arranged marriages and the boundaries of Danishness', *Journal of Ethnic and Migration Studies*, 37(2): 257–75.

Schrooten, M. (2012) 'Moving ethnography online: Researching Brazilian migrants' online togetherness', *Ethnic and Racial Studies*, 35(10): 1794–809.

Schrooten, M. (2021) 'Transnational social work: Challenging and crossing borders and boundaries', *Journal of Social Work*, 21(5): 1163–81.

Schrooten, M., Salazar, N.B. and Dias, G. (2016) 'Living in mobility: Trajectories of Brazilians in Belgium and the UK', *Journal of Ethnic and Migration Studies*, 42(7): 1199–215.

Sleijpen, M., Boeije, H.R., Kleber, R.J. and Mooren, T. (2016) 'Between power and powerlessness: A meta-ethnography of sources of resilience in young refugees', *Ethnic Health*, 21(2): 158–80.

Strasser, E., Kraler, A., Bonjour, S. and Bilger, V. (2009) 'Doing family: Responses to state constructions of "the migrant family" across Europe', *The History of the Family*, 14(2): 165–76.

Vindevogel, S., Ager, A., Schiltz, J., Broekaert, E. and Derluyn, I. (2015). 'Toward a culturally sensitive conceptualization of resilience: Participatory research with war-affected communities in Northern Uganda', *Transcultural Psychiatry*, 52(3): 1–21.

Walsh, F. (2003) 'Family resilience: A framework for clinical practice', *Family Process*, 42(1): 1–18.

Withaeckx, S., Schrooten, M. and Geldof, D. (2017) 'Thinking and acting globally and locally: Developing transnational social work practices in Belgium', *Transnational Social Review*, 7(2): 143–57.

Wray, H. (2006) 'An ideal husband? Marriages of convenience, moral gatekeeping and immigration to the UK', *European Journal of Migration and Law*, 8(3–4): 303–20.

7

Open or closed doors? Accessibility of Italian social work organisations towards ethnic minorities

Elena Cabiati

Introduction

In Italian social work organisations, ethnic minority persons represent a significant share of service seekers (Caritas and Migrantes, 2013; Terre des Hommes and Cismai, 2021). The social work global statement on ethical principles considers 'challenging discrimination and institutional oppression' and 'respect for diversity' among its ethical principles (IFSW and IASSW, 2018), which are also are universally recognised as the core principles of social work (IASSW and IFSW, 2014). However, when implementing these principles to serve the needs of ethnic minorities, social workers face several challenges, wherein tolerating or respecting differences becomes insufficient, and misinterpretation and involuntarily discrimination can easily affect the perceptions and behaviours of social workers (Brotman, 2003; Hesse, 2004; Dominelli, 2008; Hodge, 2020).

Italy has only recently started realising the need for increased intercultural sensitivity and competence in social work practices. Social work education and continuing education programs still place limited priority on recognising ethnic differences, and the approaches to social work remains predominantly universalist. Therefore, addressing the needs of ethnic minority service users constitutes an important challenge.

Through the metaphor of an open/closed door, this chapter discusses the 'accessibility and inclusivity' of Italian social work organisations towards ethnic minorities. Symbolically, a door evokes a passage or a threshold whose opening and closing movements delimit the outside from the inside and vice versa. Social work organisations often undertake 'door-opening practice' that facilitate, welcome and encourage people towards the welfare system. Sometimes, the access to the system is mandated by law or forced by a referral, for example, in child protection cases. However, access to welfare system is often affected by 'door-closing factors' that discourage, limit or impede, both in the active and passive sense, the initiation of the required processes to help the people, groups and communities in need. Therefore, these circumstances warrant further research and interventions to solve the problem of accessibility.

The chapter is based on three core ideas:

- As human beings, all those in need must have the right to access welfare services and support to improve their living conditions. The implementation of these rights depends on several micro and macro factors (Tilbury and Thoburn, 2009; Valtonen, 2015).
- Social work organisations do not operate the same way for everyone and can involuntarily discriminate against ethnic minority people.
- The ways through which services and professionals react to ethnic and cultural differences are important, and even decisive in promoting or hindering access to help resources.

'Intercultural discrimination': social work organisations do not work the same way for everyone

Through the concepts of 'disproportionality', 'overrepresentation', 'underrepresentation' and 'racial disparity', social work literature has shown that compared to ethnic majorities, ethnic minorities receive different treatment from social services and have different lived experiences (Bartholet, 2009; Tilbury and Thoburn, 2009; Foster, 2012). International research is unanimous in its assessment that ethnic minorities are severely under-represented in care systems and are over-represented in the justice systems (Dominelli, 2010; Font et al, 2012; Fong et al, 2014; Caritas and Migrantes, 2016; Font Choate, 2019). The rules, procedures, professional behaviours adopted by helping systems are often discretionary and apply a 'differential treatment' for people in need based on their ethnic backgrounds.

The ethnic background of the person in need can often influence service providers to open or close the door of helping practices to such people. Typically, the intercultural discrimination in social work practices is not determined by intentional oppressive mechanisms or racist attitudes, but are the outcomes of complex hidden and unconscious dynamics. For example, when encountering a challenge, social workers can practice discriminatory behaviour against ethnic minorities in two ways:

- 'Accelerating' or initiating faster interventions with more drastic and incisive measures.
- Applying 'brakes', by glossing over or either not intervening or intervening with a reduced conviction or urgency.

Through these opposite movements, social workers implement helping activities by either showing interventionism or laxity, claim the support of welfare organisations as urgent or not urgent and either opening or closing opportunities. These movements have critical methodological and ethical consequences for both practitioners and people in need.

An immigration report by Caritas and Migrantes (2016) revealed that in Italy, people suffering from addiction problems begin their therapeutic journey through two different channels, depending on their minority or majority status. Their research data illustrates that among prison inmates, ethnic majority people received their first addiction treatment through local community centres or services, whereas most ethnic minority people began treatment only in prisons, and up to that point had never received aid from local community services or centres. This difference can be attributed to several factors, including the lack of willingness among ethnic minority people to turn to welfare services. However, there are other factors and mechanisms that close the door towards accessing the right treatment and care for ethnic minority people suffering from addiction. This example highlights the complexity of this issue, plagued by political, methodological and ethical concerns.

Objective and subjective factors of door-opening and -closing practices

Linguistic barriers

Linguistic barriers present an objective problem in social work interventions, as highlighted by studies conducted in several countries (Križ and Skivenes, 2010; Kaur, 2012; Sawrikar, 2013; Marrs Fuchsel, 2015; Puntervold Bø, 2015). Communication and having adequate channels for communication is critical for service users and social workers. Communication requires a linguistic compatibility to maximise the opportunities of interaction, enable listening and understanding among the people involved in the coping process during difficult situations. Despite this need, Italian social work organisations show a 'monolinguistic idea of help', conducting the majority of their social work interventions only in the Italian while underestimating the needs of linguistic minority people. International laws emphasise the need to respect and meet the linguistic needs of service users (Convention on the Rights of the Child, 1989; Istanbul Convention, 2011; Directive 2012/29/EU). Italy adopted these laws but translating them into social work practice remains a challenge. The lack of adequate support to manage linguistic diversity impedes the development of helping processes and represents a door-closing approach towards social work practices.

Italian social work organisations have a limited collaboration between social workers and linguistic mediators, and, even if available, in practice such collaboration involves complications, as shown by national and international research (Bhuyan and Velagapudi, 2013; Sani, 2015). According to the human rights perspective (Dominelli, 2008), communication is an essential right and it's not an ancillary support. Therefore, social workers must advocate for this right, considering that having adequate tools for communication is not only a right for ethnic minority people but is also a professional's right. Social workers have the right to work, which involves avoiding misunderstandings and mistakes, and maximising the opportunity for people's wellbeing, and providing them with adequate and timely information, as suggested by the national and international codes of ethics. While linguistic barriers are an objective problem, they are often addressed through subjective measures that sometimes stray from the possibilities to overcome the problem. For example, a person with low competence in the Italian language might be labelled as a 'person with poor personal competences or little motivation to be helped'.

Every time social workers afford a subjective meaning to linguistic differences or neglect asking for the support of a linguistic mediator, they implicitly reinforce the disadvantaged dynamics against linguistic minorities.

Legal status

Access to social work interventions can be influenced by people's legal status, which is an objective factor. Because of their legal status, immigrants may not be eligible to receive certain benefits and support. For example, the Italian income support measures are often regulated by specific criteria that exclude people without a valid residence permit or those with less than 10 years of permanent and continuous residence in the country.

According to ISTAT data, in 2019, the poverty ratio of immigrant families with children in Italy was five times higher than that of Italian families (ISTAT, 2020); however, several ethnic minority families living in poverty are excluded from income support measures or the access to aid and services because, despite their needs, they do not meet the required criteria for help.[1]

According to a recent report by the Italian NGO Group for the Convention of the Rights of the Child (2021), the registration of foreign minors with the National Health Service is still dependent on the administrative and legal status of parents. To date, in six Italian regions, the children of EU and non-EU citizens without a residence permit do not have the access to free-choice paediatricians or general doctors.

Sometimes social workers encourage ethnic minorities people to actively search for new opportunities or to approach a service agency to receive support. The rules for availing welfare services are not always clear, especially regarding their inaccessibility based on people's legal status. Not receiving or receiving less aid than required because of legal and administrative barriers may prevent early detection and prevention interventions, accelerating unfavourable developments that receive urgent and restrictive actions only when the situation is already compromised. The limit of enforceability can be exacerbated by service professionals' lack of adequate information and, consequently, by their inefficiency in supporting people to navigate the welfare system.

Obstacles inherent in interventions and support

Social work interventions driven by an ethnocentric idea of welfare can become inaccessible to ethnic minorities, because of, for example, the difficulty of customising the interventions based on the religious, spiritual or dietary needs (Holloway, 2007) of those other than the ethnic majority.

Research shows that standardising help and the 'one size fits all' approach (Miller and Gaston, 2003) disadvantages all people because their needs are unique and are only partially similar to that of others. Nevertheless, it is important to note that most Italian social work organisations show a 'colour-blind approach' (Dominelli, 2008), premised on the principle of providing aid without factoring in people's backgrounds. However, this mindset implies that social work precludes intercultural sensitivities while planning and implementing helping interventions. Ignoring that human needs are 'same, same but different' (Harrison and Burke, 2014), service users are treated as a homogeneous category while receiving the same interventions. Consequently, there is no room for differences, and no understanding of the subjective lives and experiences of ethnic minorities, who either welcome or renounce the help because of their unsuitability for their needs. The failure of the welfare organisation to recognise and adapt with the specific needs of ethnic minorities could be misinterpreted as the people's inability or unwillingness to benefit from the support and receive help.

Therefore, Social workers must make an important distinction: it is one thing for people to not want to be helped (and close the door of help themselves), and another thing for that help or intervention to not match their specific living conditions or needs, considering not just the service users but also 'immigrant service users'. These people are at the doorway to seek help but see the door closing in the face. This distinction is crucial to avoid creating myths about the behaviour of ethnic minorities, which fuels oppressive dynamics, and in some cases, leads to interventions based on mistakes or misinterpretations.

Social workers' competences and sensitivities

Intercultural competence and sensitivity of professionals are two important factors that facilitate door-opening practices for ethnic minorities. Several studies show that the acquisition of intercultural competences is a complex journey involving cognitive, emotional and ethical dimensions (Abrams and Moio, 2009; Deardoff, 2009; Nadan, 2014; Fisher-Bourne et al, 2015), and for social work, 'cultural humility' seems more relevant than 'cultural competence' (Abell et al, 2015; Gottlieb, 2020).

Addressing the needs of ethnic minorities require that social workers (and managers, educators, and researchers) acquire new competences that refine and expand the previous ones, by increasing the learning efforts for new knowledge while simultaneously deconstructing presumed or stereotyping knowledge. In an intercultural relationship, social workers must not only learn about the Other's way of life, but also be aware of their ways of living and helping people.

The ability to provide effective help while respecting cultural differences is a prerequisite for making an intervention accessible and a realistic possibility. In this sense, the intercultural competence (or the lack thereof) of professionals can open or close the door towards helping systems for ethnic minorities. Intercultural competence also includes social workers' willingness and ability to reflect on their own work and understand the organisational and institutional forces that may facilitate or hinder the opening of doors.

To increase intercultural awareness and competence and the effective application of the anti-discrimination principle, social workers must have the right technical and critical competencies.

Despite the limited attention on this topic, social work research emphasises the need to educate and support social workers and managers of social work organisations to address the challenges and meet the needs of ethnic minorities in an intercultural world.

Ethnic minority service users' diffidence and prejudices

In this complex discourse, it is necessary to acknowledge that even ethnic minorities can end up excluding themselves from the welfare systems, as discussed by previous international studies (Chen et al, 2009; Chow et al, 2010).

Despite the presence of real difficulties, several reasons might prevent minority groups from crossing the door to access support systems, making them close the door and remain isolated with their problems instead. These reasons include the lack of perception and awareness of their state of need, their sense of pride and the fear of being judged and stigmatised because of their difficulties (Scharlach et al, 2006; Williams and Johnson, 2010).

While approaching social work organisations to seek help may seem uncomfortable or difficult, ethnic minority people could make greater efforts to do so. These efforts involve seeking knowledge and expressing trust towards the service and the social worker who wants to help them and who most likely, in their perception, appears to be a foreigner. For service seekers, opening the door may involve overcoming fears and prejudices that they may unintentionally harbour, which are distinct from those harboured by the professionals. As in the case of professionals, despite the high stakes, not all people in difficulty are able to overcome their prejudices, even when they need support.

Ethnic minority service users are equally susceptible to fears and prejudices against people of different ethnicities, even those who work as professionals within welfare organisations. Assumptions about the unpreparedness of social workers and social work organisations in meeting their specific needs are some factors that may distance people from welfare systems. As observed by international studies, for some caregivers, the recipient's unwillingness to meet a social worker of a different ethnic group presents an impassable barrier, causing them to give up the support needed (Fang, 2011; Greenwood et al, 2015).

Equivalence of care and intersectionality

In the field of social work, 'equivalence of care' implies 'differential care' because people have similar yet unique the life problems. Regarding discrimination and accessibility in social work, intersectionality is an important concept in the complex mix of objective and subjective factors for implementing equivalence of care (Crenshaw, 1989; Bubar et al, 2016). This term indicates the competition and the overlap of several identities (not only ethnic, but also gender and social class) that determine unfair treatments. Intersectionality is crucial framework for deconstructing violence, power and privilege (Bubar et al, 2016: 284).

The extant literature has represented intersectionality through several mathematical metaphors (Mehrotra, 2010) that evoke the idea of multiplication and not only of addition. However, it is important to reflect on which ethnic and cultural variables intersect with other lines of social division and how they impact the relationships and practices of social work (Lavalette and Penketh, 2014).

The culture of Italian social work organisations

In social work, the main discourse around 'culture' or 'cultural issues' is often centred around the culture of ethnic minorities and less around the culture of professionals and social work organisations. When social workers speak of 'culture', in most cases, they are referring to not their culture but that of people who need help, such as a migrant woman, an asylum seeker or an unaccompanied young boy.

To effectively challenge discrimination and institutional oppression (IFSW and IASSW, 2018), it is important to draw attention to the culture of helpers, social workers, Italian organisations and helping systems.

Social work organisations are sites of culture production, and child protection services, home care institutions, services for older adults or addiction treatment centres are culturally rooted. In other words, the culture of help they express is not neutral but is enriched with meanings, choices, principles and values that define their mission, regulations, procedures and methods of intervention. These cultures influence the way in which professionals provide help and those in need receive help.

Reflecting on their own culture, social workers can be stimulated to raise awareness on how to adapt their professional tools, intervention methods, procedures or ways of helping others to serve the needs of ethnic minorities people and not just the majority. Furthermore, social workers and managers must recognise their power to influence the culture and pathways of service provision. According to the concept of 'sensemaking' (Weick, 1995), professionals who reflect, live, think and act make sense of the identity and culture of organisations and the degree of sensitivity, accessibility and inclusivity of helping paths. A starting point for sensemaking could be the critical analysis of existing practices to develop alternatives, which is a concrete step to promote equal opportunities and eradicate discriminatory practices.

Italian social welfare organisations' need for self-reflection on their degree of accessibility and inclusivity

Challenges of intercultural social work can stimulate social workers, managers, policymakers and volunteers to critically observe social policies and social welfare organisations, whose constraints and mechanisms move the gears to facilitate or hinder caregiving actions. The needs of ethnic minorities highlight the incoherence and inequalities embodied by welfare systems, especially those beyond the individual responsibilities of social workers.

Intercultural helping relationships pose peculiar challenges to social workers that are easier to ignore (Cabiati, 2020). Social work makes more demands from professionals operating in a multicultural society than within the majority culture (Puntervold Bø, 2015: 562).

Reflecting on social work organisations' accessibility and inclusivity for ethnic, cultural and linguistic minorities reveals two key ideas: social services do not operate in the same way for everyone, and the balance between the needs of ethnic minorities and their effective participation in helping paths may be disproportionate, as confirmed by studies on disproportionality in child welfare interventions (Bartholet, 2009; Foster, 2012; Fong et al, 2014). For an ethnic minority woman, it could be more complicated to escape violence than their ethic majority counterparts; similarly, an ethnic minority child could face harsher struggles to be accepted in childcare systems for several reasons. Among the many objective and subjective variables determining these difficulties, many of these barriers and obstacles are actively or passively created, endorsed or maintained by the helping systems themselves, as evidenced in cases of institutional racism (Lea, 2000; Dominelli, 2008; Harrison and Burke, 2014). In an anti-immigration climate, seeking help from an ethnic majority becomes even more difficult (Bhuyan and Velagapudi, 2013: 74).

Therefore, managers, policymakers and practitioners must proactively examine their organisations to develop critical processes to reflect on its culture while encouraging actions to identify institutional choices, rules and mechanisms that can confirm or amplify, instead of reducing or disadvantaging the conditions of ethnic minorities. Social work organisations are involved at all levels (as educators and researchers) support to ensure accessibility and inclusivity, because working effectively while respecting ethnic and cultural differences is a collective challenge.

Anti-discrimination is not an automatic process

Providing help is not the same as being anti-discriminatory, and social workers who settle for tolerance set the bar too low. Additionally, while not discriminating is not enough for social workers, it is the bare minimum expectation while providing help. Discrimination stifles interventions and fuels dynamics and oppressive mechanisms that disadvantage people, groups and communities in need. Speaking of 'anti-racist social work', Dominelli stated that 'racism impedes social work's capacity to promote well-being' (2008: 71). As proposed by national and international codes of ethics (IFSW and IASSW, 2018), promoting people's self-determination and wellbeing through social work makes it imperative for social workers to address all forms of discriminations.

Despite their human and methodological competencies, social workers can involuntarily produce, fuel or confirm dynamics that disadvantage people for their ethnic backgrounds, often in conjunction with other variables. For social workers, anti-discrimination is not the default or an automatic mode of operation; recognising this fact is the first step in constructing a more inclusive and efficient system to address the needs of ethnic minorities. In the helping processes, identifying the elements of discrimination is not as easy as it is produced by several factors and silenced by routine practice. Even more challenging is to name and accept these elements, which requires acceptance of the idea that discrimination also affects social welfare organisations and social workers, regardless of whether it is involuntarily. Therefore, every social worker must consider whether their behaviour could be oppressive and fuel or generate inequalities.

This discourse is also connected with the concept of 'neutral' or 'value free' action (Nixon and McDermott, 2010), which is impossible in practice. Thus, if neutral means to be objective and be objective means to be without prejudices, even social workers cannot be neutral despite their intentions.

Intercultural social work requires taking a position

Because social work is not value-neutral, despite expecting social workers not to take a political stand, social work invariably involves taking a position. Ethnic minority people's experiences and needs exemplify the idea that one cannot remain ignorant of the privileges and advantages enjoyed by a country's ethnic majority. These privileges are often based on their skin colour mixed with other variables, such as gender, religion, sexuality, spirituality or economic position. Amidst the historical moment of astringent anti-immigration policies in several European countries (Valtonen, 2015; Zanker, 2019), intercultural social work highlights the need to deeply reflect on core human issues to answer 'what kind of people we are' (Boushel, 2000: 71).

Implementing social work interventions with ethnic minorities offers a great potential for reflective practice. From the origin of the social work profession, pioneers have helped people who faced the negative consequences of migration processes (Abbott, 1917; Smith, 1995). Facing these challenges in the USA, UK and France, social workers have addressed new tasks and huge workload while dealing with feelings of fear, mistrust and resistance in the societies and with unrealistic and assimilationist expectations from the governments. Early practitioners worked without specific training and tools in the context of stringent policies and laws against migrant people. Even today, despite the challenging working conditions in welfare systems, social workers must express their commitment seriously and vigorously, because ethnic minorities who live in painful conditions need to feel welcomed, understood and supported. Sometimes, support is not just needed to face the adversities of migration, but also to successfully navigate the challenges of being an ethnic minority service seeker in a foreign country. Their encounters with asylum seekers, unaccompanied minors and migrant families present social workers with the opportunity to critically test and examine the ways through which they extend help, develop new skills and sensitivities and enhance critical thinking that is vital for their mission.

Social work organisations reflect the sensitivities of social workers, managers, volunteers and towards ethnic minorities, and their commitment to effectively implement the principles affirmed in the international arena (IFSW and IASSW, 2018). Intercultural helping relationships encourage social workers to disclose personal representations and their own sensitive areas while discovering that is not easy to resist, emotionally and cognitively, the temptation to essentialise oneself, one's lifestyle and way of helping.

Conclusions

In intercultural contexts, social workers are potentially prone to make more mistakes in their assessment and interventions, especially when they lack the required support to do effective work. Intercultural relationships provide greater exposure to social workers to reflect on their practices through an ongoing learning process enriched by discoveries and humility. The mission to help ethnic minority people while effectively respecting cultural differences is an important step to help social workers explore their own culture, observe one's limits and address one's biases as well as one's own resources. To successfully meet the needs of ethnic minorities, social work practitioners and organisations must recognise and respect differences, ensure equitable access, communication, understanding and active participation of people by providing the necessary tools and support to overcome any obstacles that may disadvantage or obstruct the possibilities of giving and receiving help.

The word 'actively' implies that tolerance and non-discrimination are essential but not sufficient for social workers. Even without the ability to act directly to remove the barriers encountered by ethnic minority children, families and groups, it is important to recognise these barriers and their impact on their lives and their helping paths. Thompson said that 'in many respects, social work reflects life: full of challenges, but also full of rewards' (Thompson, 2020: xiii). In the backdrop of an undeniable ontological equity, social work experiences of ethnic minority people reveal what our differences and similarities tell us about ourselves as human beings.

Note

[1] It's clear that not all ethnic minority people don't have these requirements but these are based on mechanism of inclusion/exclusion who potentially affect more ethnic minority people in need.

References

Abbott, G. (1917) *The Immigrant and the Community*, New York: The Century Co.

Abell M.L., Manuel J. and Schoeneman, A. (2015) 'Student attitudes toward religious diversity and implications for multicultural competence', *Journal of Religion and Spirituality in Social Work: Social Thought*, 34(1): 91–104.

Abrams, L.S. and Moio, J.A. (2009) 'Critical race theory and the cultural competence dilemma in social work education', *Journal of Social Work Education*, 45(2): 245–61.

Bartholet, E. (2009) 'The racial disproportionality movement in child welfare. False facts and dangerous directions', Harvard Law School Faculty Scholarship Series, Paper 26, Harvard Law School.

Bhuyan, R. and Velagapudi, K. (2013) 'From one "Dragon Sleigh" to another: Advocating for immigrant women facing violence in Kansas', *Affilia. Journal of Women and Social Work*, 28(1): 65–78.

Boushel, M. (2000) 'What kind of people are we? Race, anti-racism and social welfare research', *British Journal of Social Work*, 30: 71–89.

Brotman, S. (2003) 'The limits of multiculturalism in elder care services', *Journal of Aging Studies*, 17: 209–29.

Bubar, R., Cespedes, K. and Bundy-Fazioli, K. (2016) 'Intersectionality and social work: Omissions of race, class, and sexuality in graduate school education', *Journal of Social Work Education*, 52(3): 283–96.

Cabiati, E. (2020) *Intercultura e social work. Teoria e metodo per le relazioni di aiuto*, Trento: Centro studi Erickson.

Caritas and Migrantes (2016) 'XXVI Rapporto immigrazione. Nuove generazioni a confronto'. http://s2ew.caritasitaliana.it/materiali/Rapporto_immigrazione/2017/Sintesi_RICM2016.pdf

Chen, A.W., Kazanjian, A. and Wong, H. (2009) 'Why do Chinese Canadians not consult mental health services: Health status, language or culture?', *Transcultural Psychiatry*, 46(4): 623–41.

Choate, P. (2019) 'The call to decolonise: Social work's challenge for working with Indigenous Peoples', *British Journal of Social Work*, 49(4): 1081–99.

Chow, C.C.J., Auh, E.Y., Scharlach, A.E., Lehning, A.J. and Goldstein, C. (2010) 'Types and sources of support received by family caregivers of older adults from diverse racial and ethnic groups', *Journal of Ethnic and Cultural Diversity in Social Work*, 19(3): 175–94.

Crenshaw, K. (1989) 'Demarginalizing the intersection of race and sex: A Black feminist critique of antidiscrimination doctrine, feminist theory and antiracist politics', *University of Chicago Legal Forum*, 1(8): 139–67.

Deardoff, D.K. (2009) *The Sage Handbook of Intercultural Competence*, Thousand Oaks, CA: Sage.

Dominelli, L. (2008) *Anti-racist Social Work*, London: Palgrave.

Dominelli, L. (2010) *Social Work in a Globalizing World*, Cambridge: Polity.

European Parliament and the Council (2012) Directive 2012/29/EU of the European Parliament and of the Council of 25 October 2012 establishing minimum standards on the rights, support and protection of victims of crime. https://eur-lex.europa.eu/legal-content/EN/TXT/PDF/?uri=CELEX:52020DC0188&from=EN

Fang, L. (2011) 'A sociocultural perspective of mental health service use by Chinese immigrants', *Canadian Social Work Journal*, 12(1): 152–60.

Fisher-Bourne, M., Cain, M.J. and Martin, S.L. (2015) 'From mastery to accountability: Cultural humility as an alternative to cultural competence', *Social Work Education*, 34(2): 165–81.

Fong, R., McRoy, R. and Dettlaff, A. (2014) *Disproportionality and Disparities. Encyclopedia of Social Work*, New York: National Association of Social Workers and Oxford University Press.

Font, S.A., Berger, L.M. and Slack, K.S. (2012) 'Examining racial disproportionality in child protective services case decisions', *Children and Youth Service Review*, 34(11): 2188–200.

Foster, C.H. (2012) 'Race and child welfare policy: State-level variations in disproportionality', *Race and Social Problems Journal*, 4: 93–101.

Gottlieb, M. (2020) 'The Case for a cultural humility framework in social work practice', *Journal of Ethnic & Cultural Diversity in Social Work*, 30(6): 463–81.

Greenwood, N., Habibi, R., Smith R. and Manthorpe, J. (2015) 'Barriers to access and minority ethnic carers' satisfaction with social care services in the community: A systematic review of qualitative and quantitative literature, *Health and Social Care in the Community*, 23(1): 64–78.

Harrison, P. and Burke, B. (2014) 'Same, same, but different', in M. Lavalette and L. Penketh (eds) *Race, Racism and Social Work: Contemporary Issues and Debates*, London: Policy Press.

Hesse, B. (2004) 'Im/plausible deniability: Racism's conceptual double bind', *Social Identities*, 10(1): 9–29.

Hodge, D. (2020) 'Spiritual microaggressions: Understanding the subtle messages that foster religious discrimination', *Journal of Ethnic & Cultural Diversity in Social Work*, 29(6): 473–89.

ISTAT (2020) 'Le statistiche dell'Istat sulla povertà. Anno 2019, Report Statistiche – 16 giugno'. www.istat.it/it/archivio/244415

Kaur, J. (2012) 'Cultural diversity and child protection. Australian research review on the needs of culturally and linguistically diverse (CALD) and refugee children and families', Report, Queensland.

Križ, K. and Skivenes, M. (2010) 'Lost in translation: How child welfare workers in Norway and England experience language difficulties when working with minority ethnic families', *British Journal of Social Work*, 40(5): 1353–67.

Holloway, M. (2007) 'Spiritual need and the core business of social work', *British Journal of Social Work*, 37(2): 265–80.

IASSW and IFSW (2014) 'Global definition of the social work profession'. http://ifsw.org/get-involved/global-definition-of-social-work/

IFSW and IASSW (2018) 'Global social work statement of ethical principles'. www.ifsw.org/wp-content/uploads/2018/07/Global-Social-Work-Statement-of-Ethical-Principles-IASSW-27-April-2018-1.pdf

Lavalette, M. and Penketh, L. (2014) *Race, Racism and Social Work*, Bristol: Policy Press.

Lea J. (2000) 'The Macpherson Report and the question of institutional racism', *The Howard Journal*, 39(3): 219–33.

Marrs Fuchsel, C.L. (2015) 'Spanish-English bilingual social workers: Meeting the linguistic needs of Latino/a clients', *Journal of Ethnic & Cultural Diversity in Social Work: Innovation in Theory, Research & Practice*, 24(3): 251–5.

Mehrotra, G. (2010) 'Toward a continuum of intersectionality theorizing for feminist social work scholarship', *Affilia: Journal of Women and Social Work*, 25(4): 417–30.

Miller, O.A. and Gaston, R.J. (2003) 'A model of culture-centered child welfare practice', *Child Welfare*, 82(2): 235–50.

Nadan, Y. (2014) 'Rethinking cultural competence in international social work', *International Social Work*, 60(1): 74–83.

Nixon, J. and McDermott, D. (2010) 'Teaching race in social work education', *Enhancing Learning in the Social Sciences*, 2(3): 1–14.

Puntervold, Bø, B. (2015) 'Social work in a multicultural society: New challenges and needs for competence', *International Social Work*, 58(4): 562–74.

Sani, S. (2015) 'The profession and the roles of the intercultural mediator in Italy', *Procedia. Social and Behavioral Sciences*, 191: 2546–8.

Sawrikar, P. (2013) 'A qualitative study on the pros and cons of ethnically matching culturally and linguistically diverse (CALD) client families and child protection caseworkers', *Children & Youth Services Review*, 35(2): 321–31.

Scharlach, A.E., Kellman, R., Ong, N., Baskin, A., Goldstein, C. and Fox, P.J. (2006) 'Cultural attitudes and caregiver service use: Lessons from focus groups with racially and ethnically diverse family caregivers', *Journal of Gerontological Social Work*, 47(1/2): 133–56.

Smith, R.F. (1995) 'Settlements and neighborhood centers', *Encyclopedia of Social Work*, 19(3): 2129–35.

Terre des Hommes and Cismai (2021) 'Indagine nazionale sul maltrattamento dei bambini e degli adolescenti in Italia', *Risultati e Prospettive*. https://terredeshommes.it/dnload/Indagine-Maltrattamento-bambini-TDH-Cismai-Garante.pdf

Thompson, N. (2020) *Understanding Social Work: Preparing for Practice*, London: Red Globe Press.

Tilbury, C. and Thoburn, J. (2009) 'Using racial disproportionality and disparity indicators to measure child welfare outcomes', *Children & Youth Services Review*, 31: 1101–6.

United Nations of Human Rights (1989) *Convention on the Rights of the Child*. www.ohchr.org/Documents/ProfessionalInterest/crc.pdf

Valtonen, H. (2015) *Social Work and Integration in Immigrants Communities*, Aldershot: Ashgate.

Weick, K.E. (1995) *Sensemaking in Organizations*, Thousand Oaks, CA: Sage.

Williams, C. and Johnson, M.R.D. (2010) *Race and Ethnicity in a Welfare Society*, London: Open University Press.

Zanker, F. (2019) 'Managing or restricting movement? Diverging approaches of African and European migration governance', *Comparative Migration Studies*, 7(17): 1–18.

8

Refugee children and families in the Republic of Ireland: the response of social work

Muireann Ní Raghallaigh

Introduction

Ireland was traditionally a country of outward migration. However, this changed in the mid-1990s when the number migrating into Ireland became greater than the numbers emigrating (Christie, 2002a). During this period also, the numbers of people arriving as asylum seekers increased, with Mac Éinrí (2001) estimating that about 10 per cent of immigrants arriving in Ireland between 1995 and 2000 were asylum seekers.[1] Prior to this less than 50 people per year sought asylum in Ireland (Cullen, 2000, cited in Christie, 2002a) with the state also occasionally welcoming small groups of programme refugees, following Ireland's signing of the 1951 UN Convention Relating to the Status of Refugees in 1956. Since the mid-1990s the trends vis-à-vis the arrival of asylum seekers and refugees have fluctuated at different points in time. While Ireland's peripheral location at the Western edge of Europe means that it doesn't receive the numbers of asylum and international protection applicants that countries such as Greece and Italy do, it nonetheless has a steady number arriving and in recent years has developed its resettlement programme substantially through the establishment of the Irish Refugee Protection Programme. Due to the multiple challenges that these individuals and families face both pre and post migration, it is evident that many could benefit from a social work service. Indeed, Christie (2002a) argues that 'with the arrival of asylum seekers in Ireland since the mid-1990s, social workers have been increasingly drawn into more explicit "policing" of the internal and external boundaries of the state'. He goes on to state that 'this relatively small profession has access to material resources and expertise that may benefit asylum seekers' (p. 14).

This chapter will explore the role of social work in relation to children and families from forced migration backgrounds in the Republic of Ireland. To begin with, it will set the context by discussing social work generally in the Irish context. Following this, four different (though overlapping) cohorts of people from a forced migration background will be identified and discussed: Those who arrive independently/ 'spontaneously' and seek asylum or international protection ('asylum seekers' or 'international protection applicants'); refugees who arrive through organised government resettlement or relocation schemes; unaccompanied minors who arrive through one of the aforementioned routes and who are placed in the care of the state child welfare and protection agency (Tusla); and people – usually from a forced migration background themselves – who arrive to be reunited with refugee family members who are already in Ireland. The chapter will examine the policy context and discuss the role of social work with each of these cohorts, highlighting both the important contributions made by social workers, the limitations of current social work practice and the possibilities for the future. Drawing on Irish and international research, the chapter will argue that social workers in Ireland and elsewhere are very well placed to work with refugee children and their families in a systemic way. Doing so requires professionals that are skilled and self-aware and who, vitally, are committed to anti-racist and anti-oppressive practice.

Social work in the Irish context

Social workers in Ireland are regulated by CORU, 'Ireland's multi-professional health regulator' (CORU, n.d.), which was established under the Health and Social Care Professionals Act (2005). Anyone using the title of 'Social Worker' must register with the Social Workers' Registration Board (which is part of CORU) and CORU also assesses, approves and monitors social work training courses. Social workers in Ireland qualify via either one of two 4-year degree programmes or via one of six 2-year postgraduate programmes. It is important to note that 'social worker' and 'social care worker' are two distinct professional titles, with different qualifications applying. Social care workers work in a range of settings, including in residential care (for example, in children's residential homes (or 'group homes') or in residential settings for people with intellectual disabilities). Some social care workers return to education to pursue a career in social work.

In Ireland there is no nationally available data on the number of social workers who are employed at a given point in time. However, as of the 11 October 2021, 4,941 social workers were registered with the Social Workers' Registration Board (CORU, 2011). An edited book on Social Work in Ireland from 2015 (Christie et al, 2015) show the range of settings in which social workers work, including child welfare and protection, fostering and adoption, hospitals and primary care settings, mental health services, older people's services, the probation service, addiction services, services responding to family violence and services for people with intellectual disabilities. Of note is the fact that there is not a specific chapter in this comprehensive book on social work with refugees and those seeking international protection, although one chapter focuses on social work in a globalised Ireland (Christie and Walsh, 2015) with content on social work with asylum seekers included within it. Nonetheless, the lack of a specific chapter on this population points to the small number of social workers working in designated roles related to this cohort and to the sometimes-hidden nature of the role of social workers with this client group in other mainstream social work services. Indeed, Christie and Walsh (2015) argue, in relation to asylum seekers in direct provision accommodation centres in Ireland (discussed further next), that such centres tend to remain 'largely outside of the concern of social work services' (p. 25).

While there is a dearth of recent data regarding the social work workforce, research by Walsh et al (2009) suggests that the workforce in Ireland has become increasingly diverse. This is related to internationally trained social workers coming to Ireland as a result of international recruitment drives and more general inward migration, as well as to the increasing diversity of the Irish population over recent decades. This increased diversity includes more students from Black and ethnic minority backgrounds undertaking social work training. Of relevance to this chapter is the fact that the author is aware, from her experience of teaching on a social work training programme, that some social work students are from a refugee background themselves: again no data is available on precisely how many. In tandem with the diversification of the social work workforce, the service user population has also become increasingly diverse. Yet, despite these changes, various authors have argued that there has been a lack of attention to anti-racist or anti-oppressive policy and practice (Christie, 2002a) with Walsh et al (2009: 1984) arguing that 'the lack of attention to cultural difference in both child protection guidelines and child welfare legislation is one tangible example of a continuing inertia'. However, more recently, particularly given the increasing global attention to racism and anti-racism in the wake of the Black Lives Matter movement, issues of race, racism, anti-racism and cultural sensitivity have been given increasing attention by the social work profession in Ireland. For example, in 2021 the Irish Association of Social Workers (IASW) launched its first Anti-Racism Strategy (IASW, 2021) and in the same year social work educators across the island of Ireland (North and South) formed an anti-racism subgroup of the All-Ireland Social Work Educators Forum. Academic work is also being done in this area (for example, McGregor et al, 2020; Olusa, 2018). This (potential) awakening to the realities of racism in the context of social work in the Republic of Ireland is of significance when we consider social work with refugee children and families, given both the interpersonal and institutional racism that many from a forced migration background are likely to experience. It is to social work with these populations that we now turn.

Children and families in direct provision

The vast majority of families that arrive in Ireland to seek international protection are accommodated, first, on a temporary basis in Balseskin Reception Centre in north county Dublin before then being dispersed and accommodated in one of the 'direct provision' centres scattered across the country, often in rural locations. The direct provision system has been in operation since 2000. Within this system, international protection applicants receive minimum support, including a weekly allowance and accommodation usually in a former hotel or similar setting designated for international protection applicants. For most of its existence direct provision centres have provided meals rather than having self-catering facilities, meaning that families could not cook for themselves. This has changed to a considerable extent in recent years. The negative impact of direct provision on international protection applicants has been widely documented (for example, Ní Raghallaigh et al, 2016; O'Reilly, 2018; Movement of Asylum Seekers in Ireland, 2019; Dunbar et al, 2020), with the particularly negative impact on children and families highlighted frequently, including by social work researchers (for example, Christie and Walsh, 2015; Foreman and Ní Raghallaigh, 2015; Ogbu et al, 2014). From early on, significant concerns about poverty, deprivation, social exclusion and social isolation were voiced (for example, Fanning et al, 2001; Dolan and Sherlock, 2010; Ombudsman for Children's Office, 2020). Concerns have frequently been raised about the welfare and development of children living in this system for prolonged periods (for example, Arnold, 2012; Ombudsman for Children's Office, 2021), including repeated concerns expressed by Ireland's then Special Rapporteur for Child Protection Dr Geoffrey Shannon who, in his final report, stated: '[a]s noted in numerous other Rapporteur reports, the system of Direct Provision for asylum seekers in Ireland should be abolished' (Shannon, 2019: 33). Concern has been expressed about the negative impact of direct provision on mental health (Crumlish and Bracken, 2011; Conlan, 2014; Ní Raghallaigh et al, 2016) and, aligned to this, it has been well documented that many parents feel a sense of powerlessness and lack of agency due to living in a system where many parenting tasks and responsibilities are outside of your control (Ogbu et al, 2014; Moran et al, 2019). For example, decisions about what and when to eat are often dictated by management of the centres; centre rules govern who can visit; limited weekly allowances and a ban on the right to work (until very recently) mean that enabling children to participate in society is often curtailed. Indeed, a recent human right's analysis of the impact of direct provision on children (Dunbar et al, 2020) states that 'Ireland's practice of institutionalising children and families in private, commercially operated Direct Provision settings is systematically infringing children's rights to health and development, education and respect for private and family life' (p. iii).

The role of social work in relation to these centres and their residents has been relatively limited. This is despite the fact that, in the Irish context, a resource book for social workers working with asylum seekers and refugees was published in 2001, a year after direct provision came into being (Torode et al, 2001). It is also despite the obvious roles that social workers could play, as is evident from international social work scholarship on working with refugees and asylum seekers (for example, Boccagni and Righard, 2020; Wroe et al, 2019). Unlike accommodation centres in some European countries which may have social workers employed or designated to them (see Hagues et al, 2019; Lintner, 2020), direct provision centres generally don't have social work staff either working within them or designated to the centres but working externally. While residents could access social workers in generic services (such as primary care teams or community mental health teams), social workers in these services don't have a specific remit vis-à-vis the direct provision centres. In addition, residents may not even know that these social work services are available in the local community or may assume that they are not eligible to avail of them, given their exclusion from many other aspects of society (Foreman, 2009), or they may face significant barriers in accessing these services (Foreman and Ní Raghallaigh, 2015). Direct provision centres are generally staffed by employees who often have a background in the hospitality sector rather than in health or social services. As such, however well-meaning these staff might be, they have a limited capacity to engage in the complex work involved in supporting those from a refugee background – individuals and families from various cultural and religious backgrounds, many of whom have experienced trauma prior to arrival and who are also dealing with the often-significant challenges of adjusting to a new society. An exception is the initial reception centre (Balseskin), where there are now two full-time social workers and one half-time social work team leader employed. In addition to this, the government department which oversees the accommodation service for international protection applicants has a senior level social worker employed who manages the work of the Child and Family Services Unit within the International Protection Accommodation Service (IPAS). It is envisaged that four more social work posts within this unit will come on stream in the near future. The social workers involved within IPAS conduct initial vulnerability assessments and, where needed, link international protection applicants with relevant services (including other social work services) and provide follow-up support where needed. They also serve as points of contact for Direct Provision centre managers and staff where concerns about residents arise or where there are child protection concerns. The recent move of responsibility for IPAS from the Department of Justice and Equality (which has responsibility for assessing asylum claims) to the Department of Children, Equality, Disability, Integration and Youth has been seen as a significant and positive one. As well as these state-employed social workers, to the author's knowledge, there are five other social workers working in non-governmental organisations (NGOs) who provide services to refugees and those seeking international protection. These individuals are employed by three NGOs (the Irish Society for the Prevention of Cruelty to Children, Nasc (a migrant and refugee rights organisation)) and Crosscare. Although social work trained, most of these social workers are not employed in social work posts. They nonetheless bring their social works skill to these roles, which focus primarily on providing support and engaging in advocacy in relation to a range of issues, including transitioning from the direct provision system, family reunification and integration.

Of course, social workers in Ireland also come across international protection applicants in other generic social work settings which the general population also access – for example in mental health services, in primary care settings, in medical social work and in child protection and welfare services. Most services in which social workers are employed are accessible to all members of the community, irrespective of their immigration status. There is little knowledge about the work of mainstream social work teams as regards international protection applicants, although a submission by Foreman and Ní Raghallaigh (2015) to the Working Group on the Protection Process provides some important data. The submission was based on a survey completed by 149 social workers and interviews with 15 social workers working in various social work settings. The majority of participants worked in child protection and welfare services and in adult mental health services. In keeping with the broader literature on direct provision, social workers highlighted concerns about the short- and long-term impact of direct provision on child development and welfare, the negative impact of direct provision on parents' capacity to parent to their full potential, the additional challenges faced by families dealing with physical or mental illness or intellectual disability and the difficulties social workers faced 'attempting to deliver an equitable service to asylum seekers' (p. 3). Regarding the latter, and as already mentioned, social workers pointed to difficulties experienced by international protection applicants in accessing social work services, with financial barriers being particularly evident, as well as issues regarding asylum seekers being moved to new accommodation, not having childcare in order to allow them to attend appointments, and language and transport barriers. While no national policy on social work service delivery to international protection applicants exists, participants' accounts highlighted examples of good practice. These included proactive practice where social workers provided information sessions to newly arrived asylum seekers in relation to child protection and welfare in the Irish context and examples of mental health social workers forming good working relationships with staff of direct provision centres which helped to encourage asylum seekers to access their services.

In other jurisdictions, children of Black, ethnic minority and migrant backgrounds are frequently over-represented in child protection and welfare systems (Boatswain-Kyte et al, 2020; Cénat et al, 2021; Johansson, 2010) and there is evidence of a fear of child protection services among refugees (Levi, 2014). In the Irish context there is no available national data regarding such representation. However, research by Dalikeni (2021) which looked at the interactions of Black African asylum-seeking families with white child protection/welfare social workers highlighted that African asylum-seeking families are 'at risk of being over-represented in the child protection system when ethnocentrism and racism rather than culturally appropriate assessment criteria are used to judge whether maltreatment has occurred' (p. 12). In addition, data from the Health Information and Quality Authority (HIQA), an independent body which inspects 'some of the social care services children access to determine if they are meeting National Standards' (HIQA, n.d.), suggests that this might be the case. HIQA inspected child protection and welfare services offered to children in direct provision in several regions (HIQA, 2015). They found that in the period studied, between August 2013 and 2014, 209 referrals of child protection and welfare concerns were made in relation to about 229 children living in direct provision. Of children living in direct provision, this represented 14 per cent, a referral rate which was significantly higher than the rate in relation to the general population of children (1.6 per cent) (HIQA, 2015). The reasons for referral were varied with roughly half relating to child protection concerns and half relating to child welfare concerns. While space limitations preclude detailed discussion here, it is worthy of note that HIQA expressed concern about referrals 'arising from children's living conditions that were outside of the control of the Child and Family Agency (Tusla) but had resulted in referrals to their service' (HIQA, 2015: 4). These included, for example, referrals in relation to children being left alone while parents queued for food or injuries sustained at least partly due to cramped living conditions. The report highlights examples of both excellent practice from social work teams and poor practice where action was not taken to protect children. Overall, the report highlights the crucial need for data on the interaction between international protection applicants and child welfare and protection services, as well as the need for social workers to understand both the context in which referrals from direct provision are made as well as the living situations and experiences of international protection applicants.

Resettled and relocated children and families

In the Irish context, children and families arriving through organised resettlement and relocation schemes are generally accommodated in emergency reception and orientation centres (EROCs) upon arrival. These EROCs are generally former hotels where it is planned that refugees would live for approximately three months before moving to housing within communities around Ireland (Ní Raghallaigh et al, 2019).

In many ways EROCS are similar to direct provision. However, the length of time spent in them is shorter – though longer than the envisaged three-month period (Ní Raghallaigh et al, 2019) – and those living there have certainty about their immigration status as they have refugee status at the point of arrival. In addition, the support provided in these centres is greater than in direct provision. Again though, the role of social work here is not well established. There are no social workers employed to work directly in these centres although some social workers employed elsewhere may engage in outreach with these centres, even though it is not an explicit part of their role. For example, Ní Raghallaigh et al (2019) gives the example of a social worker from the state child protection and welfare agency who engaged in outreach in one EROC, providing initial information sessions to new arrivals and operating follow-on clinics which focused on providing information, family support, advocacy and signposting to other services. Where the staff of the centre wished to make referrals regarding child protection and welfare concerns, these referrals were sent to different personnel in the child protection agency, with the separation of roles deemed very important in terms of allowing supportive relationships to be formed with residents. This is significant given the previously mentioned fear that refugees may have of child protection services (Levi, 2014). In addition, establishing trust between social workers and refugee populations is frequently challenging (Dalikeni, 2016; Ní Raghallaigh, 2014), this being at least partly related to what Boccagni and Righard (2020) term 'institutional ambiguity' whereby 'asylum seekers do not necessarily have a sense of the division of labour between social workers in local reception or integration initiatives and the office in charge of the legal assessment of their case' (p. 379). Such outreach and support may be particularly important given the evidence that staff in the EROCs – who again tended to have a background in hospitality rather than in social care or social work – appear to assume a regulatory role over parenting practices of residents and tend to problematise the parenting that they observe, with research findings suggesting that parents were 'subject to intrusive observations and interventions within reception centres' (Ní Raghallaigh et al, 2020: 1).

There is a potential role for social workers too following resettlement from the EROCs to local communities throughout the country. In Ireland, resettlement support workers support refugee families after they have moved out of EROCs for a period of 18 months or two years. Typically, these workers are employed by local development organisations or NGOs contracted by local authorities. They are employed on fixed-term contracts, resulting in significant loss of expertise when their contacts come to an end at the end of a resettlement period (Ní Raghallaigh et al, 2019). In addition, they generally do not have social work qualifications. While various professional backgrounds would be suited to this work, the social work role – particularly with its emphasis on adopting a systemic and ecological perspective – could make a significant contribution. This is especially important given the evidence of the multiple barriers to integration that many refugees face, including the evidence in Ireland that resettled young people face challenges creating friendships with young people from the receiving society (Smith et al, 2020). The international literature points to the potential of social work to make a positive difference in relation to resettlement and integration (Ran et al, 2020; Valtonen, 2001). Having permanent and professionally qualified resettlement social workers situated throughout the country would mean that the issues surrounding the precarity experienced by resettlement support workers in NGO's would be resolved and the resettlement 'sector' would potentially benefit from the professional social work background of the workers.

Unaccompanied minors

Records suggest that the first unaccompanied minor to arrive in Ireland presented to authorities in 1996 (Mac Neice and Almirall, 1999). At that time, the Office of the Refugee Application Commissioner referred unaccompanied minors to the local Health Board (which had responsibility for child protection prior to the establishment of Tusla). The Health Board's child protection team based in the area in which asylum applications were made assumed responsibility initially, before a dedicated team for unaccompanied minors/separated children seeking asylum was established in Dublin, with social workers in the Cork and Clare regions also beginning to work with young people presenting in those areas (Christie, 2002b). However, the vast majority of unaccompanied minors presented to the Dublin team (henceforth 'the unaccompanied minors' team'). This team comprised professionally qualified social workers,[2] as well as project workers, and was developed at a time when the social work profession in Ireland was under-resourced (Christie, 2003) (as it still is). It is widely recognised and accepted that initially the care provision for these children was hugely inadequate (Christie, 2002b, 2003; Mac Neice and Almirall, 1999). At the very beginning children were placed in 'Bed and Breakfast' homeless accommodation in which adult asylum seekers also lived. Subsequently, dedicated 'hostels' for unaccompanied minors were opened: These hostels frequently accommodated 30 or 40 unaccompanied minors, males and females, with the 'worst' hostels having up to 12 young people sharing a room. The hostels were not staffed by professionally trained individuals: in most cases they were privately run and staffed by security personnel. Each hostel had a project worker attached to it who visited the hostel frequently, linked young people to schools and provided a range of other supports. The more vulnerable or younger unaccompanied minors were allocated a social worker. Allocation of social workers to all young people was deemed not possible given the numbers of young people arriving at the time and an insufficient number of social workers employed. In the main, only a basic service could be provided (Christie, 2002b) and there were significant concerns about children going missing (Quinn et al, 2014). While a very small number of unaccompanied minors were placed in approved foster care or residential care, with these young people receiving a much higher quality of care provision, overall Christie (2002b) argued that social workers at the time 'were placed in the position of providing services that would be judged as grossly inadequate for Irish children' (p. 194).

The care provision provided to unaccompanied minors received extensive criticism – from non-government organisations, from international organisations and from social workers themselves (Veale et al, 2003; Mooten, 2006; Commissioner for Human Rights, 2008; Corbett, 2008; Charles, 2009) – and the pressure to change the service mounted. In a paper which outlines the history of the service provided by the unaccompanied minors' team Richason (2018) describes 'the quest' to provide 'sustainable solutions' in relation to the care of unaccompanied minors in Ireland as 'difficult and nonlinear' (p. 403). In the early 2000s improvements to services were made – larger hostels were closed, social care workers were employed in some hostels and new, approved residential units specifically for unaccompanied minors were established. By 2010, an 'equity of care' policy was implemented whereby all hostels were closed, and a system was put in place that was deemed to provide care on a par with the care provided to Irish children in the care of the state (Arnold and Ní Raghallaigh, 2017). In general, this involves unaccompanied minors under the age of 12 being accommodated in foster care or supported lodgings (another form of family care) upon arrival. However, the vast majority of unaccompanied minors are over 12 and they are accommodated in residential care upon arrival before then moving to live with foster families if this is deemed to be in their best interest (Ní Raghallaigh, 2013).

In sharp contrast with the initial provision for unaccompanied minors, the current policies and practice in place for this cohort are widely viewed – both nationally and internationally – as representing best practice across many domains. The unaccompanied minors' team currently employs five social work team leaders, eight social workers and seven after care workers (with the latter having qualifications in social care and other disciplines). The role of social work vis-à-vis unaccompanied minors in Ireland is now firmly established, with significant expertise having developed, particularly on this

Dublin-based team. Holistic risk and needs assessments are conducted at the outset to establish the best interests of young people and their care needs (Tusla, n.d.) In particular, the extensive use of foster care, and the initial evidence that this is working well (Ní Raghallaigh, 2013; Ní Raghallaigh and Sirriyeh, 2015), is internationally recognised (de Ruijter de Wildt, 2015).

Of course, current social work policy and practice in this area is not without criticism. Two areas of practice have been the subject of particular critique: the practice of delaying applications for asylum (Groarke and Arnold, 2018) and the practice of some unaccompanied minors entering the direct provision system upon turning 18 (Thornton and Ní Raghallaigh, 2017). Regarding the first of these, while the unaccompanied minors' team argues that it is important to wait for young people to be ready to enter into the asylum process, legal experts have highlighted the potentially detrimental impact of this on the young people, particularly as delayed outcomes to their asylum claim may negatively impact on their right to family reunification (Groarke and Arnold, 2018). In addition, Christie (2002a: 14) argues that the initial interviews or assessments that social worker conduct with children and the decision they make regarding whether or not to make an application for refugee status 'draw social workers into an immigration assessment process'. This is of concern given the obvious conflicts between the values of social work and the values of immigration and border policies.

The practice of some unaccompanied minors being placed in the direct provision system as a form of aftercare has also been widely criticised. For example, in an analysis of this practice Ní Raghallaigh and Thornton (2017) state: 'while aftercare planning is (usually) conducted, aged-out separated children are regarded as migrants first and foremost who have to fit in within the highly punitive direct provision system upon turning 18' (p. 399). This is a very concerning practice, given the extensive evidence about the negative impact of direct provision on those seeking international protection (as discussed earlier) and given the international literature on the risks posed for those leaving care (Mayock and Vekic, 2006; Stein, 2006; Cameron et al, 2018). This practice places social workers in an untenable position. It also poses significant risks to the success of foster care given the huge uncertainties that hang over young people in foster care as they approach the age of 18 (Ní Raghallaigh, 2013; Ní Raghallaigh and Sirriyeh, 2015). Two recent reports – one from the Joint Committee on Justice and Equality (2019) and one from Advisory Group on the Provision of Support including Accommodation to Persons in the International Protection Process (2020) – recommended that this practice should end and that Tusla should continue to hold responsibility for unaccompanied minors when they turn 18 if their asylum applicants are still being processed. The government's plan to end direct provision envisages that, as well as the supports that unaccompanied minors leaving care already receive, the housing supports available to all international protection applicants under the new accommodation model will be available to those in aftercare and indeed that they will be given priority in relation to these supports (Department of Children, Equality, Integration, Disability and Youth, 2021).

Family reunification

The literature on refugee family reunification suggests the multiple challenges experienced by refugees who apply to have family reunited with them and the many challenges experienced by reunified family members (Marsden and Harris, 2015; Crosscare Refugee Service, 2018). Despite the joy that many refugees experience upon reunification with their family members, challenges are often encountered at various stages from prior to applying for reunification right through to the months and years after family members arrive. These stresses include: difficulties navigating bureaucratic processes with rigid eligibility criteria; financial difficulties in relation to accessing processes and funding visas and travels; the stress of securing housing; the challenges of re-establishing relationships in a very new cultural context when family members may have changed due to migration and acculturation; the challenges of adjusting to a new cultural context, including learning a new language; the un-ending worry about family members still in danger who were not eligible to be reunited (Smith et al, 2020). Within the Irish context the state support available to refugee 'sponsors' (those who apply to have family members reunited with them) and the support available to reunified family members is largely non-existent. Indeed, Smith et al (2020) state, in relation to reunified families, 'no programmes of orientation and support exist for their benefit' (p. 116). They proceed to argue that 'this places a heavy burden on refugee sponsors – who may already be living in quite precarious circumstances – to assist family member in navigating the complex bureaucratic tasks involved in initially getting settled in Ireland' (Smith et al, 2020: 116). In addition, NGOs attempt to fill the gaps but usually with very limited resources, with these resources already stretched.

Currently, in the Irish context, social workers working on the unaccompanied minors' team are involved in this area to some extent – they assist young people to apply for family reunification and support young people and their family members when they arrive (Smith et al, 2020). After the point of arrival, unaccompanied minors are no longer actually 'unaccompanied' and therefore, strictly speaking, continuing to support these young people and their families is probably beyond the remit of this team. However, due to the critical shortage of support for individual and families in this situation, social workers on this team as well as aftercare workers often fill the gaps. Apart from the unaccompanied minors' team, the information available to the author would suggest that one of the previously mentioned social workers employed by Nasc has a remit which includes work with newly reunited families. Other social workers in mainstream social work services may also support reunited families who come to their attention, but currently there is no data or research in relation to this work. It most likely occurs on an ad hoc basis.

There is huge potential here for increased social work involvement, despite a dearth of international research on this topic. Given the training that social workers have in working systemically with families, particularly families experiencing transitions, social workers are ideally placed to support families to re-establish their relationships and navigate resettlement. Social Workers can bring their unique skills where they work with individuals and families within their social and community contexts and these skills can be leveraged to support refugee sponsors and reunified family members. As mentioned, the existing research suggests that family reunification results in huge stresses for all involved. While no data exists in Ireland on the extent to which this stress results in referrals to child welfare and protection services or to mental health services, it is reasonable to assume that increased early support, from a suitably qualified individual, might help to prevent crises arising in the future. Social Workers are ideally positioned to provide this support.

Discussion and conclusion

The discussion here points to the important role social workers can play in responding to the needs of and recognising the rights of refugees and international protection applicants in the Republic of Ireland. While it is only in relation to unaccompanied minors that social work currently occupies a central position as regards refugees in the Irish context, with few specific social work posts existing in relation to other cohorts of refugees, social workers nonetheless will frequently come across refugees and international protection applicants in the course of their work across various areas of practice. Currently, the potential of social work practice in these areas is not only thwarted by the existence of the oppressive reception system of direct provision, but also by multiple other factors. For example, the inadequate resourcing of social work teams and high caseloads mean that crisis work frequently take precedence and that the kind of outreach work that might be needed to engage refugee families often cannot be prioritised. These factors also mean that the extra time required to provide an equitable service to many refugees and international protection applicants is not available. In addition, a lack of availability of appropriately trained interpreters and the lack of training that social workers have in working with interpreters is a significant further barrier. Added to this is the fact that many social workers may lack sufficient knowledge about working with refugees and international protection applicants, particularly if they rarely encounter this cohort of clients in their work, and many may be in need of additional training in cultural competence and anti-racist practice.

Notwithstanding these challenges – all of which are surmountable – the long-overdue commencement of vulnerability assessments in the Irish context, as well as the government's commitment to establish a new model for the reception of international protection applicants, suggests a timely opportunity for social workers to play a more central role in the years to come. The new model of reception will be centred on a human rights approach, which is, of course, entirely consistent with social work's mission. Indeed, the International Federation of Social Workers identifies social justice, human rights, collective responsibility and respect for diversity as the principles central to social work. Each of these principles is crucially important in work with refugees and international protection applicants. Boaccagni and Righard (2020: 378) eloquently argue that:

> the label refugee cannot say all about the person who bears it. Being or becoming an asylum seeker, or a refugee, is a critical life event. It is not the only one though, and it cannot subsume all of the identities, interests, life projects and concerns of people who are also asylum seekers or refugees.

This points to the need to view refugees holistically, something which is a key characteristic of social work practice. Through doing so, and by adopting a human rights perspective and a client-centred approach, and crucially, by ensuring practice is underpinned by an anti-oppressive and anti-racist approach, social workers in Ireland and elsewhere have the potential to make a significant and positive difference in the lives of clients from a forced migration background. However, the system in which social workers work needs to be organised in a way that enables this to happen. Policy and system levels flaws and failures need to be addressed and social work services need to be adequately resourced, whether specialised services for refugees and international protection applicants or more generic services. Hence, in the years that lie ahead, the social work profession in Ireland should attempt to position itself more centrally not only in service provision but also in policy development and in research in this sphere. Doing so is likely to enhance the support that refugees and international protection applicants receive as they face the challenges and opportunities in navigating resettlement and rebuilding their lives.

Acknowledgements

I would like to acknowledge my research collaborations with Maeve Foreman and with Dr Karen Smith, the learning from which has informed this paper. I'd like to also acknowledge the information provided by Anna Deneher, Emma Maguire, Susan Mackey, Bernard Cantillon and Brian Davis.

Notes

[1] In the Irish context the term 'asylum seeker' was until very recent years used to describe someone seeking refuge or asylum. More recently the term 'international protection applicant' has been used to also encompass those seeking subsidiary protection. In this chapter they are both used, with the most appropriate term selected for the context. In addition, 'people of a refugee background' is used to refer to those who are applying for asylum or international protection or those who have already been granted refugee status or subsidiary protection. The word 'migrant' is used to refer to broader cohorts of people who migrate to Ireland, including those from a refugee background but also including others such as economic migrants.

[2] The author was one of the social workers on this team from 2001 to 2003.

References

Advisory Group on the Provision of Support including Accommodation to Persons in the International Protection Process (2020) 'Report of the advisory group on the provision of support including accommodation to persons in the international protection process'. Dublin: Government of Ireland. www.gov.ie/en/publication/634ad-report-of-the-advisory-group-on-the-provision-of-support-including-accommodation-to-persons-in-the-international-protection-process/#

Arnold, S.K. (2012) 'State sanctioned child poverty and exclusion: The case of children in state accommodation for asylum seekers'. Dublin: Irish Refugee Council. www.irishrefugeecouncil.ie/children-and-young-people/children-in-direct-provision-accommodation/attachment/state-sanctioned-child-poverty-and-exclusion

Arnold, S. and Ní Raghallaigh, M. (2017) 'Unaccompanied minors in Ireland: Current law, policy and practice', *Social Work & Society*, 5(1).

Boaccagni, P. and Righard, R. (2020) 'Social work with refugee and displaced populations in Europe: (Dis)Continuities, dilemmas, developments', *European Journal of Social Work*, 23(3): 375–83.

Boatswain-Kyte, A., Esposito, T., Trocmé, N. and Boatswain-Kyte, A. (2020) 'A longitudinal jurisdictional study of black children reported to child protection services in Quebec, Canada', *Children and Youth Services Review*, 116: 1–13

Cameron, C., Hollingworth, K., Schoon, I., van Santen, E., Schröer, W., Ristikari, T., Heino, T. and Pekkarinen, E. (2018) 'Care leavers in early adulthood: How do they fare in Britain, Finland and Germany?' *Children and Youth Services Review*, 87: 163–72.

Cénat, J.M., McIntee, S.-E., Mukunzi, J.N. and Noorishad, P.-G. (2021) 'Overrepresentation of black children in the child welfare system: A systematic review to understand and better act' *Child and Youth Services Review*, 120: 1–16.

Charles, K. (2009) *Separated Children Living in Ireland: A Report by the Ombudsman for Children's Office*, Dublin: Office of the Ombudsman for Children.

Christie, A. (2002a) 'Asylum seekers and refugees in Ireland: Questions of racism and social work', *Social Work in Europe*, 9(9): 10–17.

Christie, A. (2002b) 'Responses of the social work profession to unaccompanied children seeking asylum in the Republic of Ireland', *European Journal of Social Work*, 5(2): 187–98.

Christie, A. (2003) 'Unsettling the "social" in social work: Responses to asylum seeking children in Ireland', *Child and Family Social Work*, 8(3): 223–32.

Christie, A. and Walsh, T. (2015) 'Social work in a globalised world', in A. Christie, B. Featherston, S. Quin and T. Walsh (eds) *Social Work in Ireland: Changes and Continuities*, London: Palgrave, pp 18–35.

Christie, A., Featherstone, B., Quin, S. and Walsh, T. (eds) (2015) *Social Work in Ireland: Changes and Continuities*, London: Palgrave.

Commissioner for Human Rights (2008) *Report by the Commissioner for Human Rights, Mr. Thomas Hammarberg on His Visit to Ireland*, Brussels: Council of Europe. https://wcd.coe.int/wcd/ViewDoc.jsp?id=1283555

Conlan, S. (2014) *Counting the Cost: Barriers to Employment after Direct Provision*, Dublin: Irish Refugee Council.

Corbett, M. (2008) 'Hidden children: The story of state care for separated children', *Working Notes*, 59: 18–24.

CORU (2011) 'CORU registration statistics October 2021'. https://coru.ie/news/news-for-health-social-care-professionals/coru-registration-statistics-october-2021.html

CORU (n.d.). 'About us'. https://coru.ie/about-us/what-is-coru/

Crosscare Refugee Service (2018). 'Reunified refugee families and homelessness: Submission to the Minister for Justice and Equality'. https://www.migrantproject.ie/2018/07/02/crosscare-submission-on-homelessnessand-reunified-family-members-ofrefugees/

Crumlish, N. and Bracken, P. (2011) 'Mental health and the asylum process', *Irish Journal of Psychological Medicine*, 28(2): 57–60.

Cullen, P. (2000) *Refugees and Asylum Seekers in Ireland*, Cork: Cork University Press.

Dalikeni, C. (2016) 'Voices from practice: Narratives of interrelated factors leading to mutual mistrust in social work encounters with asylum-seeking families, *The Irish Social Worker: Practitioner Research Edition*, Winter: 35–40.

Dalikeni, C. (2021) 'Child-rearing practices: Cross cultural perspectives of African asylum-seeking families and child protection social workers in Ireland', *European Journal of Social Work*, 34(1): 8–20.

Department of Children, Equality, Integration, Disability and Youth (2021) 'White paper to end direct provision and to establish and new international protection support service', Dublin: Government of Ireland. www.gov.ie/en/publication/7aad0-minister-ogorman-publishes-the-white-paper-on-ending-direct-provision/

de Ruijter de Wildt, L., Melin, E., Ishola, P., Dolby, P., Murk, J. and van de Pol, P. (2015) *Reception and Living in Families: Overview of Family-Based Reception for Unaccompanied Minors in the EU Member States*, Utrecht: Nidos, SALAR and CHTB.

Dolan, N. and Sherlock, C. (2010) 'Family support through childcare services: Meeting the needs of asylum-seeking and refugee families', *Child Care in Practice*, 16(2): 147–65.

Dunbar, R., Burke, L., Candon, N., Reid, M., Crivits, S., Wrenn, S. and Shilova, A. (2020) *Direct Provision's Impact on Children: A Human Rights Analysis. A Submission to the Minister for Children, Disability, Integration, Equality and Youth*, Galway: NUI Galway.

Fanning, B., Veale, A. and O'Connor, D. (2001) *Beyond the Pale: Asylum-seeking Children and Social Exclusion in Ireland*, Dublin: Irish Refugee Council.

Foreman, M. (2009) 'HIV and "Direct Provision" – Learning from the Experiences of Asylum Seekers in Ireland', *Translocations: Migration and Social Change, An Inter-Disciplinary Open Access E-Journal*, 4(1): 67–85.

Foreman, M. and Ní Raghallaigh, M. (2015) 'Submission to the working group on the protection process'. https://researchrepository.ucd.ie/handle/10197/6494

Groarke, S. and Arnold, S. (2018) *Approaches to Unaccompanied Minors Following Status Determination in Ireland*, Dublin: ESRI.

Hagues, R.J., Cecil, D. and Stoltzfus, K. (2019) 'The experiences of German social workers working with refugees', *The Journal of Social Work*, 21(1): 46–68.

Health Information and Quality Authority (HIQA) (2015). Report on Inspection of the Child Protection and Welfare Services Provided to Children Living in Direct Provision Accommodation under the National Standards of the Protection and Welfare of Children, and Section 8(1) (c) of the Health Act 2007, Dublin: Health Information and Quality Authority.

Health Information and Quality Authority (HIQA) (n.d.). 'Children's services'. www.hiqa.ie/areas-we-work/childrens-services

Irish Association of Social Workers (2021) *A New Way Forward: Dismantling Racism in 21st Century Irish Social Work: IASW Anti-Racism Strategic Plan 2021–2023*, Dublin: Irish Association of Social Workers.

Johansson, I.-M. (2010) 'The multicultural paradox: The challenge of accommodating both power and trust in child protection', *International Social Work*, 54(4): 535–49.

Joint Committee on Justice and Equality (2019) 'Report on direct provision and the international protection application process'. https://data.oireachtas.ie/ie/oireachtas/committee/dail/32/joint_committee_on_justice_and_equality/reports/2019/2019-12-12_report-on-direct-provision-and-the-international-protection-application-process_en.pdf

Levi, M. (2014) 'Mothering in transition: The experiences of Sudanese refugee women raising teenagers in Australia', *Transcultural Psychiatry*, 51(4): 479–98.

Lintner, C. (2020) 'Professionalisation for what? Reflections on social work practices with asylum seekers at the interface between spatial proximity, emotional distress and professional distance', *European Journal of Social Work*, 23(3): 449–60.

Mac Éinrí, P. (2001) 'Immigration into Ireland: Trends, policy responses, outlook', http://migration.ucc.ie/irelandfirstreport.htm

Mac Neice, S. and Almirall, L. (1999) *Separated Children Seeking Asylum in Ireland: A Report on Legal and Social Conditions*, Dublin: The Irish Refugee Council.

Marsden, R. and Harris, C. (2015) *'We Started Life Again': Integration Experiences of Refugee Families Reuniting in Glasgow*, London: British Red Cross.

Mayock, P. and Vekic, K. (2006) *Understanding Youth Homelessness in Dublin City: Key Findings from the First Phase of a Longitudinal Cohort Study*, Dublin: Stationary Office.

McGregor, C., Dalikeni, C., Devaney, C., Moran, L. and Garrity, S. (2020) 'Practice guidance for culturally sensitive practice in working with children and families who are asylum seekers: Learning from an early years study in Ireland', *Child Care in Practice*, 26(3): 243–56.

Mooten, N. (2006) *Making Separated Children Visible: The Need for a Child-Centred Approach*, Dublin: Irish Refugee Council.

Moran, L., Garrity, S., McGregor C. and Devaney, C. (2019) 'Hoping for a better tomorrow: A qualitative study of stressors, informal social support and parental coping in a direct provision centre in the West of Ireland', *Journal of Family Studies*, 25(4): 427–42.

Movement of Asylum Seekers in Ireland (2019). 'Submission to Justice and Equality Committee', www.masi.ie/wp-content/uploads/2019/09/MASI-SUBMISSION-final-original-copy-29.05.2019.pdf

Ní Raghallaigh, M. (2013) *Foster Care and Supported Lodgings for Separated Asylum Seeking Young People in Ireland: the Views of Young people, Carers and Stakeholders*, Dublin: Barnardos and the Health Service Executive.

Ní Raghallaigh, M. and Sirriyeh, A. (2015) 'The negotiation of culture in foster care placements for separated refugee and asylum seeking young people in Ireland and England', *Childhood*, 22(2): 263–77.

Ní Raghallaigh, M. and Thornton, L. (2017) 'Vulnerable childhood, vulnerable adulthood: Direct provision as aftercare for aged-out separated children seeking asylum in Ireland', *Critical Social Policy*, 37(3): 386–404.

Ní Raghallaigh M., Foreman M., Feeley, M., Moyo, S., Wenyi Mendes, G. and Bairéad, C. (2016) *Transition: from Direct Provision to Life in the Community: The Experiences of Those Who Have Been Granted Refugee Status, Subsidiary Protection or Leave to Remain in Ireland*, Dublin: UCD and the Irish Refugee Council.

Ní Raghallaigh, M. Smith, K. and Scholtz, J. (2019) *Safe Haven: The Needs of Refugee Children Arriving in Ireland through the Irish Refugee Protection Programme: An Exploratory Study*, Dublin: The Children's Rights Alliance. https://researchrepository.ucd.ie/handle/10197/11230

Ní Raghallaigh, M., Smith, K. and Scholtz, J. (2020) 'Problematised parenting: The regulation of parenting practices within reception centres for Syrian refugees in Ireland', *Journal of Refugee Studies*, 34(3): 3362–80.

O'Reilly, Z. (2018) '"Living Liminality": Everyday experiences of asylum seekers in the "Direct Provision" system in Ireland', *Gender, Place & Culture*, 25(6): 821–42.

Ogbu, H.U., Brady, B. and Kinlen, L. (2014) 'Parenting in direct provision: Parents' perspectives regarding stresses and support', *Child Care in Practice*, 20(3): 256–69.

Olusa, O. (2018) 'Experience of black social work practitioners and students: A review of the literature', *The Irish Social Worker*, Winter: 96–105.

Ombudsman for Children's Office (2020) *Direct Division: Children's Views and Experiences of Living in Direct Provision. A Report by the Ombudsman for Children's Office 2020*, Dublin: Ombudsman for Children's Office.

Ombudsman for Children's Office (2021) *Safety and Welfare of Children in Direct Provision: An Investigation by the Ombudsman for Children's Office*, Dublin: Ombudsman for Children's Office.

Quinn, E., Joyce, C. and Gusciute, E. (2014) *Policies and Practices on Unaccompanied Minors in Ireland. European Migration Network*, Dublin: Economic and Social Research Institute.

Ran, G.J. and Join-Lambert, H. (2020) 'Influence of family hosting on refugee integration and its implication on social work practice: The French case', *European Journal of Social Work*, 23(3): 461–74.

Richason, L. (2018) 'Social work for separated children seeking asylum in the Republic of Ireland: Setting the standard for child-centred care and protection', *Child Care in Practice*, 24(4): 402–12.

Shannon, G. (2019) 'Twelfth report of the special rapporteur on child protection'. www.gov.ie/en/collection/51fc67-special-rapporteur-on-child-protection-reports/

Smith, K., Ní Raghallaigh M., Johnson, D. and Izzeddin A. (2020) *Invisible People: The Integration Support Needs of Reunified Refugee Families*, Cork: Nasc.

Stein, M. (2006) 'Research review: Young people leaving care', *Child and Family Social Work*, 11(3): 273–9.

Torode, R., Walsh, T. and Woods, M. (2001) *Working with Refugees and Asylum Seekers: A Social Work Resource Book*, Dublin: Trinity College Dublin.

Tusla (n.d.) 'Separated children seeking international protection', www.tusla.ie/services/alternative-care/separated-children/

Valtonen, K. (2001) 'Immigrant integration in the welfare state: Social work's growing arena', *European Journal of Social Work*, 4(3): 247–62.

Veale, A., Palaudaries, L. and Gibbons, C. (2003) *Separated Children Seeking Asylum in Ireland*, Dublin: Irish Refugee Council.

Walsh, T., Wilson, G. and O'Connor, E. (2009) 'Local, European and global: An exploration of migration patterns of social workers into Ireland', *The British Journal of Social Work*, 40(6): 1978–95.

Wroe, L., Larkin, R. and Maglajlic, R.A. (eds) (2019) *Social Work with Refugees, Asylum Seekers and Migrants: Theory and Skills for Practice*, London: Jessica Kingsley.

9

Sense of place, migrant integration and social work

Susan Levy and Maura Daly

Introduction

From the local to the global, demographic maps have throughout history been fluid, constantly in flux. Migration has created diversity and cultural richness through the making and re-making of societies, a sense of place and identities. This porosity and global interconnectedness is ever more visible leading to the world being 'increasingly dominated by movement – of people, images and information' (Massey, 1991: 24). A canvas of 'super-diversity' (Vertovec, 2007) is being created through the intensification of movement and subsequent integration of migrants. Super-diversity invites new understanding of the complexity of and relationships between migration and integration in postmodern societies, as well as understanding of and questions on the role of social work in this dynamic process. This chapter focuses on the cultural and social dimensions of the integration of migrants, and the building of a sense of place and belonging. It uses Ager and Strang's (2004) *Indicators of Integration Framework*, and Sen's (1999) Capability Approach (CA) to explore the integration of migrants (asylum seekers and refugees) in Scotland, contextualised within cultural social work.

The chapter is presented in two main sections: first, we address approaches to integration, a sense of place and the CA. The opening section discusses integration as a relational, two-way process (Berry, 1997). Ager and Strang's (2004) *Indicators of Integration Framework* is introduced, and we explore the role of building a sense of place, the ways that meanings are ascribed and created to turn the unfamiliar into the familiar, and connections to social work are made visible. The CA (Sen, 1999) frames discussion on conceptualising the integration of migrants, and the evolving sense of place, wellbeing, and identity; of embedding hope in precarious lives. We highlight the relational dimensions of the CA as a way of conceiving of and working to create a society that is tolerant and inclusive of difference for 'living well together' (Deneulin and McGregor, 2010). Second, we situate the chapter geographically within Scottish refugee integration policy and social work practice. The *New Scots Integration Strategy, 2018–22* (Scottish Government,

2017) is shaping the process of integration in Scotland. At the core of the Strategy is a vision of 'a welcoming Scotland where refugees and asylum seekers are able to rebuild their lives from the day they arrive' (Scottish Government, 2017: 11). The chapter explores how this vision and policy is reflected in social work practice and in the everyday lives of migrants.

Integration: building a sense of place and belonging

Integration, as Berry (1997) notes, is essentially a two-way and relational process, and should be understood as distinct from assimilation. The latter refers to a unidirectional process, of migrants absorbing and assimilating into the host society, a process that dilutes outsider uniqueness and diversity. In contrast, integration is a process that requires established society and incoming migrants to adapt to each other through a 'complex process of balancing the integration of the majority culture with the preservation of one's native culture' (Sodowsky et al, 1991: 195). Adaptation requires re-imagining and expanding understanding of diversity through a curiosity and exploration of who and what the migrant is, of making space for the retention of 'strangeness' (de Shalit, 2019: 276). This relational, dialogical approach to integration creates opportunities for a new and richer sense of place. For a society to be open and inclusive, for complexity to be visible and integral to everyday life, the status quo and prevailing narrative of the city needs to be challenged (de Shalit, 2019).

Identities evolve over time, they are complex and layered by, amongst other things, ethnicity, race, language, religion and spirituality. The latter can be core to a migrant's identity, yet is inadequately covered in social work education. Students and graduates often feel unprepared for working with religion and spirituality in practice (Horwath and Lees, 2010), or lack an understanding that leads to practitioners overlooking the cultural dimensions of religion in everyday life (Daly and Smith, 2021). More generally, there is limited understanding and application of cultural competence in relation to social workers' perspectives and experiences of culturally competent practice (Dominelli, 2017; Willis et al, 2017). Embracing the cultural views of others can more fully engage social workers with cultural diversity, getting to the heart of ways to identify the markers that can orientate and support people who are struggling to read a new landscape. Inadequate exposure to different lives is 'an important factor affecting social workers' sensitivity and receptivity towards clients' cultural uniqueness' (Lee et al, 2020: 13). A pointed echoed in Shier et al's (2011) literature review on international social work and migration. They concluded that understanding of cultural competence, awareness of the subtleties of migration, and the multiple paths and integration of migrants remains limited. Ager and Strang's (2004) *Indicators of Integration Framework* is one model that acknowledges and engages with the complexity of refugee integration, encompassing the social and cultural dimensions through to the structural aspects associated with employment and housing. As Käkelä (2020) notes, the numerous structural factors that interact with the cultural and social dimensions underpinning migrants' experiences of being disempowered and marginalised, should not be overlooked.

The *Indicators of Integration Framework* (Ager and Strang, 2004) provides an holistic framework for policy makers and practitioners based around four interconnected domains: Means and Markers; Social Connections; Facilitators; and Foundations (Figure 9.1). Each domain is the 'home' of one of ten sub-areas that can underpin successful and meaningful integration. The Social Connections domain is of particular relevance to this chapter, with integration being conceived as a relational 'two-way' process between migrants and host communities. Under the Social Connections domain, the sub-areas of Social Bridges, Social Bonds and Social Links draw on Bourdieu's (1986) concept of social capital, and the social value accrued from having social relationships and networks within societies. A lack of social connections and feeling isolated is common for migrants (Strang and Quinn, 2019).

Social work, along with other relevant professionals, is well positioned to support migrants in addressing functional and tangible integration outcomes such as employment and housing, as well as supporting in the building of local, social connections and a sense of place. What does having a sense of place and belonging mean, how is it experienced and what happens when

Figure 9.1: The Indicators of Integration Framework

Means and Markers	Social Connections	Facilitators	Foundation
Employment	Social Bridges	Language and Cultural Knowledge	Rights and Citizenship
Housing	Social Bonds	Safety and Stability	
Education	Social Links		
Health			

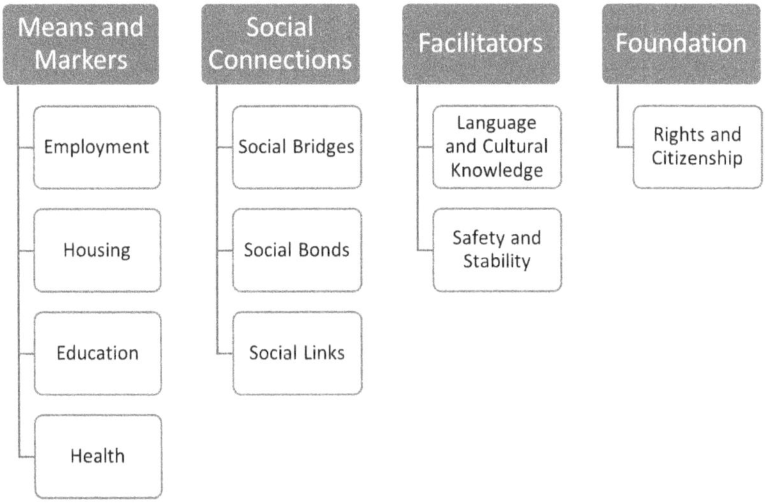

Source: Ager and Strang (2004)

it is absent in someone's life? Prevailing narratives around the integration of migrants largely centre on the impact of migrants on the local, on the host community; on what it means to situate 'difference' in established, settled lives. Asylum seekers and refugees are frequently stigmatised, portrayed as deviant, 'othered', and as problematic (Rigby et al, 2021). This narrative does not account for, nor does it make visible, the disruption, the struggles, and often trauma, that migrants themselves embody. The focus is not centred at the human level (Gottlieb, 2020), nor on the numerous push factors that have led to the dislocation from home, and embarking on an odyssey, usually into the unknown, from the familiar to the unfamiliar. In a migrant's final destination, the unfamiliar positions them as a minority, and what remains familiar to them potentially becomes distinct, different and unfamiliar to the majority population. When there are few, if any, markers to locate and ground oneself, the experience of looking around one's new 'home' is likely be disorientating and disconcerting, with multiple aspects of day-to-day life being unknown. From the mundane and deceptively obvious and simple, such as the opening times of shops, to cultural norms of how to queue and express thanks in various settings, all of which can be bewildering and unsettling. Meanings are ascribed, fostered and communicated through tangible and intangible factors, including through the purpose and aesthetic of buildings; the emotional and functional aspects of food (Daly and Smith, 2021); and the informal and formal norms associated with social interactions. This process of meaning making relies on understanding integration as a two-way relational process (Berry, 1997), a process that is open to learning and adaptation taking place between established communities and incomers. Humanising the migrant experience and seeing the person first, rather than the application of legislation in practice (UNISON Scotland and Scottish Association of Social Work, 2017), is a starting point for nurturing a sense of place and identity for migrants in their new home.

A sense of place is not a fixed entity but porous, open to change over time, and importantly, a point of intersection. That is a meeting of 'relations, experiences and understandings' (Massey, 1991: 28); in the case of migrants, de Shalit (2019) argues, they bring a plurality to a city. The extent to which a city embodies this plurality, of being multi-layered and in a constant flux, determines the extent to which diversity will be supported as integral to the life of the city and wider society. Having a sense of place, Amelina et al (2021) argue, is intertwined with a relational understanding of belonging, premised on social relationships that are conducive to feeling 'more self-assured, more positive … [and] capable of doing more things' (de Shalit, 2019: 269). An individual's 'freedom' to take part and flourish in society, in the words of Sen (2009: 246) and the CA, requires holding a mirror up to society: 'valuing a person's ability to take part in the life of society, there is an implicit valuation of the life of the society itself'.

Capability Approach and flourishing lives

Freedom is conceived in Sen's (1992: 31) Capability Approach (CA), as 'the real opportunity that we have to accomplish what we value'. Framed within the context of migration, the CA supports understanding the integration experience from a migrant's perspective, providing insight into how opportunities are presented and accessed to achieve a sense of belonging and facilitate for flourishing and fulfilling lives. The CA consists of *Functionings, Capabilities*, and *Adaptive Preferences*, with *Functionings* referring to the life that someone wants to lead, the activities they want to pursue to enhance their wellbeing. These activities will be unique to each person and could include access to healthcare; employment; freedom to meet and socialise; and to feel safe. Combined these factors contribute to a sense of place and belonging, which de Shalit (2019: 268) points out 'is an important functioning'.

Capabilities refer to the freedom to enact *Functionings*, the freedom to be and do (Sen, 1999). In practice, *Capabilities* refer to the supports and resources, including social capital (Bourdieu, 1986), to enable someone to achieve their *Functionings*. Importantly these resources must respond to and be in a form that are accessible and relevant to individual lives. At the core of the CA is an understanding of difference and context. For example, supporting a migrant to achieve the *Functioning* of employment necessitates a different approach from someone from a host community. The application of the CA requires a relational approach to practice that centres the voice of the user, to excavate and bring to the fore their life experiences, ambitions and thoughts on current and future wellbeing, alongside the practical aspects of resources and individual support that is required.

Adaptive Preferences refers to how people can, consciously and unconsciously, adapt, accept and embody social norms even when this translates into limiting their ability to lead a life of their own choosing. 'Adaptive preferences should not however be conceived of as static and unchangeable … they can be challenged and transformed' (Levy et al, 2017: 256). Wellbeing and fulfilment in life is one area that can lead to misunderstanding and the adoption and assimilation of local norms. Drawing on Eudemonic and Hedonic notions of wellbeing, Deneulin and McGregor (2010) argue that *Adaptive Preferences* provide insight into the contextual nature of wellbeing, and therefore the need for cultural sensitivity when working with the wellbeing of migrants. Eudemonic wellbeing, which stems from Aristotle's concept of eudaimonia, refers to the self-realisation of individual potential which in turn leads to the greatest fulfilment, or the experience of eudaimonia. Eudemonic wellbeing is derived from doing, from having a purpose and meaning in one's life, and is more associated with non-Western cultures. This is contrasted with a hedonic approach to wellbeing, which is more aligned with individualistic Western societies, where happiness is derived from enjoyment, maximising pleasure and avoiding negative experiences. A fundamental distinction here relates to process and outcome, for hedonists happiness is the desired outcome, whereas for eudemonics, the process of doing and being translates into wellbeing. This is just one example of embodied cultural differences that require understanding when working to support migrants to retain their 'nature', their personal ways of being and doing, as a foundation to 'live well together' (Deneulin and McGregor, 2010).

For a society to 'live well' in relation to others, the tapestry of cultural diversity needs to be flexible, to stretch and be re-made through co-creating and sharing what 'people have reason to value' (Sen, 1992: 81). While social connections, relationships and valuing difference are all essential for integration, the success of this is also dependent on migrants having the capacity to access and utilise the 'conditions for integration' (Strang et al, 2018: 199) as set out in the *Indictors of Integration Framework* (Ager and Strang, 2004). Places and spaces are never neutral, they harbour opportunities and visions, but they also reflect and reinforce prevailing power relations, outsider/insider privileges and normative practices. Finding ways to disrupt and unlock this binary thinking is essential in achieving a 'creative city' (Yencken, 1988), that is a sustainable city that supports belonging across the spectrum of people living together. Contradictions can and will exist, but should be exposed to make space for a sense of place for all.

We now turn to look at the policy and practice context of the integration of migrants (asylum seekers and refugees) in Scotland, UK.

Scottish context

The Scottish Parliament, located in Edinburgh, was established in 1999, and has responsibility for devolved matters, largely social policy covering social services; health; education; children's services; housing; criminal justice and policing. Responsibility for immigration, foreign policy and social security are reserved matters, and remain the responsibility of the UK government based in London. The rights and access to public/state support for refugees and asylum seekers is therefore determined by the UK government (Home Office). This duality of responsibility and policy frameworks is a distinguishing and contested feature of the integration landscape in Scotland. Before moving on to address what this means in policy and practice terms, we offer some definitions of key terms used within a Scottish context.

A refugee includes anyone who has successfully applied for asylum and been granted leave to remain, usually for a period of five years, after which an application for indefinite leave to remain can be made. Refugee status provides the right to services from the welfare state, including access to social services; social security (Universal Credit) and housing benefit; support if homeless and access to social housing along with help to pay for rent. Refugees have the right to work, study and access healthcare through the National Health Service (NHS). Unaccompanied Asylum-Seeking Children (UASC) refers to a child or young person aged up to 18 years, who has arrived in the UK seeking asylum without an adult carer. Social workers are involved in age assessments for UASC which has become a controversial part of social work assessments over recent years (UNISON Scotland and Scottish Association of Social Work, 2017). An asylum seeker refers to an adult that has made a claim for asylum but has not yet had a decision. During the application process asylum seekers, under immigration legislation, are not eligible to welfare services, although local authorities, at their discretion, can provide assistance. The risk of being destitute is very real for asylum seekers, as a Scottish Government report highlights, 'the asylum and immigration system is peppered with points at which the risk of destitution becomes likely' (Scottish Parliament, 2017: 3). The UK government's immigration system, and in particular, the No Recourse to Public Funds (NRPF) policy, can lock asylum seekers out of being able to meet their basic needs for, amongst other things, food and housing. The Scottish Government's *Ending Destitution Together* (Scottish Government, 2021) is a strategy to mitigate against destitution for people with No Recourse to Public Funds (NRPF) with asylum and insecure immigration status in Scotland.

The 1999 Asylum and Immigration Act, led to the establishment of the National Asylum Support Service Dispersal Scheme, the first nationwide system for the reception and resettlement of asylum seekers. Through the UK government's resettlement scheme, asylum seekers are eligible to accommodation in dispersal areas throughout the UK, including in Glasgow, Scotland. The 'housing led' focus (Wren, 2004: 1) of the resettlement programme has led to asylum seekers being placed in housing on a no-choice basis, in areas of high social deprivation, where resources and the capacity to support the development of a sense of place and belonging are exacerbated, especially within areas of little ethnic diversity.

Scotland has historically been largely monocultural, this is beginning to change with a doubling since the start of the twenty-first century of the number of people in every local authority, who do not identify as 'White Scottish' (Simpson, 2014). The population of Scotland is 5.5 million, little changed from 5.2 million in 1970. With a fertility rate that has fallen from 2.5 in 1971, to 1.37 in 2019, the stability of this population is largely due to immigration. In 2019, 87,400 migrants made Scotland their new home, which was higher than emigration at 57,100 people (National Records of Scotland, 2021). The capital city, Edinburgh, has a population of 543,000, 8 per cent identify as non-white. Glasgow is the largest city in Scotland (fifth in the UK), with a population of 1.6 million, 29 per cent of the Scottish population, and the country's most ethnically diverse city. Migrants settling in Glasgow is not a new phenomenon, the city has a long and rich history of people from across the world shaping and reshaping the city. This includes a large Scottish/Irish population, descendants from the Irish Potato Famine of the 1840s, as well as Scottish/Indians, Scottish/Italians, and many others who hold hybrid identities. More recently, through Glasgow's involvement in the UK wide National Asylum Support Service Dispersal Scheme, around 10,000 asylum seekers from 70 countries have settled in Glasgow, the largest concentration in Scotland. Through the dispersal scheme the city's Black, Asian and Minority Ethnic (BAME) population has increased by 60 per cent, more than doubling ethnic diversity from 7.2 per cent in 2001 to 15.5 per cent in 2011 (Population and Migration Office of National Statistics, 2021).

Demographic stability and growth is needed for sustainable economic growth in Scotland, and immigration is viewed as a means through which this can be achieved (McCollum et al, 2014), along with valuing the opportunities inherent in a multicultural and inclusive society. In contrast to the UK government's 'hostile environment policy' (Grierson, 2018), the issue of immigration has not been politicised in Scotland to the same extent as it has been in England. Devolution has passed power and decision making to Scotland, enabling the country to take a different, more benign approach to the integration of migrants. Relatively positive attitudes towards migration exists in Scotland (Lewis, 2006), along with broad political consensus that Scotland 'needs' and 'welcomes' immigration. This discourse is visible in the *New Scots Refugee Integration Strategy 2018–2022*, the policy framework underpinning the Scottish Government's commitment to nurturing diverse and integrated communities (Figure 9.2).

Figure 9.2: New Scots Refugee Integration Strategy 2018–2022

Vision
For a welcoming Scotland where refugees and asylum seekers are able to rebuild their lives from the day they arrive.
To achieve this vision, we will work to ensure that Scotland: • Is a place of safety for everyone, where people are able to live free from persecution as valued members of communities. • Enables everyone to pursue their ambitions through education, employment, culture and leisure activities. • Has strong, inclusive and resilient communities, where everyone is able to access the support and services they need and is able to exercise their rights. • Is a country that values diversity, where people are able to use and share their culture, skills and experiences, as they build strong relationships and connections.
The New Scots strategy sees integration as a long-term, two-way process, involving positive change in both individuals and host communities, which leads to cohesive, diverse communities.

Source: Scottish Government (2017: 10)

Now in its second four-year iteration, the ambitions of the Scottish Government's integration strategies are centred around intersectoral working and nurturing meaningful relationships that are responsive to the needs of refugees and asylum seekers (Scottish Government, 2017). The *Indicators of Integration Framework* (Ager and Strang, 2004) (Figure 9.1) has been core to driving this holistic approach and elements of the framework are visible within the strategy. As Strang notes, the *New Scots Refugee Integration Strategy 2018–2022*, is 'based on the distinct aspects of integration identified in the "Indicators of Integration" framework' (Scottish Government, 2017: 6), and a relational understanding, 'two-way process', of integration (Berry, 1997).

We now turn to social work with migrants, and how social work 'sees' and 'works' with difference while centring human relationships and retaining the profession's core values. Looking at how social work engages with difference and cultural diversity raises fundamental questions around what is 'good' practice (Baines et al, 2019)? These are issues that surface in the context of social work practice with refugees and asylum seekers in Scotland, and are explored in the next section.

Policy and social work practice: Precarious Integration

Social work in Scotland is a regulated profession, with social workers found in both statutory local authority and voluntary settings. Intersectoral and interprofessional work are now both commonplace, with collaborative working across different sectors and professions leading to co-produced, locally based support. Social work with asylum seekers and refugees is a new and emerging area of practice in Scotland. This work is integrated into mainstream practice rather than being a discreet and separate area of practice, for example, dealing directly with reception work as in Nordic countries (Käkelä, 2020). There is limited practice knowledge outside of Glasgow, and limited coverage of working with asylum seekers and refugees on social work qualifying programmes. The *Refugee and Asylum in Scotland: Social Work Support a Human Right not an Administrative Burden* (UNISON Scotland and Scottish Association of Social Work, 2017) provides social workers with practice guidance, including legal guidance, on working with asylum seekers. The guidance clarifies responsibility in the context of codes of practice and professional ethics. The Scottish Codes of Practice set out standards and expectations around culturally competent practice: a social worker should '[w]ork in a way that promotes diversity and respects different cultures and values' (Scottish Social Services Council, 2016) however, how this is to be achieved remains an amorphous topic. There are other terms that lack clarity in how they are defined, and consequently, interpreted in practice. For example, social workers have a duty, under the Social Work (Scotland) Act 1968, to assess vulnerable adults' community care needs, and arrange services if required, this applies to anyone resident in Scotland, including asylum seekers. Yet what constitutes 'vulnerable' and 'needs' is 'open to wide interpretation' (UNISON Scotland and Scottish Association of Social Work, 2017: 4) which impacts on the allocation of services.

Unaccompanied Asylum-Seeking Children (UASC) are treated in the same way as any other looked after child, as 'children in need' under the Children (Scotland) Act 1995. The United Nations Convention on the Rights of the Child (UNCRC) 1989, and its four principles: Non-discrimination; Best Interests of the Child; Right to Survival and Development; and the Views of the Child; informed the Children (Scotland) Act 1995. Alongside being part of the Scottish care system, UASC are also required to go through the UK government's asylum application process. Claiming asylum for UASC is a prolonged and arduous process. Harrowing accounts of an applicant's journey require to be retold, leading Daly and Smith (2021) to conclude that steering a course through the asylum process can be one of the greatest challenges for UASC. Rigby et al (2020) come to a similar conclusion, highlighting the salience of relationships, and developing a sense of place:

> It was clear that young people especially focused on the time it took to develop trusting relationships, suggesting that disclosing painful and distressing background details cannot always be the priority. In this respect there is a tension between the 'system' needing to understand the situation, gather information, and provide appropriate support and protection immediately (based on the past), and young people's attempts to look forward and develop a clearer sense of self in their new environment, and their future. (Rigby et al, 2020: 55)

Adult asylum seekers, as with USAC, are required to go through the parallel processes of Scottish social services and the (UK government) asylum application process. The latter is complex and 'inaccessible' (Scottish Parliament, 2017) which can place asylum seekers at risk of becoming destitute at a critical time (Farmer, 2017). Support from social work to navigate the way through this bureaucratic system is often lacking, as social workers themselves are often unfamiliar with the system. The tensions between 'conflicting' (Wren, 2004) UK government immigration legislation and Scottish welfare approaches are increasing the challenges for migrants to build trusting relationships (Rigby et al, 2021), and for social work to achieve change in people's lives. A 'punitive policy framework' emerging from the UK government sits uncomfortably alongside the 'more positive messages' from Scotland (Wren, 2004: 3). This talks to a dissonance between a policy framework that problematises migrants, and one that is based on promoting social justice, human rights and cultural humility, leading Rigby et al (2020) to call for social work to have a stronger presence as a lead agency driving the integration agenda. Current tensions between UK immigration legislation and Scottish Government welfare legislation, are exacerbated by the Scottish context of work with asylum seekers being situated within mainstream social work practice, rather than as a discreet area of practice. Wells (2011) questions whether positioning UASC within mainstream policy and practice, risks overlooking their personal challenges and the unique support needs of those seeking asylum, including the sociocultural dimensions of their needs. The Scottish system of mainstreaming working with asylum seekers and refugees, may go some way in explaining the unpreparedness of social workers for working with cultural diversity and meeting the needs of asylum seekers in Glasgow (Wren, 2004).

In this final section, the focus is on Glasgow, the city with the largest concentration of migrants in Scotland, and recent work that has explored the integration of migrants. We start with Kirkwood et al's (2014) study on how integration is being understood, defined and experienced. Findings from their study point to integration being misconceived as 'assimilation' leading to refugees being 'blamed' for a lack of integration. Kirkwood et al (2014) call for (re)focusing attention on integration as a two-way and relational process (Berry, 1997), requiring adaptation and change by the host society and incoming migrants. Their work highlights the absence of crucial aspects of working with diversity and supporting the development of social connections. The need to 'provide greater opportunities for new arrivals to build social connections across communities' emerges out of the work of Mulvey et al (2018: 2), and that of Strang et al (2018). Using the *Indicators of Integration Framework*, Strang et al's (2018) study looked at the transition from asylum seeker to refugee in Glasgow. They found the cumulative demands of transition to be disempowering, highlighting that refugees' desire to be independent was frequently thwarted by limited social networks, coupled with inaccessible systems and structural factors. Here they are referring to systems that were insensitive to language and cultural barriers, exacerbated by a prevalence of racism, poverty and inadequate accommodation. Käkelä (2020) also reminds us not to lose sight of the structural factors underpinning the oppression and powerlessness experienced by migrants. Through exploring social workers' experiences of applying cultural competence in practice in Glasgow, Käkelä (2020) highlights the multi-layered aspects of integration through which the lives of migrants are mediated, and power imbalances navigated.

The precariousness of migrant integration in Scotland is a common narrative woven through the studies just outlined. The context of this is captured in the words of Wren (2004: 3), that statutory agencies, including social work, are 'not geared up to meet the needs of asylum seekers across the city'. Through the lens of the CA 'not geared up' can be understood within the context of *Capabilities*. That is, the supports and resources that can enable or inhibit the freedom of migrants to enact *Functionings*, what they what to be and do (Sen, 1999), and facilitate for the building of a sense of place and familiarity in their new home.

Conclusion

This chapter has explored approaches to the integration of migrants broadly and specifically within Scotland. This has been contextualised within cultural social work, working with difference, and developing a sense of place and wellbeing to achieve sustainable and 'creative cities' (Yencken, 1988). The *Indicators of Integration Framework* (Ager and Strang, 2004), a relational approach to integration and the CA (Sen, 1999) have been used to conceptualise the work, which we argue, usefully frame practice with migrants and facilitate for building a sense of place and wellbeing.

Working with cultural diversity, and specifically asylum seekers and refugees, is an emerging field of practice in Scottish social work, little covered in social work education. This chapter has highlighted that the journey so far into this new area of practice faces multiple challenges and tensions. These include balancing working with UK government immigration legislation and Scottish welfare legislation; social work practice with asylum seekers and refugees being located within mainstream practice; and finally, a lack of preparedness for working with cultural diversity and the complexity of issues associated with supporting migrants to transform the unfamiliar into the familiar.

A central thread running through the chapter is a call to change the narrative on integration through working more effectively with cultural differences and putting a human face on the challenges encountered in building a new life in an unfamiliar country. Migrants, like anyone else, want to establish roots and develop a sense of place (Forrest and Kearns, 2001), but, as de Shalit (2019) reminds us, they often can't. As a profession based on social justice, anti-oppressive practice and working with diversity, social work is well positioned to work to achieve change in the lives of migrants. Yet despite promoting culturally competent practice, social workers time and again appear to be unable to connect, understand and access the lives of migrants (Daly and Smith, 2021). Balancing curiosity and respect are called for when working with migrants. Engagement at a human level should be prioritised along with re-imagining how to work with diversity through an approach that is inclusive of a migrant's evolving sense of place and belonging.

References

Ager, A. and Strang, A. (2004) 'Indicators of integration: Final report, *Home Office Development and Practice Report 28*, London: Home Office.

Amelina, A., Schäfer, J. and Trzeciak, M.F. (2021) 'Classificatory struggles revisited: Theorizing current conflicts over migration, belonging and membership', *Journal of Immigrant and Refugee Studies*, 19(1): 1–8.

Baines, D., Bennett, B. Goodwin, S. and Rawsthorne, M. (eds) (2019) *Working Across Difference: Social Work, Social Policy and Social Justice*, London: Macmillan International/Red Globe Press.

Berry, J.W. (1997) 'Immigration, acculturation and adaptation', *Applied Psychology*, 46: 5–6.

Bourdieu, P. (1986) 'The forms of capital', in J.G. Richardson (ed) *Handbook of Theory and Research for the Sociology of Education*, New York: Greenwood, pp 241–58.

Daly, M. and Smith, M. (2021) '"We need to talk about Bona": An autoethnographic account of fostering an unaccompanied asylum seeker', *International Journal of Social Pedagogy*, 10(1).

de Shalit, A. (2019) 'The functioning of having a sense of place: Cities and immigrants', *Journal of Human Development and Capabilities*, 20(3): 267–79.

Deneulin, S. and McGregor, A. (2010) 'The Capability Approach and the politics of a social conception of wellbeing', *European Journal of Social Theory*, 13(4): 501–19.

Dominelli, L. (2017) 'Lena Dominelli, 2012', in G.A. Askeland and M. Payne (eds) *Internationalizing Social Work Education: Insights from Leading Figures across the Globe*, Bristol: Policy Press, pp 183–94.

Farmer, N.J. (2017) '"No recourse to public funds", insecure immigration status and destitution: The role of social work?', *Critical and Radical Social Work*, 5(3): 357–67.

Forrest, R. and Kearns, A. (2001) 'Social cohesion, social capital and the neighbourhood', *Urban Studies*, 38(12): 2125–43.

Gottlieb, M. (2020) 'The case for a cultural humility framework in social work practice', *Journal of Ethnic and Cultural Diversity in Social Work*, 9(1): 1–19.

Grierson, J. (2018) 'Hostile environment: Anatomy of a policy disaster', *Guardian*, 27 August.

Horwath, J. and Lees, J. (2010) 'Assessing the influence of religious beliefs and practices on parenting capacity: The challenges for social work practitioners', *British Journal of Social Work*, 40(1): 82–99.

Käkelä, E. (2020) 'Narratives of power and powerlessness: Cultural competence in social work with asylum seekers and refugees', *European Journal of Social Work*, 23(3): 425–36.

Kirkwood, S., McKinlay, A. and McVittie, A. (2014) '"He's a cracking wee geezer from Pakistan": Lay accounts of refugee integration failure and success in Scotland', *Journal of Refugee Studies*, 28: 1.

Lee, V.W.P., Lai, D.W. and Ruan, Y. (2020) 'Receptivity and readiness for cultural competence training amongst the social workers in Hong Kong', *British Journal of Social Work*, 1–20.

Levy, S., Robb, A. and Jindal-Snape, D. (2017) 'Disability, personalisation and community arts: Exploring the spatial dynamics of children with disabilities participating in inclusive music classes', *Disability and Society*, 32(2): 254–68.

Lewis, M. (2006) *Warm Welcome? Understanding Public Attitudes towards Asylum Seekers in Scotland*, London: IPPR.

Massey, D. (1991) 'A global sense of place', *Marxism Today*, 38, 24–29.

McCollum, D., Nowok, B. and Tindal, S. (2014) 'Public attitudes towards migration in Scotland: Exceptionality and possible Implications', *Scottish Affairs*, 23(1): 79–102.

Mulvey, G., Bynner, C., Murray, N. and Watson, N. (2018). 'Resettlement of Syrian refugees in West Dunbartonshire', What Works Scotland. http://whatworksscotland.ac.uk/publications/resettlement-of-syrian-refugees-in-west-dunbartonshire/

National Records of Scotland (2021) 'Scotland's net migration'. https://statistics.gov.scot/data/net-migration

Population and Migration Office of National Statistics (2021) 'Scotland population mid-year estimate'. https://www.nrscotland.gov.uk/statistics-and-data/statistics/statistics-by-theme/population/population-estimates/mid-year-population-estimates

Rigby, P., Malloch, M., Beetham, T. and Callaghan, J. (2020) 'Child trafficking in Scotland', Scottish Government. https://www.gov.scot/binaries/content/documents/govscot/publications/research-and-analysis/2020/10/child-trafficking-scotland-research/documents/child-trafficking-scotland/child-trafficking-scotland/govscot%3Adocument/child-trafficking-scotland.pdf

Rigby, P., Fotopoulou, M., Rogers, A. Manta, A. and Dikaiou, M. (2021) 'Problematising separated children: A policy analysis of the UK Safeguarding Strategy: Unaccompanied asylum seeking and refugee children', *Journal of Ethnic and Migration Studies*, 47(3): 501–18.

Scottish Government (2017) 'New Scots integration strategy, 2018–22'. https://www.gov.scot/publications/new-scots-refugee-integration-strategy-2018-2022/

Scottish Government (2021) 'Ending destitution together: Strategy'. https://www.gov.scot/publications/ending-destitution-together/

Scottish Parliament (2017) 'Hidden lives – new beginnings: Destitution, asylum and insecure immigration status in Scotland', Edinburgh: Scottish Parliament.

Scottish Social Services Council (2016) 'Codes of practice', Scottish Social Services Council. www.sssc.uk.com/the-scottish-social-services-council/sssc-codes-of-practice/

Sen, A. (1992) *Inequality Re-examined*, Oxford: Clarendon Press.
Sen, A. (1999) *Development as Freedom*, New York: Alfred Knopf.
Sen, A. (2009) *The Idea of Justice*, Cambridge: Harvard University of Press.
Shier, M.L., Engstrom, S. and Graham, J.R. (2011) 'International migration and social work: A review of the literature', *Journal of Immigrant and Refugee Studies*, 9: 38–56.
Simpson, L. (2014) 'How has ethnic diversity changed in Scotland? Dynamics of diversity: Evidence from the 2011 census'. http://hummedia.manchester.ac.uk/institutes/code/briefings/ dynamicsofdiversity/code-census-briefing-scotland_v2.pdf
Sodowsky, G.R. Lai, E.W.M. and Plake, B.S. (1991) 'Moderating effects of sociocultural variables on acculturation attitudes of Hispanics and Asian Americans', *Journal of Counselling and Development*, 70(1): 194–204.
Strang, A.B. and Quinn, N. (2019) 'Integration or isolation? Refugees' social connections and wellbeing', *Journal of Refugee Studies*, 34(1): 328–53.
Strang, A.B., Baillot, H. and Mignard, E. (2018) '"I want to participate": Transition experiences of new refugees in Glasgow', *Journal of Ethnic and Migration Studies*, 44(2): 197–214.
UNCRC (1989) *The United Nations Convention on the Rights of the Child*, New York: UNICEF.
UNISON Scotland and Scottish Association of Social Work (2017) 'Refugee and asylum in Scotland: Social work support a human right not an administrative burden'. https://unison-scotland.org/asylum-seekers-in-scotland-are-denied-social-work-services-say-unison-and-scottish-association-of-social-work/
Vertovec, S. (2007) 'Super-diversity and its implications', *Ethnic and Racial Studies*, 30(6): 1024–54.
Wells, K. (2011) 'The politics of life: Governing childhood', *Global Studies of Childhood*, 1(1): 15–25.
Willis, R., Pathak, P., Khambhaita, P. and Evandrou, M. (2017) 'Complexities of cultural difference in social care work in England', *European Journal of Social Work*, 20(5): 685–96.
Wren, K. (2004) *Building Bridges: Local Responses to the Resettlement of Asylum Seekers in Glasgow*, Glasgow: Scottish Centre for Research on Social Justice.
Yencken, D. (1988) 'The creative city', *Meanjin Quarterly*, 47(Summer): 4.

10

"If not now, when?": Reclaiming activism into social work education – the case of an intercultural student-academic project with refugees in the UK and Greece

Sofia Dedotsi and Ruth Hamilton

Introduction

In the years of the refugee crisis (2015 and onwards),[1] more than 1.8 million refugees and migrants (UNCHR, 2021) arrived in Europe fleeing war-affected countries and persecution. Migration to Europe is not a new and sudden phenomenon, yet its policies have been historically anti-migratory and repressive, driven by 'securitanianism' and exclusion (Vitus and Lidén, 2010; Teloni et al, 2020). This has resulted in catastrophic human casualties – 16,668 people dying or gone missing so far in the Mediterranean Sea (UNCHR, 2021).

The context that refugees face upon arrival involves a further brutal reality by being detained in overcrowded camps such as Calais (France) and the Aegean islands (Greece), with inhumane conditions and limited resources to respond to peoples' needs (Kourachanis, 2018, 2019; GNCHR, 2019). Commenting on the cruel conditions of 'slow death' at the Calais camp, Davies et al (2017) concluded that the brutality that refugees suffer becomes a 'necropolitical experience': structural dehumanisation, where suffering is normalised through a deliberate and violent series of (in)actions by the European and national institutions. Similar 'necropolitical' experiences have been discussed for the Scottish context (Farmer, 2020) where notions of 'illegality' exclude refugees from public resources and support.

In contrast, numerous anti-racist and solidarity initiatives flourished across Europe during the refugee crisis. In Greece, while the country was already seven years into deep recession, a movement mobilised to respond to the immediate refugee needs (that is, rescues from the sea, provision of food and dry clothes, medical help, shelter, access to phones). In addition, there was resistance and challenges to institutions and legal frameworks through collective action and engaging in advocacy for refugee rights, campaigns and demonstrations (Teloni and Mantanika, 2015; Oikonomakis, 2018; Dedotsi et al, 2019).

In this contradictory context of structural repression and grassroots solidarity, social workers are among the key professionals in the frontline responding to refugee needs. Considering the limited resources for refugees and the anti-immigration policies, social workers have been found to struggle between being agents of control[2] and protecting service users (Humphries, 2004; Guhan and Liebling-Kalifani, 2011; Masocha, 2014; Robinson, 2014; Hagues et al, 2021). The instrumentalisation of bureaucratic and repressive migratory frameworks by professionals has been characterised as 'everyday bordering', where othering takes place in multi-layered professional practices (that is, assessments) for entitlement to rights and access to services between 'deserving' and 'undeserving' populations (Cassidy, 2019; Yuval-Davis et al, 2019). Yet, there are examples of activism in social work practice with refugees, based on advocacy for refugee rights and resistance to bordering policies through collective action and community engagement (Lavalette and Ferguson, 2007; Marston and McDonald, 2012; Lavallette and Penketh, 2014; Ottosdottir and Evans, 2014; Robinson, 2014; Teloni and Mantanika, 2015; Teloni, 2017; Wroe, 2018, 2019; Briskman, 2020). However, these practices do not seem to be the mainstream approaches to working with refugees (Jönsson, 2014; Masocha, 2014; Fennig and Denov, 2019) and, primarily, this has been rooted in the content and context of social work education.[3] The focus in social work education is arguably more on the acquisition of technical skills and/or individualised perspectives with an apolitical approach which does not provide social workers with knowledge and consciousness for structural perspectives and understandings, collectivist practices and resistance (Gray and Gibbons, 2007; Morley, 2008; Park and Bhuyan, 2012; Strier and Bershtling, 2016; Dedotsi and Young, 2019a).

The last revision of the Global Definition of Social Work (IFSW, 2014) and the new Global Standards for Social Work Education and Training (IFSW and IASSW, 2020) strongly emphasise the political dimension of social work as a global profession that develops critical consciousness and strategies for action that build solidarity with the disadvantaged and the oppressed. In social work there is a breadth of scholarly work exploring if and how social work students can undertake anti-oppressive practices with vulnerable and oppressed populations such as refugees and migrants. Suggestions vary in relation to the theories used to critically teach about these such as cultural competence approaches (Potocky-Tripodi, 2002; Lum, 2003); anti-oppressive models (Cemlyn and Briskman, 2003; Sakamoto, 2007); socio-ecological theories (Miller and Rasmussen, 2016; Hagues et al, 2021); critical race and whiteness theories (Abrams and Moio, 2009; Olcoń et al, 2020); postcolonial approaches (Yee and Wagner, 2013; Mapp and

Rice, 2019); and anti-racist social work (Dominelli, 1997, 2018; Lavalette and Penketh, 2014; Singh, 2014, 2019).

Similarly, a breadth of teaching methods/strategies are offered in literature in order to stimulate students' critical thinking and challenge understandings such as the use of case studies and role playing (Milner and Wolfer, 2014; Swank and Fahs, 2014); class debate (Hafford-Letchfield, 2010); narrative techniques, such as reflective essays and portfolios (Collins and Wilkie, 2010; Preston and Aslett, 2014); groupwork and game-based exercises (Das and Carter Anand, 2014); participation of refugees in lectures (Allegri et al, 2020); and artistic approaches such as photovoice, poetry, theatre/drama and crafts (Cramer et al, 2012; Peabody, 2013; Papouli, 2017) as creative tools to examine experiences, express deep emotions and liberate critical awareness.

These accounts on theories and teaching methods for social work practice with refugees can be inspirational for an anti-oppressive and emancipatory social work education. Yet, it is argued that education also needs to expand beyond the walls of a classroom, connecting with the wider community and political struggles, and engage in the collective participation of academics and students against the violation of human rights and oppressive policies (Dedotsi et al, 2016; Morley et al, 2020; Martínez Herrero and Charnley, 2021). There are some inspiring examples of activism in literature for social work education, where staff and students mobilised together. These included participating in advocacy/community action projects, grassroots initiatives for social and political issues, connecting with social movements such as Black Lives Matter, attending political meetings as well as protesting/attending demonstrations with service users for their rights and/or challenging oppressive policies (Lane et al, 2012, 2017; Mizrahi and Dodd, 2013; Preston and Aslett, 2014; Swank and Fahs, 2014).

In addition, some international study trips have been used with an activist and anti-oppressive approach that centres on people's human rights and needs with attention to the privileges and power relations that are involved, rather than a framework based on a recipient/donor dichotomy (Gammonley et al, 2013; Fisher and Grettenberger, 2015; Bell et al, 2017; Mapp and Rice, 2019). What is interesting here is that these trips were not one-off events; instead, they were used as resources for *co-learning* and *action* before, during and after the trip with the involvement of students and academics in advocacy and community engagement (Gammonley et al, 2013; Jönsson and Lian Flem, 2018; Mapp and Rice, 2019).

However, activism in social work education is a rather contested site of struggle and not always supported or welcomed. The neoliberal context of social work education – higher education's policies and functionalities – is infiltrated by corporate ideals, where the pressure to marginalise and perhaps sacrifice social justice issues over students' technical and marketable skills is rising (Yee and Wagner, 2013; Bhuyan et al, 2017; Dedotsi and Young,

2019a). This 'hidden curriculum' (Tsang, 2011) has led to a depoliticised (Giroux, 2010) learning environment, that intentionally and unintentionally may isolate, alienate and consequently weaken/silence any potential resistance (Wilson and Campbell, 2013; Preston and Aslett, 2014; Dedotsi and Panić, 2020).

There is no doubt that resisting the neoliberal regime of academia and the involved tensions may feel at times isolating and exhausting (Caron et al, 2020); however, in times of crisis, it is more critical than ever to respond to 'whose side are we on' (Becker, 1967) and what position do we take as social work educators? In an attempt to provide our own response to these questions, we were involved in the project that we describe and reflect on shortly.

The project

The project involved a group of students and us (academic staff) from the Social Work Department at a university in the North East of England with a long history of social work education spanning over five decades. The university has undergraduate and postgraduate (PG) qualifying social work degree programmes,[4] well-established links within the community and largely recruits from its local population.

Within this setting, both of us were senior lecturers at the university in 2019, and taught the students across the curricula, including anti-oppressive practice and international contexts of social work. These subject areas were focused upon in the different academic years using a variety of critical theories and strategies such as class debates, case studies and group work as triggers for critical reflection. The educational philosophy underpinning our general approach, however, varied between lecturers but, for us, was informed by critical pedagogy and, more specifically, Paulo Freire's (1970, 1993) writings for education. His concept of *critical consciousness* as 'learning to perceive social, political, and economic contradictions and to take action against the oppressive elements of reality' (1970: 35) is closely aligned to social work's values. More specifically, Freire himself highlighted that social work is 'educational-pedagogical' (Moch, 2009: 93), and, therefore, raising social work students' critical consciousness is a core component of anti-oppressive praxis (Dominelli, 2002; Clifford and Burke, 2005; Mackay and Woodward, 2010). Critical pedagogy in this sense is, as Carroll and Minkler argue, compatible with the 'methodological underpinnings of social work practice' (2000: 22).

While teaching about the political context of social work and reflecting on social issues (that is, the refugee crisis, Black Lives Matter) with students enabled a process of 'critical consciousness', it was limited in terms of students' abilities to critically reflect and act on these as global issues. However, the limitations are not only because students may not 'experience' a social issue such as the refugee crisis in UK in similar ways as in other contexts (that is, Greece), but mostly because the content and context of education is structurally driven by a technical and neoliberal approach based on the acquisition of skills, which does not leave enough space for collective action and political engagement. In order to promote international understandings for our students on social issues and anti-oppressive practices, we have been gradually developing a range of international collaborations including organised study trips to Northern Ireland and Istanbul (Turkey), where students met with other peers and professionals to discuss and reflect on social work as a global anti-oppressive profession.

Within this context, a lecture on anti-oppressive practice and the refugee crisis, discussing in particular the Greek case, sparked further interest and we explored with students the idea of developing our understandings and engagement in activism within the refugee crisis within local and international contexts. This was informed by Kolb and Kolb's (2009) concepts of 'experiential learning' and 'learning spaces' and the value of these to the learner. Athens (Greece) was chosen as the destination of our study trip for various reasons: (1) it is one of the main EU entrance and host countries during the refugee crisis; (2) it has been a place of interest for the development and response to the crisis by various social movements; and (3) it covers matters of access and convenience as one of us has experience and networks in the field. Our aim was to use this trip as an opportunity to engage in anti-oppressive critical consciousness– both reflection and action – before, during and after the trip about the current refugee crisis.

Reflection and action before the trip

Postgraduate students were notified in classes about the trip proposal and, following expressions of interest, a final small group of students from year one of the programme was formed to further plan the trip. All participants, including both academic members of staff, were women. Of the students, three were White British and one was mixed White British and Black African, both academics were White European and the ages in the group varied from mid-20s to mid-50s. The students' first degrees were in the arts and humanities.

Prior to the study trip, the group met four times, not only for organisational and administrative matters (that is, division of planning tasks; travel logistics) but also for learning and reflecting on the refugee crisis both in the UK and Greece. The discussions at this stage included learning from the literature about the structural roots of migration such as poverty, war and persecution, how and why refugees are disenfranchised, oppressed and excluded through oppressive discourses in policies and media as well as the contested role of social work. Students recognised that their understanding of the refugee crisis had been shaped to varying extents by narratives such as those promoted in the British press and wanted to challenge this further. Finding out more information about Greece – the impact of the financial crisis on welfare, the solidarity movements during the crisis as well as social work initiatives – helped all the participants to identify areas of interest for further learning and reflection and prepare for the trip.

The learning and reflection process during these meetings led to students taking a number of initiatives to raise awareness on refugee issues and advocate for their rights across the university. These included designing an information leaflet that was disseminated, presenting at a social work event before the trip, using social media and being on a stand at the university library to raise consciousness amongst the wider learning community. In addition, they decided to fundraise – using a crowdfunding website and by selling cakes and small crafts at the university – for humanitarian aid for one self-organised activist refugee group in Athens that we visited. It is important to say here that these actions and the funds that were raised were not driven by a 'charitable' approach (Mapp and Rice, 2019); instead, using an anti-oppressive framework of recognising issues of privilege and power, these were actions of solidarity and support. Last but not least, students' expenses for the trip were self-covered.

Reflection and action during the trip

The trip took place over five days in October/November 2019 and a few visits were arranged to meet professionals, refugee activists and social work students. It is important to say here that following each visit, we met as a group to discuss and reflect on the experience as co-learners and connect our shared learning with social work's anti-oppressive principles and values.

The first visit was to a Social Work Department in Athens, where students and staff from both programmes debated the social work role and social justice matters during the refugee crisis in an (inter-)national context. The shared learning about the similarities and differences in national contexts of practice provided an important opportunity for everyone to develop their understanding of social work as a global profession. The contrast in contexts of practice and especially the experience of living, studying and working under multiple crises (financial and refugee crises) were sources of deep reflection. The English students were especially struck by how politicised the student group were in Athens compared to the English context and how Greek social work educators included in their teaching a strong political perspective. It was echoed in our students' feedback[5] that social work education in comparison is less politicised in the English context and we explored the potential impact this has on practice.

The second visit was to a refugee children and families centre, where we met with social workers and other professionals who provided advice and support for children trying to gain legal status that gave them access to vital resources and facilities. Professionals outlined their roles and the challenges they faced trying to advocate for refugees and provide both housing, legal and medical support for homeless children and within a number of refugee camps with extremely limited resources. They shared a number of disheartening stories; for example children being left at police cells for days as the only way to offer protected housing amidst limited resources and a complex and dysfunctional legal process of protection. Such stories and experiences stimulated reflections on the limited resources available and restricted, even punitive, migration policies that are imposed on social workers to implement 'everyday bordering' strategies (Cassidy, 2019) that reproduce structural dehumanisation and inequalities. Children's rights, refugee and human rights were discussed and professionals expressed how they try to resist the violation of these through collective action and through connection with social movements for political pressure.

Last but not least was a visit to a self-organised refugee community centre in a politically active neighbourhood in Athens, where we met with a member (we will call him 'N') who is a refugee and political activist. 'N' shared his story with us, his struggle to obtain asylum as well as the story and work of the centre itself – a safe space for refugees – which provides practical support such as language classes, a community kitchen and a housing project. 'N' explained how the anti-racist and solidarity movement in Greece has developed with actions not only at a micro level (providing practical and immediate help) but at a macro level too by engaging in policy analysis, demonstrations and advocacy in the community as well as lobbying for refugee rights. We debated if and how close social work is connected with social movements and reflected on the learning that social work can take by their multilevel actions in resisting oppressive policies and advocating for human rights. These discussions as well as the poverty and homelessness of refugees visible on the streets of Athens, sparked deep emotions and reflections on a range of issues – the direct impact of social policies on the lives of migrating populations; the response by European Member States; the differences in the daily and professional struggles in southern and Northern Europe; as well as the urgent need for social work to resist and challenge refugees' dehumanisation and oppression as a global human and emancipatory profession.

Reflection and action after the trip

The shared images, learning and reflections following the trip provided us with rich understandings about how and why the refugee crisis is constructed and managed as well as hopeful examples of resistance and empowerment. It was felt that this co-learning needed to be shared widely as an opportunity for further reflection and action in our context and local communities (Fisher and Grettenberger, 2015). Therefore, a public event was arranged at the university, by a unanimous decision, bringing together refugees, activists, students, practitioners and academics from mainly the North East of England. The event offered a space to share our learning, connect with activist groups and social movements in the area and explore social work's (anti-) oppressive practice and bordering policies.

An outcome of this public event was to formulate a network of people (students, professionals, academics, activists) that would be in contact for further action in the area in relation to refugee rights and events and contribute to the teaching of social work students. In addition, the communication and links with the people that we met in Athens continue as a further space for activism for refugee rights and collaborative social work education. At the same time, the COVID-19 pandemic happened and changed our living and teaching reality; however, we keep trying to extend learning environments further and encourage the need for critical consciousness – constant reflection and action – by both students and academics on social work's role with vulnerable populations and oppressive policies (Boccagni and Righard, 2020).

Conclusions

This project was a mutual attempt by students and ourselves to understand more about refugee issues within a (inter)national context, migration policies, the violation of refugee rights, issues of power and privilege and engaging in activism outside the walls of the classroom. Through a dialogic process of de-construction and co-construction of knowledge with an emphasis on critical and political analysis of migration, the self and the institutions in which we are situated as social workers, the project proved to be a good opportunity to reclaim activism into our teaching.

It needs to be acknowledged that the neoliberal corporate ideals of the context of social work education encourage narrow individualism rather than collective concerns and responses (Yee and Wagner, 2013). However, social work (education) cannot lag behind current social needs. Anti-oppressive praxis for Freire (1970, 1993) includes both action and reflection, and, therefore, social work education needs to be a learning environment that challenges the oppressive reality and the structural roots of dehumanisation and oppression, nurture critical reflection and inspire activism.

Such an activist approach would need to conceptualise the classroom as a 'living' (Lane et al, 2017) site of transformation, where human rights and social justice perspectives are prioritised in the curriculum as well as provide the space for social and collective actions (Preston and Aslett, 2014; Martínez Herrero and Charnley, 2021). This safe space for activism, even within neoliberal universities, would mean that educators need to develop strong and active links with the community and mobilise with students against the violation of human rights through social movements and professional associations.

The co-production of this learning opportunity with students, other academics, social workers and community activists created a space for us to reflect on our role as educators. Through this pedagogic partnership (Cook-Sather et al, 2014) we emphasised the importance of learning from the voices and reality of the people we work with and alongside our students. We also created a dynamic space to be open and critical about our own privileges and power as white Europeans and as social work academics. As educators who are often confined to classrooms, we witnessed the value of fostering dialogue through study trips and pedagogic partnerships that span the global social work community. It is through this dialogue where individual and collective critical consciousness and anti-oppressive praxis could thrive.

Considering the criticality of the times in which we live with multiple crises (austerity, refugee crisis, pandemic) and our profession's mandate for standing in solidarity with the oppressed, it's an urgent need to reclaim activism into social work education. If not now, when?

Acknowledgement

This project was partially funded by Northumbria University, UK.

Notes

[1] In this chapter, we have used the term 'refugee crisis' to refer to a specific time period and context, the crisis of 2015 and onwards spurred by the war in Syria. However, these refugee waves have not been a new phenomenon for Europe; increasing numbers of people have been seeking asylum to Greece (and Europe) especially since the early 1990s from Eastern Europe and in the 2000s as a result of the wars in Iraq and Afghanistan. At the time of writing this chapter, another 'crisis' has been developed following the war in Ukraine since February 2022, which has resulted in large refugee movements seeking shelter and protection to other European countries. It is beyond the scope of this chapter to debate and explore critically the term 'crisis'; however, it is important to note that the term has been suggested to have been appropriated and used by political discourses as a tool to securitisation instead of long-term inclusive reception policies. For further analysis see Carastathis (2018), Kapsalis et al (2022).

[2] We refer here to the perception of social control as disempowering for people using social work services (Humphries, 2004).

[3] Further explanations include the organisational context, more specifically the dominant target culture in professional settings as well as job descriptions that

may construct more bureaucratic and/or individualised approaches to social work practice (Strier and Bershtling, 2016; Gal and Weiss-Gal, 2015).
4 The qualifying programmes, mapped against professional standards and frameworks (Social Work England, 2019a, 2019b; BASW, 2018), are approved by the regulatory body, Social Work England. These frameworks prescribe the core curriculum of qualifying programmes.
5 Students' reflections and learning journey will be presented in a forthcoming paper.

References

Abrams, L.S. and Moio, J.A. (2009) 'Critical race theory and the cultural competence dilemma in social work education', *Journal of Social Work Education*, 45(2): 245–61.

Allegri, E., Eve, M., Mazzola, R., Perino, M. and Pogliano, A. (2020) 'Other "Lenses": A training programme for social workers and others working with asylum seekers and migrants in Italy', *European Journal of Social Work*, 23(3): 529–40.

Becker, H.S. (1967) 'Whose side are we on?' *Social Problems*, 14(3): 239–47.

Bell, K., Moorhead, B. and Boetto, H. (2017) 'Social work students' reflections on gender, social justice and human rights during a short-term study programme to India', *International Social Work*, 60(1): 32–44.

Bhuyan, R., Bejan, R. and Jeyapal, D. (2017) 'Social workers' perspectives on social justice in social work education: When mainstreaming social justice masks structural inequalities', *Social Work Education*, 36(4): 373–90.

Boccagni, P. and Righard, E. (2020) 'Social work with refugee and displaced populations in Europe: (Dis)Continuities, dilemmas, developments', *European Journal of Social Work*, 23(3): 375–83.

Briskman, L. (2020) 'The people's inquiry into detention: Social work activism for asylum seeker rights', *Journal of Sociology*, 56(1): 100–114.

British Association of Social Workers (BASW) (2018) 'Professional capabilities framework'. www.basw.co.uk/social-work-training/professional-capabilities-framework-pcf

Carastathis, A. (2018) 'Nesting crises', *Women's Studies International Forum*, 68: 142–8.

Caron, R., Lee, E.O.J. and Pullen Sansfaçon, A. (2020) 'Transformative disruptions and collective knowledge building: Social work professors building anti-oppressive ethical frameworks for research, teaching, practice and activism', *Ethics and Social Welfare*, 14(3): 298–314.

Carroll, J. and Minkler, M. (2000) 'Freire's message for social workers: Looking back, looking ahead', *Journal of Community Practice*, 8(1): 21–36.

Cassidy, K. (2019). 'Everyday bordering: The internal reach of the UK's borders', *Geography*, 104(2): 100–2.

Cemlyn, S. and Briskman, L. (2003) 'Asylum, children's rights and social work', *Child and Family Social Work*, 8: 163–78.

Clifford, D. and Burke, B. (2005) 'Developing anti-oppressive ethics in the new curriculum', *Social Work Education*, 24(6): 677–92.

Collins, S. and Wilkie, L. (2010) 'Anti-oppressive practice and social work students' portfolios in Scotland', *Social Work Education*, 29: 760–77.

Cook-Sather, A., Bovill, C. and Felten, P. (2014) *Engaging Students as Partners in Learning and Teaching: A Guide for Faculty*, San Francisco, CA: Jossey-Bass.

Cramer, E.P., Ryosho, N. and Nguyen, P.V. (2012) 'Using experiential exercises to teach about diversity, oppression, and social justice', *Journal of Teaching in Social Work*, 32(1): 1–13.

Das, C. and Carter Anand, J. (2014) 'Strategies for critical reflection in international contexts for social work students', *International Social Work*, 57(2): 109–20.

Davies, T., Isakjee, A. and Dhesi, S. (2017) 'Violent inaction: The necropolitical experience of refugees in Europe', *Antipode: A Radical Journal of Geography*, 49(5): 1263–84.

Dedotsi, S. and Panić, G. (2020) 'Resisting within the neoliberalising academy: Reflections on doing transformative doctoral research', *Emotion, Space and Society*, 35: 1–4.

Dedotsi, S. and Young, A. (2019) 'Educating against all odds: The context and content of social work education in times of national crisis in Greece', *International Journal of Social Work*, 62(2): 849–63.

Dedotsi, S., Young, A. and Broadhurst, K. (2016) 'Social work education in a time of national crisis in Greece: educating the workforce to combat inequalities', *European Journal of Social Work*, 19(3–4): 368–84.

Dedotsi, S., Ioakimidis, V. and Teloni, DD. (2019) 'Refugee crisis in Greece: The development of racism, anti-racist responses and implications for social work', *Communitarian-International Journal of Social Work and Social Sciences*, 17: 59–69.

Dominelli, L. (1997) *Anti-racist Social Work: A Challenge for White Practitioners and Educators* (2nd edn), London: Macmillan.

Dominelli, L. (2002) *Anti-Oppressive Social Work Theory and Practice*, Basingstoke: Palgrave Macmillan.

Dominelli, L. (2018) *Anti-racist Social Work* (4th edn), London: Red Globe Press.

Farmer, N. (2021) '"I never felt like an illegal immigrant until social work turned up at the hospital": No recourse to public funds as necropolitical exception', *The British Journal of Social Work*, 51(8): 3301–18.

Fennig, M. and Denov, M. (2019) Regime of truth: Rethinking the dominance of the bio-medical model in mental health social work with refugee youth', *British Journal of Social Work*, 49: 300–17.

Fisher, C.M. and Grettenberger, S.E. (2015) 'Community-based participatory study abroad: A proposed model for social work education', *Journal of Social Work Education*, 51: 566–82.

Freire, P. (1970) *Pedagogy of the Oppressed*, New York: Continuum.
Freire, P. (1993) *Pedagogy of the Oppressed*, 20th anniversary edn, London: Penguin.
Gal, J. and Weiss-Gal, I. (2015) 'The "why" and the "how" of policy practice: an eight-country comparison', *British Journal of Social Work*, 45: 1083–101.
Gammonley, D., Rotabi, K.S., Forte, J. and Martin, A. (2013) 'Beyond study abroad: A human rights delegation to teach policy advocacy', *Journal of Social Work Education*, 49: 619–34.
Giroux, H.A. (2010) 'Bare pedagogy and the scourge of neoliberalism: Rethinking higher education as a democratic public sphere', *The Educational Forum*, 74: 184–96.
GNCHR (2019) 'Reference report on the refugee and migrant issue'. www.nchr.gr/en/news/1131-gnchr-reference-report-on-the-refugee-and-migrant-issue.html
Gray, M. and Gibbons, J. (2007) 'There are no answers, only choices: Teaching ethical decision making in social work', *Australian Social Work*, 60(2): 222–38.
Guhan, R. and Liebling-Kalifani, H. (2011) 'The experiences of staff working with refugees and asylum seekers in the United Kingdom: A grounded theory exploration', *Journal of Immigrant & Refugee Studies*, 9(3): 205–28.
Hafford-Letchfield, T. (2010) 'A glimpse of the truth: Evaluating "debate" and "role play" as pedagogical tools for learning about sexuality issues on a law and ethics module', *Social Work Education*, 29(3): 244–58.
Hagues, R.J., Cecil, D. and Stoltzfus, K. (2021) 'The experiences of German social workers working with refugees', *Journal of Social Work*, 21(1): 46–68.
Humphries, B. (2004) 'An unacceptable role for social work: Implementing immigration policy', *British Journal of Social Work*, 34(1): 93–107.
IFSW (2014) 'Global definition of social work'. www.ifsw.org/what-is-social-work/global-definition-of-social-work/
IFSW and IASSW (2020) 'Global standards for social work education and training'. www.ifsw.org/global-standards-for-social-work-education-and-training/
Jönsson, J. (2014) 'Local reactions to global problems: Undocumented immigrants and social work', *British Journal of Social Work*, 44(1): 33–52.
Jönsson, J. and Lian Flem, A. (2018) 'International field training in social work education: Beyond colonial divides', *Social Work Education*, 37: 895–908.
Kapsalis, A., Kourachanis, N. and Koumarianos V. (2022) *Κοινωνική Πολιτική, Αυταρχικός Νεοφιλελευθερισμός και Πανδημία* [*Social Policy, Authoritarian Neoliberalism and Pandemic*], Athens: Topos.
Kasparek, B. (2016) *Migration Politics and Policy in the European Union*, Athens: Rosa Luxembourg Stiftung Office in Greece. https://rosalux.gr/sites/default/files/publications/migration_politics_kasparek.pdf

Khiabany, G. (2016) 'Refugee crisis, imperialism and pitiless wars on the poor', *Media, Culture and Society*, 38(5): 755–62.

Kolb, A. and Kolb, D. (2009) 'The learning way: Meta-cognitive aspects of experiential learning', *Simulation & Gaming*, 40(3): 297–327.

Kourachanis, N. (2018) 'Asylum seekers, hotspot approach, and anti-social policy responses in Greece (2015–2017)', *International Migration & Integration*, 19(4): 1153–67.

Kourachanis, N. (2019) *Housing Policies for Refugees: Social Integration or Welfare Dependence?*, Athens: Topos.

Lane, S.R., Cooper Altman, J., Schaffner Goldberg, G., Kagotho, N., Palley, E. and Paul, M.S. (2012) 'Inspiring and training students for social action: Renewing a needed tradition', *Journal of Teaching in Social Work*, 32(5): 532–49.

Lane, T.Y., Chiarelli-Helminiak, C., Bohrman, C. and Lewis, T. (2017) 'The teachable moment: Engaging students in social justice movements', *Social Work Education*, 36(4): 359–72.

Lavalette, M. and Ferguson, I. (2007) 'Towards a social work of resistance: International social work and the radical tradition', in M. Lavalette and I. Ferguson (eds), *International Social Work and the Radical Tradition*, Birmingham: Venture Press.

Lavalette, M. and Penketh, L. (2014) 'Conclusion: Race, racism and social work today: Some concluding thoughts', in M. Lavalette and L. Penketh (eds), *Race, Racism and Social Work: Contemporary Issues and Debates*, Bristol: Policy Press, pp 257–67.

Lum, D. (2003) *Culturally Competent Practice: A Framework for Understanding Diverse Groups and Social Justice Issues*, Pacific Grove, CA: Brooks/Cole.

Mackay, K. and Woodward, R. (2010) 'Exploring the place of values in the new social work degree in Scotland', *Social Work Education*, 29(6): 633–45.

Mapp, S. and Rice, K. (2019) 'Conducting rights-based short-term study abroad experiences', *Social Work Education*, 38(4): 427–38.

Marston, G. and McDonald, C. (2012) 'Getting beyond "heroic agency" in conceptualizing social workers as policy actors in the twenty-first century', *British Journal of Social Work*, 42(6): 1022–38.

Martínez Herrero, M.I. and Charnley, H. (2021) 'Resisting neoliberalism in social work education: Learning, teaching, and performing human rights and social justice in England and Spain', *Social Work Education*, 40(1): 44–57.

Masocha, S. (2014) 'We do the best we can: Accounting practices in social work discourses of asylum seekers', *British Journal of Social Work*, 44(6): 1621–36.

Miller, K.E. and Rasmussen, A. (2016) 'The mental health of civilians displaced by armed conflict: An ecological model of refugee distress', *Epidemiology and Psychiatric Sciences*, 26(2): 1–10.

Milner, M. and Wolfer, T. (2014) 'The use of decision cases to foster critical thinking in social work students', *Journal of Teaching in Social Work*, 34(3): 269–84.

Mizrahi, T. and Dodd, S-J. (2013) 'MSW students' perspectives on social work goals and social activism before and after completing graduate education', *Journal of Social Work Education*, 49: 580–600.

Moch, M. (2009) 'A critical understanding of social work by Paolo Freire', *Journal of Progressive Human Services*, 20(1): 92–7.

Morley, C. (2008) 'Teaching critical practice: Resisting structural domination through critical reflection', *Social Work Education*, 27(4): 407–21.

Morley, C., Le, C. and Briskman, L. (2020) 'The role of critical social work education in improving ethical practice with refugees and asylum seekers', *Social Work Education*, 39(4): 403–16.

Oikonomakis, L. (2018) 'Solidarity in transition: The case of Greece', in D. della Porta (ed.), *Solidarity Mobilizations in the 'Refugee Crisis'*, Cham: Palgrave Macmillan, pp 65–98.

Olcoń, K., Gilbert, D.J. and Pulliam, R.M. (2020) 'Teaching about racial and ethnic diversity in social work education: A systematic review', *Journal of Social Work Education*, 56(2): 215–37.

Ottosdottir, G. and Evans, R. (2014) 'Ethics of care in supporting disabled forced migrants: Interactions with professionals and ethical dilemmas in health and social care in the South-East of England', *British Journal of Social Work*, 44(1): 53–69.

Papouli, E. (2017) 'The role of arts in raising ethical awareness and knowledge of the European refugee crisis among social work students: An example from the classroom', *Social Work Education*, 36(7): 775–93.

Park, Y. and Bhuyan, R. (2012) 'Whom should we serve? A discourse analysis of social workers' commentary on undocumented immigrants', *Journal of Progressive Human Services*, 23(1): 18–40.

Peabody, C.G. (2013) 'Using photovoice as a tool to engage social work students in social justice', *Journal of Teaching in Social Work*, 33(3): 251–65.

Potocky-Tripodi, M. (2002) *Best Practices for Social Work with Refugees and Immigrants*, New York: Columbia University Press.

Preston, S. and Aslett, J. (2014) 'Resisting neoliberalism from within the academy: Subversion through an activist pedagogy', *Social Work Education: The International Journal*, 33(4): 502–18.

Robinson, K. (2014) 'Voices from the front line: Social work with refugees and asylum seekers in Australia and the UK', *British Journal of Social Work*, 44(6): 1602–20.

Sakamoto, I. (2007) 'A critical examination of immigrant acculturation: Toward an anti-oppressive social work model with immigrant adults in a pluralistic society, *British Journal of Social Work*, 37: 515–35.

Schuster, L. (2011) 'Turning refugees into "illegal migrants": Afghan asylum seekers in Europe', *Ethnic and Racial Studies*, 34(8): 1392–407.

Singh, G. (2014) 'Rethinking anti-racist social work in a neoliberal age', in M. Lavalette and L. Penketh (eds), *Race, Racism and Social Work: Contemporary Issues and Debates*, Bristol: Policy Press, pp 17–33.

Singh, S. (2019) 'What do we know about the experiences and outcomes of anti-racist social work education? An empirical case study evidencing contested engagement and transformative learning', *Social Work Education*, 38(5): 631–53.

Social Work England (2019a) 'Professional standards'. www.socialworkengland.org.uk/standards/professional-standards/

Social Work England (2019b) 'Education and training standards'. www.socialworkengland.org.uk/standards/education-and-training-standards/

Strier, R. and Bershtling, O. (2016) 'Professional resistance in social work: Counterpractice assemblages', *Social Work*, 61(2): 111–18.

Swank, E. and Fahs, B. (2014) 'Predictors of feminist activism among social work students in the United States', *Social Work Education: The International Journal*, 33(4): 519–32.

Teloni, D.D. (2017) 'Let us try to make another social work possible …: A report on the Greek social work action network, 2008–16', *Critical and Radical Social Work*, 5(2): 257–60.

Teloni, D.D. (2020) 'Anti-immigration policy and social work: Questions and challenges according to radical and critical social work perspectives', in I. Psimmenos (ed.), *Immigration and Immigration Policy*, Athens: Dionikos.

Teloni, D.D. and Mantanika, R. (2015) '"This is a cage for migrants": The rise of racism and the challenges for social work in the Greek context', *Critical and Radical Social Work*, 3(2): 189–206.

Teloni, DD., Dedotsi, S. and Telonis, A. (2020) 'Refugee "crisis" and social services in Greece: Social workers' profile and working conditions', *European Journal of Social Work*, 23(6): 1005–18.

Tsang, A.K.L. (2011) 'Students as evolving professionals: Turning the hidden curriculum around through the threshold concept pedagogy', *Transformative Dialogues: Teaching and Learning Journal*, 4(3): 1–11.

UNHCR (2021) 'Operational portal, mediterranean situation'. https://data2.unhcr.org/en/situations/mediterranean/location/5179

Vitus, K. and Lidén, G. (2010) 'The status of the asylum-seeking child in Norway and Denmark: Comparing discourses, politics and practices', *Journal of Refugee Studies*, 23(1): 61–81.

Wilson, G. and Campbell, A. (2013) 'Developing social work education: Academic perspectives', *British Journal of Social Work*, 43(5): 1005–23.

Wroe, L.E. (2018) '"It really is about telling people who asylum seekers really are, because we are human like anybody else": Negotiating victimhood in refugee advocacy work', *Discourse & Society*, 29(3): 324–43.

Wroe, L.E. (2019) 'Social working without borders: Challenging privatisation and complicity with the hostile environment', *Critical and Radical Social Work*, 7(2): 251–5.

Ying Yee, J. and Wagner, A.E. (2013) 'Is anti-oppression teaching in Canadian social work classrooms a form of neo-liberalism?', *Social Work Education*, 32(3): 331–48.

Yuval-Davis, N., Wemyss, G. and Cassidy, K. (2019) *Bordering*, Cambridge: Polity.

11

EU border migration policy and unaccompanied refugee minors in Greece: the example of Lesvos and Samos hotspots

Marina Rota, Ine Lietaert and Ilse Derluyn

Introduction

The hotspot approach

So much ink has been spilled about the so-called 'refugee crisis' of 2015 that it is almost impossible to refer to it without the fear of falling into endless repetition. Reports from international organisations state that in the period between January 2015 and September 2015, the largest number of refugees since World War II moved into Europe. During those months, an estimated 1,000,000 refugees arrived in Europe, about 850,000 of whom via Greece as gateway and mainly via the islands of Lesvos and Samos. Among them, there were thousands of unaccompanied minors; minors travelling without their parent/legal guardian. In May of the same year, the European Commission introduced 'The hotspot approach to managing exceptional migratory flows' as defined in the European Agenda on Migration and formally endorsed by the European Council on 25–26 June 2015. In early 2016, Greece legally introduced the establishment of these centres with Law L4375/2016. Under this law, five so-called hotspots, officially titled 'Registration and Identification Centres' (RICs), were created on the islands of Lesvos, Samos, Kos, Leros and Chios.[1] A few days before the Greek law, the ratification of the EU-Turkey Statement came into effect stating that:

> All migrants arriving in the Greek islands would continue to be duly registered, and the Greek authorities would process all applications individually at the hotspot in accordance with the Asylum Procedures Directive. Migrants not applying for asylum, or whose application was held to be unfounded or inadmissible under the directive would be returned to Turkey.

With this agreement, 'the corresponding regimes, which have long been criticized by Europeans for their infringements of human rights and the rule of law, would now be seen as guaranteeing sufficient protection for refugees' (Fassin, 2016: 1).

The impact of the 'hotspots' in Greece on the migration management was immediate and severe (Afouxenidis et al, 2017; Kourachanis, 2018). Suddenly, Greece changed from being one of the main gateways – together with Italy and Spain – towards Northern Europe, to being the main migrant detention centre in the EU. Thousands of people kept arriving to the Greek islands, only to find out that they were no longer allowed to leave, but had to proceed with their asylum application at the RICs. If they refused to apply for asylum at the 'hotspot', they were immediately subject of deportation to Turkey.

As more people arrived on the Greek islands of Lesvos and Samos than those leaving them, the already difficult living conditions at the centres became inhumane (Perkowski, 2016; Fili and Xythali, 2017). Many international organisations and NGOs began to issue warnings about the conditions in the RICs, pointing to the lack of safety, food, water, privacy and access to medical care (see for example, ECRE, 2016; FRA, 2016; HRW, 2016, 2018). Modified cargo containers, which were meant to be used as temporary accommodation for a few hundred people, proved inadequate to house the thousands needing shelter while they were waiting for their asylum procedure being processed. Ad hoc shelters started to appear at the perimeter of the hotspots in the nearby fields and woods.

International organisations, NGOs and human rights observatories have repeatedly called for European and national actions towards the improvement of the living conditions in Greek RICs (see for example, ECRE, 2016; FRA, 2016; HRW, 2016, 2018; Avocats Sans Frontières, 2019). In their press release for the three-year anniversary of the EU-Turkey agreement, MSF stated that:

> What was once touted as a 'refugee emergency' has given way to inexcusable levels of human suffering across the Greek islands and on mainland Greece. The EU and Greek authorities continue to rob vulnerable people of their dignity and health, seemingly in an effort to deter others from coming. This policy is cruel, inhumane and cynical, and it needs to end. (Emmanuel Goué, MSF's Head of Mission in Greece, March 2019)

Among the people who found themselves detained in the 'hotspots', there were hundreds of unaccompanied refugee minors (URMs) (Fili and Xythali, 2017). There is not a single answer on why children travel alone. Many start the journey on their own, while others are separated from their families during the journey. The reasons vary and should not be relevant when granting them protection in a host country. The need for protection and care for URMs has been extensively argued for (see for example, Derluyn and Broekaert 2008; De Graeve et al, 2017; Zijlstra et al, 2018), together with these young people's higher risk for multiple traumatic experiences (Derluyn, 2009; Vervliet et al, 2014), and the importance of an adequate institutional response (Derluyn, 2007; Lietaert et al, 2020). As stated by the UN General Assembly, Guidelines for the Alternative Care of Children, 'every child and young person should live in a supportive, protective and caring environment that promotes his/her full potential. Children with inadequate or no parental care are at special risk of being denied such a nurturing environment' (UNGA: 24 February 2010). However, living conditions in the RICs did not address of all those needs, resulting in these URMs having almost no access to basic rights such as security, family reunification, education, legal aid and guardianship.

The purpose of this chapter is to see how international, European and national legislation on unaccompanied minors are translated into actual reception practices in the RICs on the Greek islands. We hereto, first, give a short overview of the relevant international, EU and Greek legislation, then, second, describe the evolution of the Greek refugee camps on the islands of Lesvos and Samos, and, last, look at how URMs experience their living situation based on a thematic analysis of interviews with URMs within the framework of the ERC ChildMove project. As such, we will try to illuminate the possible gaps between policy and practice.

Legislation for the protection of unaccompanied minors

According to the UNHCR Guidelines on 'Policies and Procedures in Dealing with Unaccompanied Children Seeking Asylum', 'an unaccompanied child is a person who is under the age of eighteen ... and who is separated from both parents and is not being cared for by an adult who by law or custom has responsibility to do so', a definition also shared in Greek policy.

Article 3 of the Convention on the Rights of the Child (UNCRC) and Article 24 of the Charter of Fundamental Rights of the European Union state the principle of the best interest of the child,

> The well-being of a child in a broad sense which includes their basic material, physical, educational and emotional needs as well as needs for affection and safety. The best interest principle applies to all children without discrimination, to children not only as individuals, but also in general or as a group.

In addition, Art. 2 of the UNCRC states that, while protecting the rights of a child, 'there shall be no discrimination on the grounds of race, colour, sex, language, religion, political or other opinions, national, ethnic or social origin, property, disability, birth or other status'. According to this, every public or private body that is called to make a decision concerning a minor must always operate with the best interest of the child in mind.

Also EU-Regulation No 604/2013 (Art. 6) sets the best interests of the child as a primary consideration and calls for the allocation of qualified representatives as advocates for the minors. Indeed, various EU-instruments include special provisions for unaccompanied or separated children that entitle them to early identification, legal aid, guardianship, family reunification, safe accommodation and non-detention. Due to their increased risk of abuse and exploitation as well as their need for protection, unaccompanied children automatically fall under the definition of person in vulnerable situation of the EU Reception Conditions Directive (Article 21) and the EU Return Directive (Article 3).

The overall legal framework for the protection of children in Greece is designed in line with the Convention on the Rights of the Child that was merged into Greek legislation with Law 2101/1992 and refers to all children on Greek territory, irrespective of their nationality or ethnic origin (Fili and Xythali, 2017). Greek legislation is also in accordance with the EU Directives on the protection and rights of children on the move (UNICEF, 2016b). Article 60 of Law 4760/2020 regulates international protection procedures for unaccompanied minors, safeguarding their rights, always having the 'best interest of the child' in mind.

The evolution of the 'hotspot' approach in Moria, Lesvos and Vathi, Samos

Although the RIC of Moria only became widely known after 2015, both this RIC and the Samos hotspot were created in the space of already existing smaller detention/reception facilities. Specifically, the centre in Moria had been operating since 2013 as a Screening Center with a maximum capacity of 98 people, and was converted into a First Reception Center starting from January 2015. Likewise, a small First Reception Center at the Vathi area of Samos, designed to temporarily meet the needs of about 650 people, would be transformed into one of the largest reception facilities – what we call human warehouses – in the EU.

Even before the 2015 'refugee crisis', the treatment of migrants by the Greek state had caused a series of negative reports by international organisations and convictions by European Courts. The country's migration policy included, among others, closed centres with inhumane living conditions, long delays in the processing of asylum applications and the establishment of a special police force dedicated to the street-level prosecution of migrants which was found to work based on racial profiling rather than the migrants' legal status.

Long before the creation of Moria, Lesvos housed the infamous 'Pagani' structure where hundreds of people ended up imprisoned for an indefinite period of time with no access to basic human rights. For this reason, the establishment of the First Reception Service in June 2013 was met by those working in the field of immigration and asylum in Greece with a degree of scepticism and distrust. The year 2015 found Greece in social turmoil and on the verge of bankruptcy (Zambarloukou, 2015), with its new government in open confrontation with the EU and a war that was raging a few hundred kilometres away, causing thousands to take flight towards Europe in search for protection. Being on the most common route to the European Union during this period, Greece served as passageway for hundreds of thousands of people, while thousands of others lost their lives while trying to cross the Greek seas.

Very soon, migration gained a high position on the political agenda of both the Greek government and the rest of Europe, with mixed results. Within a year, the EU went through various phases from the famous 'Refugees Welcome' to the closure of the borders, and from solidarity and humanitarian action to public outrage and racist ravings (Benček and Strasheim, 2016). The closure of the so-called 'Balkan Route' in February 2016 and the subsequent EU-Turkey agreement sent a clear message to both Greece and Italy: 'We are willing to pay for you to keep them there'.[2]

In April 2016, just a few days after the EU-Turkey agreement, the Greek immigration law stipulated the creation and operation of 'hotspots' or – according to their Greek title – 'reception and identification centres'. Overnight, the first reception centres in Moria, Lesvos and in Vathi, Samos were converted to centres for long-stay and return/deportation, responsible for accepting and processing asylum requests. To anyone watching, the only visible difference in the camps was the installation of new containers to accommodate European services, such as EASO, Frontex and Europol, since this was also the first time that European institutions would be involved in a Member State's procedures of processing and granting asylum requests.

The hotspot of Moria, Lesvos

> We now have but one choice. We must face the long dark of Moria. Be on your guard.
> Lord of the Rings, The Fellowship of the Ring[3]

Moria was already operating as a 'pilot' for the Greek hotspots since October 2015. At that time, the total hosting capacity of the two Lesvos centres – Moria and Kara Tepe – was 2,800. According to the UNHCR, in October 2015, the two centres were already hosting, for registration procedures, more than 10,000 people, and already exhibiting severe shortages in basic necessities. The closure of the 'Balkan Route' with North Macedonia on February 2016 and the EU–Turkey agreement in March of the same year led to thousands of people arriving in Greece being held as hostages in an already overcrowded and understaffed structure. Amnesty International's report in the same period of February–March 2016 stated that:

> Even on Lesvos, where the Service had a First Reception Center within Moria camp ... the majority of the arrivals ... were screened by the police only to determine their nationality and registered by the police without receiving information on their rights and obligations, including the right to asylum and the relocation scheme. (Amnesty International, 2016: 26)

Although the RIC in Moria had already expanded its capacity to 3,000 people, the number of people trapped there was more than double. Gradually, the centre began to expand into adjacent olive groves, creating an informal settlement called the 'Jungle of Moria', with reference to the Calais settlement at the French-UK border. In August 2018, the field coordinator of Doctors Without Borders, Luca Fontana, described it as "the worst refugee camp on earth", adding that he had "never seen the level of suffering we are witnessing [there] every day". Two years later, Jean Ziegler (2020) would describe Moria as 'the recreation of a concentration camp on European soil'.

On 8 and 10 September 2020, the centre was completely destroyed by two consecutive fires. Although the official announcement of the Greek State was that the burning happened as a protest for the lockdown against the spread of the COVID-19 pandemic, the unacknowledged truth in everyone's minds was that there was no other way for Moria to cease to exist. At the time of the burning, Moria was 'home' to approximately 12,000 people, among whom there were 406 unaccompanied minors. The whole of Europe was watching 'in shock' what was an inevitable outcome of the overcrowding, while thousands of people, including families and young children, were standing in the midst of the rubble fearing even then to leave the centre without official permission. In its five years of operation as a hotspot, the centre of Moria became a symbol of the complete failure of the European migration policy. These policy shortcomings included

> the rejection of responsibility to accept a share of asylum seekers by a growing number of EU members; the adoption of draconian border exclusion policies, including inhumane push-backs out to sea; and an acceptance of degrading and inhumane camp conditions threatening the basic safety and health of inhabitants. (Digidiki and Bhabha, 2018: 1)

The hotspot of Vathi Samos

> All hope abandon, ye who enter here.
> Dante Alighieri, The Divine Comedy[4]

The situation at the Vathi RIC in Samos was no better. The centre, which was set up at a former military base, initially had a maximum capacity of 650 people. In no time, the number of people living there doubled. By 2017, it had reached 2,000, by 2018, it was 4,000, and in early 2019, it was 8,000. Since the capacity of the centre remained the same, an informal settlement started growing in the forest just outside of it. Thousands of people ended up living in the mountains above the centre amidst rubbish, mud and sewage. Their lodgings were summer camping tents, makeshift shacks made from plastic parts or just canvas sheets tied between the trees. In a statement of September 2020, MSF denounced that 'according to (their) medical teams, rats, scorpions and snakes are biting children and adults … at the … inhumane reception and identification centre, in Vathi on Samos island'. International and non-governmental organisations issued reports describing the appalling living conditions in the centre as they tried to raise awareness of the Greek and European authorities, while the Court of Human Rights acknowledged the violations of the rights of minors in Vathi.[5] Just ten days after the complete destruction of Moria, and following the assurances of EU countries that the unaccompanied minors of the camp would be transported to other European countries, a fire broke out at the minors' section of the Vathi camp, failing to provide the 'successful development' of Moria, meaning the destruction of the camp and the relocation of the URMs.

Although the RIC of Samos was less present in the media than the one of Moria, conditions there were no less horrible. As an officer from MSF Germany stated after her visit in Samos and Lesvos: "[In Samos] … I can hardly imagine that somewhere in Europe there is a place where people have to live under even worse conditions. … I didn't think it could get worse until I visited Moria", describing the situation in both camps and continued wondering: "How could the appalling conditions – under which tens of thousands of people seeking protection in Europe have to survive – become a kind of normality? People who are being ignored year after year are living between rats and rubbish". Dozens of reports (see for example, Amnesty International, 2016; HRW, 2016, 2018; MSF, 2016, 2018, 2020) and newspaper articles were published about the miserable living conditions of the people there, but both the EU and the respective Greek Governments chose to let the situation continue as it was.

On the 23 September 2020 – thus a few days after the fires in Moria and Vathi – the new EU Pact on Asylum and Migration was announced. Rather than acknowledging the failure of the hotspots policy, it introduced stricter border controls,[6] and pre-screening closed centres at border regions. Anticipating the new Pact on Migration and Asylum, the Greek government had already announced the creation of closed EU-funded camps on the islands, starting from Samos.

Method

This research is part of the European Research Council (ERC) funded ChildMove project, a large longitudinal study looking at the evolutions in the psychosocial wellbeing of unaccompanied refugee minors in relation to the experiences they have before migrating, in transit from home to the host country, and, where possible, after settlement. We started our research in Greece in October 2017, armed with a quiver full of quantitative and qualitative research tools. These included participant observations and semi-structured interviews (including socio-demographic questions about age, family and education) and self-report questionnaires related to the prevalence of the participants' psychosocial wellbeing, past traumatic experiences, current daily stressors, social support and ways of coping.

In Greece, a total of 44 initial interviews were conducted with minors aged 14 to 18 years old, two girls and 42 boys; a proportionate amount given the Greek statistics on gender differences in URMs at the time of the survey (EKKA, National Centre for Social Solidarity, October 2017).[7] These interviews took place in different parts of the country (that is, Athens, Samos and Thessaloniki) and in different contexts (that is, first reception and identification centres, unaccompanied minors' shelters and a detention centre), and they were conducted using an interpreter when necessary. Prior to each interview, the first author explained the objectives of the research, the confidentiality and anonymity of the participants, as well as the possibility of withdrawing from the research at any time without having to justify their decision.

This chapter is based on participant observations and interviews with minors that have been in these centres. From a total number of 44 participants in the project, 23 minors passed from one of the islands' hotspots, while two of them where in the hotspot of Samos during the interview. The length of stay in the hotspots varied from a couple of weeks to 13 months.

Participant observation in the hotspots took place inside the RIC of Vathi, Samos in November 2017 and February 2019. Additionally, a field visit at the ad hoc camp in Vathi took place in March 2018. As for the RIC of Moria, two field visits took place in the 'jungle' on March 2018 and March 2019.

We used thematic analysis (Braun and Clarke, 2006), creating codes based on EU and Greek legislation for the protection of URMs. Using NVivo12 as a tool, we highlighted the sections in our texts – usually phrases or sentences – whose content was directly linked with basic rights. We ended up with the following recurring themes: reception and identification (including age assessment), legal procedures (including family reunification), living conditions, safe environment, and state/police violence. Our notes from the participant observations strongly confirmed the findings coming from our interviews.

Results

Since the EU-Turkey agreement came into force, the situation started to deteriorate in the RICs of Moria and Vathi. In just a few months, tens of thousands of people were trapped in and around the hotspots. The continuous arrivals, in combination with the longer stay of people in the centres, led to ad hoc reception solutions, lengthy procedures for the identification of URMs and lack of access to basic rights. During our research, we faced the problems of misidentification of minors as adults, inhumane living conditions, lack of safety and incidents of violence.

Identification of URMs

Many minors were incorrectly identified as adults and were therefore left vulnerable to abuse and devoid of access to the provisions the law specifies for unaccompanied children (HRW, 2017). In some cases, they chose to declare a false age themselves in order not to be detained due to their minority in the reception centre while waiting to be placed in a shelter.

> 'At the beginning, I said I was an adult, I was afraid that they would keep me in the camp forever … but then I was with the adults. I was so scared. I had my Afghan ID, I was 15. Then I went to the UNHCR and showed them the paper. And they told me "You need to wait. We are obliged to send this to our headquarters in Athens. If they say yes, then it's fine." I received a reply after three months saying that they've accepted … three months, yes! They had accepted me as a minor. Until then I was living with the adults.' (Boy, 16 years old, Moria)

> 'My situation was different than the others. The first day I arrived in Mitilini. Upon arrival in Greece, they were separating the adults from the minors. I had papers proving I am a minor. But the papers were all lost on the boat. They ended up in the sea. I arrived in Mitilini, they ask me how old I am, and I say: "I am 18." What is the reason I declared I am 18? The people who arrived before me, they said: "If you say you are a minor, you are going to have a really bad time." They were many people who were minors, but they declared they are adults. And I did the same.' (Boy, 16 years old, Moria)

The absence of trained staff and the permanent shortage of resources combined with the large number of minors finding themselves in the hotspots, turned timely identification almost impossible.

Legal proceedings: asylum application and family reunification

Minors are required to apply for asylum in the hotspot according to the EU-Turkey agreement. The geographical constraint of the agreement forces them to stay in these hotspots until their application is evaluated. At the time of our visit, minors could apply for asylum – according to Law 4375/2016 – either through their legal representative if they were under 15 years old, or independently otherwise. In practice, none of the children that we have met had a legal representative or a guardian while staying at the hotspots. All the minors we interviewed based their decision to apply for asylum on information from the police, and cited incidents of deception and intimidation.

> 'When you arrive in Greece and you say you will not apply for asylum, they say "We will deport you back to Turkey or Afghanistan". When someone thinks about the effort he has put into this trip, the money he has paid and the life he used to have in Afghanistan or all the trouble he has been through, he decides to stay in Greece. Instead of deporting him back to Afghanistan.' (Boy, 16 years old, Samos)

> 'I showed them my ID. They had told me do it, so we can apply for asylum, the age in the paper is right, but if you do not apply for asylum, you will stay here forever and you will not be able to get away from here. They said you will stay forever here if you do not apply.' (Boy, 16 years old, Samos)

> 'Before they took you and put you in Moria, the interpreter with the policeman, they told you when they came and pick you up that we are going to take you somewhere, that you will have a room, food, Wi-Fi … like a king. … Well, let us say, they did not have Wi-Fi.' (Boy, 17 years old, Moria)

In many cases, unaccompanied minors arrived in Greece with the aim of reuniting with their family in other EU countries. Delays in the registration process often undermined procedures for family reunification. None of our participants was able to start the family reunification procedure inside the hotspots, mostly due to late identification and lack of legal representation.

> 'We were told back in Mitilini that in order to apply for family reunification, you need to spend at least six months at the camp. That

camp was in such bad condition that I did not want to stay there. When I went to the asylum services, I spoke to the translator and he told me that the process (for family reunification) will take six to seven months. That is why I did not do it.' (Boy, 16 years old, Moria)

For all our participants, the process of family reunification only started after they had left the centres for a shelter. For many of them, family reunification took place after they had reached adulthood, wasting valuable time and favourable conditions such as access to international protection as minors in vulnerable situation.

Living conditions

Since the initial phases of Moria's conversion into a hotspot, unaccompanied minors were kept in a separate section in what was the area of the First Reception Service. The minors' section was relatively isolated, and surrounded by barbed wire. Even before the closing of the Greek-North Macedonia border and the implementation of the EU-Turkey agreement, unaccompanied minors were required to stay in this isolated area until a suitable shelter could be found for them on the mainland (Rozakou, 2017). Gradually the situation changed, due to the increasing number of minors. During our field visit to the Moria 'jungle' in March 2019, the fences around the minors' section were destroyed, while many minors were living in tents in the informal settlement. Since the number of children waiting for a place in one of the shelters outnumbered the available places by hundreds, many of them had to live in these conditions for several months.

> 'The first day they put me in a container together with 30 other people. The situation inside the container was difficult ... life there was difficult. After that ... because the circumstances were not good in the container ... in that space there were 30 people, but it was really small ... I found two to three people I could trust, together we decided to go and buy a tent. And we were sleeping together in the tent.' (Boy, 16 years old, Moria)

Samos was not much different. In February 2019, during a visit by the ChildMove project team, we noticed that there were improvised tents around the containers of the minors' department. The toilets and bathrooms did not work, and there were minors who simply slept under makeshift awnings. Many children ended up living outside the centre, in the ad hoc camp on the mountain.

> 'From the beginning, we were five and then seven and then ten, eleven, and then there wasn't enough space. When we told them that

there isn't enough space, they put more children inside the container, and they told us "whether you like it or not you will find space". … Only if we squeeze, we could fit in that place. Then when we see that we can't fit as the people were increasing, some people left and went to the mountains to sleep, in a tent, anywhere we could find. Each person found a place for himself. One was saying that "I will go after the forest that I have found an abandoned car and I sleep in there." … I was there. … They told us that five to six months you will stay in this place, it wasn't sure.' (Boy, 17 years old, Samos)

According to the law, the responsible authorities must consider the specific conditions experienced by persons in vulnerable situations, such as URMs, when applying the provisions on reception conditions. However, our research, as well as multiple reports, has shown that this was not the case in the hotspots of Lesvos and Samos. Only two out of the 23 participants attended school while staying in the hotspots, and only for a few days per week. None of them had a guardian, and they had limited access to medical and psychological care, clothing, food and safety. Due to the overcrowded conditions in the camps, the minors were forced to live either in cramped, destroyed containers inside the camps or in tents in the ad hoc settlements.

> 'In the camp, I do not have a bed or something, you just sleep on the floor … no bathroom, no water. We are in the tent, you see the tent when people are coming new. … I lost my phone, my money, my clothes, they steal it, I still there, and then we were super disgusting. No one could sit with us because we smell. Yeah, like 20 days after the boss of the camp comes and then she cried because she saw us like that.' (Boy, 17 years old, Moria)

> 'One day in Samos, people came and told us that we are from UNHCR, we told them that where we are staying the situation is really bad, in the container that where we were there was no light, there was no bathroom. When it was raining, the roof was dripping, the wind was going through the tent, no window, no light.' (Boy, 16 years old, Samos)

> 'In Mitilini, in Moria, the situation was not good. It was really bad. At the tent in Mitilini, things were pretty bad. We were inside the tent, and it was snowing. When it was raining, our blankets would be soaking wet. We were going to change and get other blankets. We were sleeping at night, and we were waking up and see that we were soaking wet. The situation was not good.' (Boy, 16 years old, Moria)

Lack of safety

Although EU legislation and the Greek laws guarantee URMs' access to basic needs, such as 'material, physical, educational and emotional needs as well as needs for affection and safety', none of these standards were met inside the hotspots of Moria and Vathi. The living conditions were inhumane, and the minors lived in constant fear:

> 'there were days, in general, at nights when we were about to go to sleep, in order not to steal us, we were hiding our personal belongings in places that you should not hide things, in our underwear.' (Boy, 17 years old, Moria)

> 'We were in the tent, we were six days there in the tent, more than 50 people. In my opinion now that I have seen all that in Moria, they do not give any attention to the unaccompanied minors. I was two months there, every night robbery, fight, arguing. ... The food was not good, was awful.' (Boy, 15 years old, Moria)

> 'You couldn't keep anything safe there. When you were leaving the container, you had to take everything with you ... your clothes. If you lost sight of your belongings for only a minute, you would lose everything.' (Boy, 16 years old, Moria)

Violence among residents

During our research, the impression of the hotspots as a hostile and violent environment towards the minors was constant, both during participant observations and the interviews. URMs in the hotspots were facing a high risk of experiencing violence, of being involved in tensions between groups of different origins or being victims of violent behaviours.

> 'In Moria, when a fight was happening, everyone was in the audience till a head will be broken, a nose or someone fell down, then they were coming and were picking up the dead bodies. The policemen did not come to separate us.' (Boy, 17 years old, Moria)

> 'The fire in Moria. ... I was there. The situation was really bad. You could not sleep after 12 at night. Everyone was fighting. ... They were drinking alcohol and then they were fighting ... every night. No one could sleep at night there. You could only sleep during the day.' (Boy, 16 years old, Moria)

'To be honest with you, life is difficult here. The last four days, I have only slept about four hours. I get nightmares at 5 am, I get scared. ... Our container has no door, no windows. In the night, drunk men are coming to the minors' section, and they hit the containers with sticks to scare us. I am always afraid to sleep. We went to the police and we asked them to address the situation. We waited and waited ... no one came.' (Boy, 17 years old, Samos)

Police violence before arriving at the hotspot

Many of our participants stated the degrading conditions and the abusive treatment, including ill-treatment by police the moment they arrived in Greece, even before entering the hotspots.

'[The police] put us in jail. ... To wake us up, actually I have still here in my legs, my feet, excuse me, they hit my feet, they fire my feet with electricity, I still have the scars here.' (Boy, 17 years old, Moria)

'We walk like in line to get inside the (police) bus to take us to the camp and they were beating us. ... And we get there, because actually the island is beautiful, you know. ... I said, oh my God, I found a good life, then we were on the bus, and then I get to the camp. ... I get super scared, super scared.' (Boy, 17 years old, Moria)

'At the port, at the port, outside and then inside a police bus. Inside the bus, they forced us to enter. I'm afraid, also hungry. Nobody gave us something to eat, to keep us alive. It was just like that. At 7 or 8 o'clock, we arrived in Moria. I look at Moria like that with my mouth open. I thought: this is what they call Europe?' (Boy, 17 years old, Moria)

Police violence inside the hotspots

Our participants talked about deliberated violence from the police while in RICs, and in some cases, they linked this violence with their traumatic experiences in their home country.

'There was a problem with some other people here. And the problem was related to the unaccompanied minors. The police came to separate them, and they started breaking the containers, all ... the things. ... And since that night, for a while, the police was coming down to intimidate us. They were waking everyone up, they were knocking on the containers. It was like a terrorist act.' (Boy, 17 years old, Samos)

'For example, the police hit me here (in the camp). The same thing happened in Syria, they hit me. I haven't seen any difference. To show some interest. … The only difference is that in Syria, there is war, but here, there isn't. I was hit many times from the police, in the container, in the line for food … because they push each other sometimes they hit us.' (Boy, 17 years old, Samos)

According to an MSF research, people who arrived on Samos after the EU-Turkey deal was signed in March 2016 reported more violence in Turkey and Greece than those who arrived before the deal came into force. Between 50 and 70 per cent of that violence was allegedly committed by state authorities.

Mental health of URMs in the hotspots

During the participant observations in Samos in November 2017, we recorded some incidents of self-harm by minors. Similar incidents at the Moria camp were reported to us by our interviewees. URMs often present feelings of stress and anxiety, as well as depressive behaviours (Derluyn and Broekaert, 2007). Reports from the Greek hotspots provide information about the struggle of URMs that have often led them to suicide attempts.

'All of these guys there had like psychological problems. All of them. Like they stand, they sit, they cut themselves, one took too much pills to kill himself, one is jumping the, how is called, the fence, one put in the window to cut his head.' (Boy, 17 years old, Moria)

The longer the URMs were stuck in the hotspots, the more vulnerable to violent incidents they became. Our participants complained about recurring nightmares, anxiety and aggressiveness even after they left the camps. In accordance with our findings, Human Rights Watch reported from Moria that most of the children were experiencing psychological distress, including symptoms such as anxiety, depression, headaches and insomnia, while many of them were sleeping in overcrowded and unhygienic conditions that put their physical and mental health at risk.

Discussion

In this chapter, we attempt to address the European hotspots approach in Greece through the prism of children's rights. Using an overview of international, European and national legislation, as well as scientific articles and reports, combined with our own findings from the ChildMove project, we uncovered the contrast between the legal framework regulating URMs' protection and the daily practices in the centres of Moria and Samos. Our aim was to highlight the problem at its core: it is not the lack of laws and political decisions that lead to the non-protection of URMs, but the conscious choice not to implement them.

Both European and Greek legislation guarantee the rights of refugee children based on the best interests of the child. Nevertheless, the hotspots policy left no room for the exercise of their rights. URMs had no protection inside the RICs. Hundreds of them were living in inhumane conditions in or around the camps, while their applications for international protection or family reunification (under Dublin III) were often delayed to the point that they were receiving a decision after they reached adulthood. The implementation of hotspots in Lesvos and Samos also left no room for personalised care for URMs or even the possibility of early detection of minority. Fear of detention pushed many children to report false age, which the responsible authorities were just accepting, even when it was obvious that they were minors.

In Greece, many URMs remain in detention, even today, under the euphemistic term of 'protective custody', despite the fact that Article 43 of Law 4760/2020 officially put an end to this practice.

None of the minors in our sample had an appointed guardian while in the centres. Most of them did not even have a guardian during their stay in the shelters. Although the law on guardianship was voted in 2018, it hasn't been implemented yet, even today. The law clearly defines the right of URMs to education, access to medical care, safe accommodation and protection, as well access to basic needs such as food and clothing. In both the RICs of Moria and Vathi, none of these rights were respected. More often than not, minors stood in line for food with adults for more than two hours just to be informed when it was their turn that there was no more food left. Many minors said they were being beaten by the police while queuing for food. Many of our participants compared the violence they experienced or saw in the hotspots with the violence in the war zones of their homeland, while most reported symptoms of depression, anxiety and aggression during their stay there.

In July 2019, MEP Pietro Bartolo stated at the European Parliament that:

> 'the Samos hotspot is seriously overcrowded. Toilet facilities and the provision of basic necessities, such as food and medicines, are insufficient, with consequent health risks. In addition, the registration and age verification system, as well as the systems for protecting and safeguarding children from adults unknown to them, are inadequate. The complaint also refers to cases of violence against children, serious self-harm incidents and cases of unaccompanied foreign siblings and cousins being separated.'

Bartolo then posed the following questions:

> 'Is the Commission aware of the situation in the Samos hotspot? What measures will it take to ensure decent living conditions and genuine protection for unaccompanied minors in the Samos hotspot? How does the Commission intend to check whether the EU funds that Greece is receiving are being used in an efficient way to improve reception conditions in hotspots such as the one in Samos?'

Such questions fell on deaf ears. 'In response', the new Pact for Migration and Asylum constitutes the continuation of the hotspot logic with even stricter border controls. Unaccompanied children are required to stay in the new, closed detention centres for as long as the pre-entry screening lasts, with a maximum stay of ten days. Bearing in mind that the maximum stay in the hotspots – according to the legal provisions – was 25 days, and the minors were in fact forgotten there for months, we can only worry, since this means that, for the first time under EU law, detention of migrant children will become the rule rather than a measure of last resort. To be fair, both the Pact for Migration and Asylum and the Greek law 4756/2020 include all the compatible provisions for the protection of the rights of unaccompanied minors. Unfortunately, so far, experience has shown that this is not enough. According to Article 8 of the new Ministerial Decision (no. 23/13532) on the function of the new RICs, access to these closed centres will be strictly regulated, which will render control of the conditions within by the press, academia and civil society organisations virtually impossible. If the EU has openly accepted so many blatant human rights violations in hotspots over the years, we can only wonder if the new policy is aimed at protecting people or hiding these violations from the public eye by offering a convenient excuse such as *Davon haben wir nichts gewusst*.

So far, all efforts by both the EU and Greece to protect unaccompanied minors did not even come close to reaching their goal. The necessary recommendations for improvement are already enshrined in the UNCRC and European and Greek law. These speculate that all relevant decisions by Member States should be in the best interests of the child. They guarantee unaccompanied minors the legal right to access international protection, guardianship, family reunification, a safe living environment, education, medical care, adequate nutrition and clothing. What remains is for the existing provisions of the laws to be implemented, and for the people who are responsible to make it happen to have the correct professional profile. As discussed in the chapter on social workers at the Samos refugee camp, social work is a rights-based profession whose practitioners need to be provided with the right training, appropriate working conditions and tools, in order to safeguard the rights of unaccompanied minors. With the contemporary war in Ukraine creating millions of refugees within a couple of months, among which are thousands of unaccompanied and separated children, it is essential that the new EU policy will not repeat previous mistakes and will ensure the protection of children's rights, specifically focusing on the best interests of each child.

Acknowledgements

The authors would like to thank all participants for sharing their stories with us, as well as all colleagues who contributed to this work with their valuable comments. This work was supported by the European Research Council under grant ChildMove; project number: 714222.

Disclosure statement

We have no known conflict of interest to disclose.

Notes

[1] In the following pages the interchangeable terms 'hotspots' and 'reception and identification centres' will be used in accordance to European Union and Greek terminology, respectively.
[2] https://www.theguardian.com/world/2016/feb/25/europe-braces-major-humanitarian-crisis-greece-row-refugees
[3] Fran Walsh, Philippa Boyens and Peter Jackson, 'The Lord Of The Rings – The Fellowship of the Ring', Screenplay based on the novels by J.R.R. Tolkien, p 120.
[4] Dante Alighieri (1265–1321), The Divine Comedy, Inferno, Canto III.
[5] https://www.gcr.gr/en/news/press-releases-announcements/item/1352-the-european-court-of-human-rights-provides-interim-measures-to-unaccompanied-minors-living-in-the-ric-and-the-jungle-of-samos-island
[6] https://www.hrw.org/news/2020/10/08/pact-migration-and-asylum
[7] https://reliefweb.int/report/greece/situation-update-unaccompanied-children-uac-greece-15-october-2017-enel

References

Afouxenidis, A., Petrou, M., Kandylis, G., Tramountanis, A. and Giannaki, D. (2017) 'Dealing with a humanitarian crisis: Refugees on the eastern EU border of the island of Lesvos', *Journal of Applied Security Research*, 12(1): 7–39.

Amnesty International (2016) 'Trapped in Greece: An avoidable refugee crisis'. www.amnesty.org/en/documents/eur25/3778/2016/en/

Avocats Sans Frontières France (2019) 'The hotspot approach at the service of the geographical containment of migrants: Study on violations of migrants' rights on the island of Samos. Observation Report', Mission carried out for Migreurop and by Mathilde ALBERT from 7 May 2019 to 6 October 2019. www.migreurop.org/IMG/pdf/fiche_hotspot_-_m._albert_-_en.pdf

Benček, David and Strasheim, Julia (2016) 'Refugees welcome? A dataset on anti-refugee violence in Germany', *Research & Politics*, 3(4): 1–11.

Braun V. and Clarke, V. (2006) 'Using thematic analysis in psychology, *Qualitative Research in Psychology*, 3(2): 77–101.

Charter of Fundamental Rights of the European Union (2000/C 364/01) Official Journal of the European Communities. https://www.europarl.europa.eu/charter/pdf/text_en.pdf

Convention on the Rights of the Child (1989) Treaty no. 27531, United Nations Treaty Series. https://www.ohchr.org/sites/default/files/Documents/ProfessionalInterest/crc.pdf

De Graeve, K., Vervliet, M. and Derluyn, I. (2017) 'Between immigration control and child protection: Unaccompanied minors in Belgium', *Social Work and Society*, 15(1): 1–13.

Derluyn, I. and Broekaert, E. (2007) 'Different perspectives on emotional and behavioural problems in unaccompanied refugee children and adolescents', *Ethnicity and Health*, 12(2): 141–62.

Derluyn, I. and Broekaert, E. (2008) 'Unaccompanied refugee children and adolescents: The glaring contrast between a legal and a psychological perspective', *International Journal of Law and Psychiatry*, 31(4): 319–30.

Derluyn, I., Mels, C. and Broekaert, E. (2009) 'Mental health problems in separated refugee adolescents', *Journal of Adolescent Health*, 44(3): 291–7.

Digidiki, V. and Bhabha, J. (2018) 'Sexual abuse and exploitation of unaccompanied migrant children in Greece: Identifying risk factors and gaps in services during the European migration crisis', *Children and Youth Services Review*, 92: 114–21.

Directive 2008/115/Ec of the European Parliament and of the Council of 16 December 2008 on common standards and procedures in Member States for returning illegally staying third-country nationals. https://eur-lex.europa.eu/legal-content/EN/TXT/PDF/?uri=CELEX:32008L0115&from=EN

Directive 2013/33/Eu of the European Parliament and of the Council of 26 June 2013 laying down standards for the reception of applicants for international protection. https://eur-lex.europa.eu/legal-content/EN/TXT/PDF/?uri=CELEX:32013L0033&from=EN

ECRE (2016) 'The implementation of the hotspots in Italy and Greece—a study'. www.ecre.org/wp-content/uploads/2016/12/HOTSPOTS-Report-5.12.2016.pdf

European Council (2016) 'EU-Turkey statement', Brussels, 18 March. http://www.consilium.europa.eu/en/press/press-releases/2016/03/18/eu-turkey-statement/#

Fassin D. (2016) 'Hot spots: What they mean', Fieldsights, 28 June. https://culanth.org/fieldsights/hot-spots-what-they-mean

Fili, A. and Xythali, V. (2017) 'The continuum of neglect: Unaccompanied minors in Greece', *Social Work Society International Online Journal*, 15(2): 1–14.

FRA (2016) 'Opinion of the European Union Agency for Fundamental Rights on the Fundamental Rights in the "hotspots" set up in Greece and Italy'. https://fra.europa.eu/sites/default/files/fra_uploads/fra-2019-opinion-hotspots-update-03-2019_en.pdf

Human Rights Watch (2016) '"Why are you keeping me here?" Unaccompanied children detained in Greece'. www.hrw.org/report/2016/09/08/why-are-you-keeping-me-here/unaccompanied-children-detained-greece

Human Rights Watch (2017) 'Greece: Dire refugee conditions on islands'. www.hrw.org/news/2017/01/23/greece-dire-refugee-conditions-islands

Human Rights Watch (2018) 'Greece: 13,000 still trapped on islands'. www.hrw.org/news/2018/03/06/greece-13000-still-trapped-islands

Kourachanis, N. (2018) 'Asylum seekers, hotspot approach and anti-social policy responses in Greece (2015–2017)', *Journal of International Migration and Integration*, 19(4): 1153–67.

Lietaert, I., Behrendt, M., Uzureau, O., Adeyinka, S., Rota, M., Verhaeghe, F. and Derluyn, I. (2020) 'The development of an analytical framework to compare reception structures for unaccompanied refugee minors in Europe', *European Journal of Social Work*, 23(3): 384–400.

Médecins Sans Frontières (MSF) (2016) 'Obstacle course to Europe: A policy-made humanitarian crisis at EU borders'. www.msf-me.org/article/obstacle-course-europe-eu-policies-dramatically-worsened-2015-refugee-crisis

Médecins Sans Frontières (MSF) (2018) 'Suicide attempts and self-harming among child refugees in Moria'. www.msf.org/child-refugees-lesbos-are-increasingly-self-harming-and-attempting-suicide

Médecins Sans Frontières (MSF) (2020) 'En el campo de Vathy hay 4.500 personas hacinadas como animales viviendo entre suciedad, basura y ratas'. https://msf-spain.prezly.com/en-el-campo-de-vathy-hay-4500-personas-hacinadas-como-animales-viviendo-entre-suciedad-basura-y-ratas

Office of the United Nations High Commissioner for Refugees Geneva (1997) 'Guidelines on policies and procedures in dealing with unaccompanied children seeking asylum February 1997'. https://www.unhcr.org/afr/3d4f91cf4.pdf

Perkowski, N. (2016) 'Deaths, interventions, humanitarianism and human rights in the Mediterranean "Migration Crisis"', *Mediterranean Politics*, 21(2): 331–5.

Rozakou, K. (2017) 'Nonrecording the "European refugee crisis" in Greece: Navigating through irregular bureaucracy', *Focaal*, 77: 36–49.

Special Report EU response to the refugee crisis: The 'hotspot' approach (pursuant to Article 287(4), second subparagraph, TFEU) 2017. https://www.eca.europa.eu/Lists/ECADocuments/SR17_6/SR_MIGRATION_HOTSPOTS_EN.pdf

UNHCR (2016) 'More displaced now than after WWII'. https://edition.cnn.com/2016/06/20/world/unhcr-displaced-peoples-report/index.html

UNICEF (2016) 'Unaccompanied refugee and migrant children in urgent need of protection', Press release, 6 May. www.unicef.org/media/media_91069.html

Vervliet, M., Lammertyn, J., Broekaert, E. and Derluyn, I. (2014) 'Longitudinal follow-up of the mental health of unaccompanied refugee minors', *European Child & Adolescent Psychiatry*, 23(5): 337–46.

Zambarloukou, S. (2015) 'Greece after the crisis: Still a south European welfare model?' *European Societies*, 17(5): 653–73.

Ziegler, J. (2020) 'Nous avons recréé des camps de concentration', *L'ILLUSTRÉ*, 23 January. www.illustre.ch/magazine/jean-ziegler-avons-recree-camps-concentration

Zijlstra, El., Rip, J., Beltman, D., Os, C. and Kalverboer, M (2018) 'Unaccompanied minors in the Netherlands: Legislation, policy, and care', *Social Work & Society*, 15(2): 1–20.

Epilogue: Time to listen, time to learn, time to challenge ... because there is hope

Emilio José Gómez-Ciriano, Elena Cabiati and Sofia Dedotsi

This book can be read as a series of interconnected pieces of social work research exploring social work practice in the areas of migration and asylum across Europe. However, the aim of the volume is to produce a comparative analysis of contemporary social work practice in this complex and challenging area. It is also a reflection on how effective social practice is in the field and a source of reflection on how social work education programmes can contribute to train professionals.

The volume can be viewed in four different ways:

- A *compilation*. Twenty authors and collaborators, from nine countries reflect across the pages of this volume about the richness of research in this field from different perspectives and social work traditions as well as the range of approaches across Europe. All the chapters are original pieces of work and reflect the research that has been undertaken in the fields of migration: reception, integration, education and policy-making. Certainly, the academic perspective is prevailing and it would have been desirable to include direct perspectives from migrants, refugees and asylum seekers; this is something perhaps missed in the book and that will be very present in our next publications. However, it is important to highlight that most of the authors are both academics and social workers with fieldwork experience.
- A *magnifying glass*. By reading its different chapters, it is possible to identify how authors go into depth and raise difficult issues that in most of the cases are silenced or not made public due to their high degree of controversy as they challenge the current state of the things regarding migration: policies, academia, organisations, European Union politics, institutional racism, neoliberal scheme and so on. The book sheds light on these matters and this is why this book is not only necessary but timely too.
- A *tool for comparative analysis* on how migrants and asylum seekers are being treated in the countries of transit and/or destination, on the conditions they live in, on how their rights are (or not) safeguarded, on which initiatives are developed to make their lives more 'liveable' or on which good practices could be replicated and what bad uses should be avoided

to promote their rights and dignity accordingly with the Global definition of social work.
- A *powerful material of reflection on social work identity* on the current state of social work practice with immigrants and refugees. This is a crucial issue as touches the very essence of social work identity as a profession committed to social justice.

It is important to emphasise that the situation of migrants, asylum seekers and refugees has worsened with the pandemic of COVID-19 as highlighted in the latest report of the Fundamental Rights Agency (FRA, 2022). In addition, at the time of publishing this book, the war in Ukraine (since February 2022) has resulted in large refugee waves seeking protection in other European countries. These multiple crises as well as the response policies by the European Member States result in significant challenges for people, especially migrants and refugees and the professionals in the frontline such as social workers.

Key themes

The following themes emerge:

- *Human rights*: Migrants' and refugees' needs and rights are not being met and not respected enough in Europe. There is hardly receptiveness and empathy towards their situation from the reception and integration structures of the States. Their feelings, concerns, hopes and potentialities are systematically ignored, and this makes their vulnerability, fragility and anxiety arise. The feeling of not being listened, not being understood, not being respected in their traditions and habits makes many of them feel they do not have a sense of place.
- *Social work practice*: Most social workers do not feel confident when working with migrants, refugees and asylum seekers. All authors in their chapters outline how practitioners often lack the knowledge, skills and competences that would enable them to be aware of the complexity of their job and the specificities it entails, as most have to learn on the job and blindly follow the instructions they receive from above in their organisations or by the government. As a result, they became part of a system that may oppress and violate human rights, even without practitioners being aware of this.
- *Social work education*: academia, and specifically faculties and schools of social work are not sufficiently providing in their formative programmes the contents and skills needed to have a proper knowledge of migration and asylum by promoting enough the development of critical thinking and favouring a direct contact with migrants and refugees. Migration is

still marginalised in many curricula and placed, as Van Ewijk (2020) says, in the corner of peculiarities.
- *Good practice*: Across the pages of this book it is possible to find remarkable and sound experiences that can be replicated in other contexts. The importance of arts, dialogue, close contacts of students with migrants and refugees helps to feed emphatic attitudes and to develop a critical perspective that may result in better promotion and defence of rights.
- *Social work research*: It is crucial that the findings of social work research on migration and asylum reach decision-making levels in order to influence political decisions in this field. This is something that still needs to be achieved. However, some steps are being taken and some organisations (IFSW, EASSW and ESWRA) are moving in this direction.

A sense of hope

This volume has been written by social work researchers who are conscious of the importance of social work as a profession and discipline and aware of their responsibility towards the society, the citizenry and the migrants and refugees. The authors have written all these chapters because they have previously developed a critical perspective and this has not been an easy work, as the context – as it has been explained – does not favour any alternative position that challenges the current state of the things. This is, by itself, good news and a reason for hope as it paves the way for future research and reflections in this way.

References

FRA (European Union Agency for Fundamental Rights (2022) 'Guardianship systems for unaccompanied children in the European Union', Brussels Publications Office of the European Union. https://fra.europa.eu/sites/default/files/fra_uploads/fra-2022-guardianship-systems-developments_en.pdf

Van Ewijk, H. (2020) *European Social Policy and Social Work*, New York: Routledge.

Index

References to figures appear in *italic* type.

A

academic
  culture 9–10
  institutions 12
  knowledge 9
  teaching-learning programmes 8
accelerated asylum procedure 82, 83
accessibility and inclusivity, Italian social work organisations 112
acculturation 137
activism into social work education
  anti-immigration policies 162
  anti-racist and solidarity initiatives 161–2
  collective action and community engagement 162
  consciousness and strategies for action 162
  exclusion 161
  neoliberal context 163–4
  project 164–8
  securitanianism 161
  structural repression and grassroots solidarity 162
  students' critical thinking and challenge 163
adaptation 147
adaptive preferences 150
Addams, J. 5
Adeyinka, S. 3
adult asylum seekers 155
Advisory Group on the Provision of Support 136
African asylum-seeking families 132
Ager, A. 146, 147–8
Ai Weiwei 31, 37
All-Ireland Social Work Educators Forum 128
Amelina, A. 149
anomie 36
anthropological places 84
anti-discrimination 120
anti-immigration policies 121
anti-oppressive approach 139, 163
  critical consciousness 165
  models 162–3
  policy and practice 128
  practice 127
  profession 165
  research 9
  social work practices 3–4

anti-racism 128
anti-racist approach 139
anti-racist social work 120, 127, 163
anti-racist and solidarity movement 167
anti-refugee sentiment 30
anxiety 76
Arendt, H. 80
Aristotle's concept of eudaimonia 150–1
asylum application and family reunification 186–7
Asylum and Immigration Act, 1999 152
asylum seekers 127, 128, 131–2, 152
  procedure and residency of 82–3
  and refugees 149
  shelter, coercive community 81–2
Augé, M. 84–5
Austrian National Agency 32
awareness 5–6, 9

B

Balkan refugee route 26, 29
'Balkan Route' in February 2016 181
Behrendt, M. 3
Belgium, refugees in *see* family reunification
Berardi, F. 30
Berry, J.W. 147
Berthold, T. 81
Best Interests of the Child 155
Black, Asian and Minority Ethnic (BAME) population 153
Black African asylum-seeking families 132
Black and ethnic minority 128
Black Lives Matter movement 128
Boccagni, P. 11, 139
Bombach, C. 3
border migration policy
  asylum application and family reunification 186–7
  confidentiality and anonymity of participants 184
  crossing perspective and methodological nationalism 98
  European Research Council (ERC) 184
  hotspot approach 177–9
  living conditions 187–8
  migration management 178
  Moria, Lesvos 181–2
  police violence 190–1
  safety 189

unaccompanied minors, legislation for protection 179–80
Vathi Samos 183–4
violence among residents 189–90
Bourdieu, P. 148

C

Cabiati, E. 3
Capability Approach (CA) 146, 150–1
Chen, G.M. 10
Child and Family Services Unit 130
ChildMove project 58, 184, 187
children in Swiss asylum camps
  asylum shelter, coercive community 81–2
  de-homing 89–90
  dimensions of home 84–5
  ethics 83–4
  home as an idea and feeling at home 86–8
  home as place 85–6
  homing 88–9
  methods and terminology 83
  non-places 84
  procedure and residency of asylum seekers 82–3
  see also home
Children (Scotland) Act 1995 155
child welfare interventions 119
Christie, A. 126, 128, 135
Clark-Kazak, C. 84
clients' cultural uniqueness' 147
co-learning 168
'colour-blind approach' 116
comfort zones 22
communication 8, 114
community mental health 130
concentration camps 26
Court of Human Rights 182
critical consciousness 164–5
critical pedagogy 164
critical race and whiteness theories 162–3
critical thinking 21
Crosscare 131
'cult of managerialism' 10–11
culture(al)
  anaesthesia 36–7
  competence 147–8
  competence approaches 162–3
  coping strategies 101
  diversity 147
  humility 10
  integration 67
  sensitivity 8, 128
  social work 3
Cummins, I. 10–11

D

Dalikeni, C. 132
Daly, M. 3, 155

Davies, T. 161
Debruyne, P. 3
decision-making processes 82
Dedotsi, S. 3–4
defensive social work 13
degree of intercultural sensitivity 9
degree of togetherness 100
de-homing 89–90
delegated performances 35
demographic stability and growth 153
Deneulin, S. 150
deportability 65
Derluyn, I. 3–4
Di Rosa, R.T. 10–11
discretionary space 48, 107
discrimination 118, 120
disproportionality 113
distant family 106
Divjak, Ž. 34

E

educational-pedagogical approach 164
Éinrí, M. 126
Ekstron, E. 3
emergency reception and orientation centres (EROCs) 133
emotional dysregulation 57
emotional exhaustion 56
emotional pain 74
empathy 8
Ending Destitution Together 152
enforceability 115–16
environmental turbulence 53
'equity of care' policy 135
equivalence of care and intersectionality 118
ethics, Swiss asylum camps 83–4
ethnic minorities 113, 117
  people 115–16
  service 121
  service users 117–18
etymology 8
EU border migration policy 3–4
eudemonic wellbeing 150
EU Reception Conditions Directive 180
EU-Regulation No 604/ 2013 180
Eurodac fingerprints regulation 31
European Anti-Poverty Network (EAPN) 16
European Association of Schools of Social Work 16–17
European Border and Coast Guard Agency (EBCG) 47
European Network Against Racism (ENAR) 16
European Network for Social Action (ENSACT) 17
European Research Council (ERC) 49, 184

European Social Work Research
  Association (ESWRA) 2, 14, 17–18
European Union 13
European Union Agency for Fundamental
  Rights (FRA) 16
EU-Turkey agreement 181, 187
'everyday bordering' strategies 167
experiential learning 165
expert group
  on economic migration 20
  migrants, asylum and integration 20

F

family
  fosters wellbeing 100–1
  members, conflicting roles and
    loyalties 101
  relations, level 106–7
  relationships 100
family reunification 3, 185
  definition 95–6
  European directive on 96
  methodological nationalism 97–8
  migration 96
  political level 107
  refugee families, transnational
    lives 98–105
  of refugees 3
  transnational dynamics of 95–108
  transnational social work, infrastructure
    for 105–7
Fawcett, J.T. 11
federal Immigration Department 103
first-line social field work 59
First Reception Service 57
forced migration 80, 127
Foreman, M. 131
Foucault, M. 81–2
F-permit 82
Freire, P. 164
functioning of employment 150
Furman, R. 105

G

Gal, I. 13–14
Geldof, D. 3
geographical territory 39
German camps
  as 'childhood in waiting' 80
Global Standards for Social Work
  Education and Training 162
Gómez-Ciriano, E.J. 2
Greek immigration law 181
Greek legislation 180
Greek reception and identification centres
  (RICs) 178
  emotional exhaustion 56
  lack of resources 52–4
  living conditions in 47–8

of Moria 49–50
researcher's integration in social
  space 50
research setting 51–2
of Samos 51–2
self-injury behaviour 53
social services 56
'street-level' frontline worker 53
of Vathi 49
working conditions 54–8
Guidelines for the Alternative Care of
  Children 179
Gustafsson, K. 67, 73

H

Hamilton, R. 3–4
Health and Social Care Professionals Act
  (2005) 127
Health Information and Quality Authority
  (HIQA) 132
hedonic approach to wellbeing 150–1
Herz, M. 67
Hoffnungsträger Foundation 80
home
  dimensions of 84–5
  as place 85–6
homing 88–9
'hostile environment policy' 153
housing benefit 151–2
human rights
  -based policies 4
  profession, refugee families 108
Human Rights Watch 191

I

Illinois State Bureau of Labor 7
immigrant families 115
immigrant service users 116
immigration assessment process 136
Immigration Department 104
Indicators of Integration Framework 146,
  147–8, 151, 154
individualism 36
informal volunteer social workers 105
informed consent 84
inhumane camp conditions 182
institutional ambiguity 133
institutional anaesthesia 37
institutional oppression 118
institutional racism 120
integration 147–9
  culture(al) 67
  language and 71
  migrant 156–7
  migrant girls' experiences in
    Sweden 64–6
  refugees 148
  structural and cultural 67
  as two-way relational process 149

intellectual disabilities 127–8
interconnectedness 146
intercultural
  communication 10
  competence 116–17
  discrimination 113–14
  helping relationships 121
  sensitivity 9–10
International Association of Schools of Social Work (IASSW) 14, 16
International Federation of Social Workers (IFSW) 14, 139
  at Council of Europe 15
  participation in networks and platforms 15–16
  as political actor 14
  at United Nations 14–15
International Human Rights Organisation 34–5
International Protection Accommodation Service (IPAS) 130
international protection applicants 127
intolerance 21
Irish Association of Social Workers (IASW) 128
Irish Refugee Protection Programme 126
Irish Society for the Prevention of Cruelty to Children 131
Italian Guantanamo 26
Italian NGO Group for the Convention of the Rights of the Child (2021) 115
Italian social work organisations
  accessibility and inclusivity 112
  culture 118–20
  door-opening and -closing practices 114–18
  enforceability 115–16
  equivalence of care and intersectionality 118
  ethnic minorities people 115–16
  ethnic minority service users 117–18
  immigrant families 115
  intercultural discrimination 113–14
  intercultural social work 119, 121
  legal status 115–16
  linguistic barriers 114–15
  obstacles inherent in interventions and support 116
  social workers' competences and sensitivities 116–17

J

Jaji, R. 80
Johansson, J. 67
Joint Committee on Justice and Equality (2019) 136
'Jungle of Moria' 182

K

Käkelä, E. 148, 156
Kelley, F. 7
knowledge *9*
Kočevar, M. 27, *28*
Kolb, D. 165

L

Lalander, P. 64, 67
language
  and integration 71
  of war 26
laxity 113–14
Le, C. 11
learning spaces 165
legal status, Italian social work organisations 115–16
Levi, P. 32
Levy, S. 3
Lietaert, I. 3–4
linguistic barriers, Italian social work organisations 114–15
linguistic mediators and social workers 114–15
Lipsky's streetlevel bureaucrats' theory 48–9
lobbying 7

M

McGregor, A. 150
McLaughlin, H. 12
mental health social workers 131–2
methodological nationalism 97–8
migrant girls' experiences in Sweden 3
  first-order constructs 66
  gender roles 72
  identity 71–3
  integration 64–6
  responsibility 73–6
  right to life and being worthy of protection 68–71
  second-order concept 66
  social workers' interpretation 65–6
  Swedish political discourse 66
  Swedish social work practice, integration discourses 65–7
  unaccompanied refugee minors 64–5
migration and asylum policies in Europe
  academia and social work research 11–12
  empathy, knowledge and awareness 8–11
  inspirational thoughts 5–7
  organisational culture and social work research 12–13
  research role 13–21
migratory policy 9–10
military dictatorships 36
Moria, Lesvos 181–2
Morley, C. 13

Movement of Asylum Seekers in Ireland, 2019 129
Murray-Garcia, J. 10

N

Nasc 131, 138
National Asylum Support Service Dispersal Scheme 152
National Centre for Social Solidarity 184
National Health Service (NHS) 152
national welfare state 97
Navaro-Yashin, Y. 98
necropolitical experience 161
Negi, N.J. 105
neoliberalism 9–10
neoliberal paradigm in social work 10–11
networking 8
Neue Slowenische Kunst (NSK) 37–40, *40*
New Scots Integration Strategy, 2018–22 146–7
New Scots Refugee Integration Strategy 2018–2022 *153*, 153–4
Ní Raghallaigh, M. 131, 133, 136
non-discrimination 155
No Recourse to Public Funds (NRPF) policy 152
N-permit 82
NSK passport 39–40, *40*

O

Öberg, K. 66
'one size fits all' approach 116
organisational culture 10
Organisation for Economic Co-operation and Development (OECD) 13
organisational knowledge 8
outrage and ethical commitment 5–6
overrepresentation 113

P

parentification 102
participants' psychosocial wellbeing 184
participatory art in social work
  cultural anaesthesia 36–7
  emotional experiences 35
  epistemological flexibility 32–3
  methodology 25–6
  migration through embodied reflexivity 26–32
  transdisciplinarity 33–4
Pawson, R. 8
personal competences 115
persuasiveness 8
Petersen, M.G. 85, 86, 88, 90

Pioneer labor legislation in Illinois 5
Platform for International Cooperation on Undocumented Migrants (PICUM) 15–16
police violence, border migration policy 190–1
'political culture of danger' 30
political knowledge/policy knowledge 9
postcolonial approaches 162–3
post-traumatic stress disorder 57
poverty ratio 115
practice-based research 13
practitioner knowledge 8–9
psychosocial wellbeing 49
punitive policy framework 155–6

R

racial disparity 113
racism 21, 26, 128
Raghallaigh, M.N. 3
Raoof, D. 64
reception and identification centres (RICs) 3, 177, 178, 180
  discretion 48
  emotional exhaustion 56
  lack of resources 52–4
  living conditions in 47–8
  of Moria 49–50
  research setting 51–2
  of Samos 51–2
  self-injury behaviour 53
  social services 56
  of Vathi 49
  working conditions 54–8
refugee families
  throughout reunification processes 97
  transnational lives 98–105
Refugee Heritage Project 33
Refugee Studies Centre 84
refugees
  camps 80
  crisis 180
  emergency 178
  ethnographical studies of 80
  immigration 96
  institutionalisation and spatial segregation 27
  integration 148
  in Republic of Ireland 126–39
  status 151–2
Republic of Ireland
  children and families 129–32
  family reunification 137–8
  resettled and relocated children and families 132–4
  social work in 127–8
  unaccompanied minors 134–7
reunified families 137

Richason, L. 135
Richmond, M. 5
Rigby, P. 155–6
Righard, E. 11
Righard, R. 139
Rota, M. 3–4

S

Sager, M. 66
Salvador, R. 105
Schlingensief, C. 35–6
Schrooten, M. 3
Scotland, migration and social work 151–7
  demographic stability and growth 153
  migrant integration 156–7
Scottish care system 155
Scottish welfare approaches 155
self-critique 10
self-determination and wellbeing 120
self-evaluation 10
self-evident hierarchies 33–4
self-organised refugee community centre 167
self-report questionnaires 184
sensemaking concept 118
sense of place 155
service user knowledge 9
settlement-permit (C-permit) 82
Shannon, G. 129
Shier, M.L. 147
Smith, K. 137, 155
social anaesthesia 36
social capital 148
social deprivation 152
Social Diagnosis (1917) 5
social security 151–2
social value 148
social work 22
  academics 13–14
  associations 14
  interventions with ethnic minorities 121
  in nongovernmental organisations (NGOs) 131
  research 19
  role 130
  scholarship 130
social workers 96–7, 147
Social Workers' Registration Board 127
social work research on migration and asylum (SWIM) 2
Society for Social Work Research (SSWR) 14, 17
socio-ecological theories 162–3
Special Interest Group (SIG) 2
Starosta, W. 10
state-employed social workers 131
State Secretariat for Migration 83

Strang, A. 146, 147–8
street-level bureaucracy 48
stress and anxiety 191
structural and cultural integration 67
structural dehumanisation 161
super-diversity 146
Sweden, migrant girls' experiences in
  first-order constructs 66
  gender roles 72
  identity 71–3
  integration 64–6
  political discourse 66
  unaccompanied refugee minors 64–5
Swedish norms and customs 67

T

Täubig, V. 91
Teater, B. 12
terrorism 96
Tervalon, M. 10
Thornton, L. 136
totalitarianisms 34
transdisciplinarity 33–4
(trans)national
  awareness 97
  migration law 102–3, 107
  social work, infrastructure for 105–7
Turkish and Moroccan family reunifiers 96
Twenty years at Hull House (1910) 5

U

UK government immigration legislation 155
Unaccompanied Asylum-Seeking Children (UASC) 152, 155
unaccompanied minors 81, 101, 134, 135, 136, 137
unaccompanied refugee minors (URMs) 49, 178, 185–6
underrepresentation 113
United Nations Convention on the Rights of the Child (UNCRC) 1989 155
URMs *see* unaccompanied refugee minors (URMs)
Uzureau, O. 3

V

Van Acker, K. 3
Views of the Child 155
vulnerability assessments 139

W

Walsh, T. 128
Weiss-Gal, I. 13–14
welfare state humanitarianism 26
Wells, K. 156

Werdermann, D. 81
Wernesjö, U. 67
Willkommenskultur 26
Winther, I.W. 85, 90
World Health Organisation (WHO) 13
Wren, K. 156–7

X

xenophobia 21, 26, 27, 35, 36

Z

Zaviršek, D. 2
Ziegler, J. 182

www.ingramcontent.com/pod-product-compliance
Lightning Source LLC
Chambersburg PA
CBHW070042040426
42333CB00041B/2045